GARDNER'S
guide to

Multim & Animation Studios

The Industry Directory

2nd Edition

Garth Gardner, Ph.D.

GARTH GARDNER COMPANY

GGC publishing

Washington DC, USA · London, UK

Acknowledgments

I thank the many people who have helped create, produce, and review the materials in this book, this book has been a learning experience for us all. In particular I am especially thankful to Chris and Nic for their loyalty to our shared vision of providing quality information. I thank Rachelle for working to finalize the layout on this second edition.

In addition, I thank the associates of GGC Publishing for their invaluable help, support, and devotion in building this successful business.

Associate Editor: Chris Edwards
Art Director: Nic Banks
Layout Assistant: Rachelle Painchaud-Nash
Cover Image: Wayne Gilbert, *CPU* animation still

Disclaimer

After publication of this manuscript, changes may occur. Such changes administered by the individual studios should take precedence over this book. While reasonable effort will be made to update changes in subsequent editions, the reader is encouraged to seek current information from appropriate offices at the companies.

Editorial inquiries concerning this book should be addressed to: The Editor, Garth Gardner Company, Inc. 5107 13th Street NW, Washington, DC 20011. Email comments and corrections to: info@ggcinc.com. Visit our site: http://www.gogardner.com

Copyright © 2004 by Garth Gardner, Ph.D. ISBN: 1-58965-020-4

Library of Congress Cataloging-in-Publication Data

Gardner, Garth.

Gardner's guide to multimedia and animation studios 2004 / Garth Gardner. p. cm.

Includes index.

ISBN 1-58965-020-4 (paper back)

1. Multimedia systems—Directories. 2. Computer animation—Directories.

3. Computer graphics—Directories. I. Title: Guide to multimedia and animation studios 2004. II. Title.

QA76.575.G395 2004

006.7'025—dc22

2004002910

Printed in Canada

About the Author

Garth Gardner, Ph.D.

Dr. Gardner is a graduate of the Ohio State University's Advanced Computing Center for the Arts and Design and Department of Art Education.

Dr. Gardner is former Associate Professor of Multimedia at the New Century College, George Mason University. Before his appointment at GMU Dr. Gardner was an Assistant Professor at William Paterson University where he co-directed the Center for Computer Art and Animation. A member of this university's proposed MFA degree committee, in the Spring of 1996 Dr. Gardner chaired a subcommittee responsible for developing the proposed MFA degree concentration in Computer Art and Design.

As a consultant Dr. Gardner has advised various colleges and universities in structuring their curricula for teaching computer graphics and animation. He is a member of the Professional Advisory Board for the development of a BFA degree program in Computer Graphics and Multimedia at the Fashion Institute of Technology.

Dr. Gardner's research has focused on computer-art education and he is considered one of the nation's experts in his area. Dr. Gardner has presented papers at several universities including the University of California Los Angeles' Animation Workshop, the University of Southern California, Florida A&M University and the Fashion Institute of Technology. He has been a contributing author to several national and international animation magazines and professional journals. His computer fine art images have been published and exhibited in galleries and museums nationally and in China.

Dr. Gardner is the president and publisher at GGC, Inc., A Computer Graphics, Publishing, Animation and Consulting firm. The Company's clients include Universal Records, Air Jamaica, B.A.D., and Florida A&M University. His most recent publications are Gardner's Guide to Colleges for Animation and Multimedia 2004, and Gardner's Guide to Internships in New Media 2004 the number one resource for finding and internship in computer graphics, animation and multimedia. In addition Dr. Gardner is the executive producer Gardner's Great Animation Show, a video that showcases 3D animation from some of the best animation schools in North America.

Table of Contents

Index – Listed by State or Province

Colorado

Connecticut

Delaware

Florida

Canada

Index –Listed by Company Name

C

D

E

Submit your company's information for the next edition of Gardner's Guide to Multimedia & Animation Studios.

This form is also available at **http://www.gogardner.com/bizform.html**

Company Name

Areas of Specialization

Number of Employees

Description of Company

Street Address

City, State, Zip Code

Telephone Number

Fax Number

Web Address

Mail to: GGC Studio Bk Listing

GGC publishing

5107 13th Street NW,
Washington, DC 20011
202-541-9700
202-541-9750 fax
866-GO GARDNER (toll free)
www.gogardner.com

About This Book

Introduction

This book is written for the professional or college student who wishes to pursue career in the field of multimedia which, for the purpose of simplifying this book, we have defined as the following areas: pre production, computer graphics, computer animation, traditional animation, web design, video production, digital imaging studios, visual effects, post production, and sound. In short, it is written for the person who dreams of joining the ranks of an elite group of creative artists and scientist that are in the business of creating visual effects for feature films, experimental art, or television commercials. The book is also designed for those who seek the services of an animation or multimedia studio.

Gardner's Guide to Multimedia and Animation Studios is designed to assist prospective employees of the industry to locate a specific studio that may be in search of their talents. This book will help people interested in employment or employing the services of a computer graphics studio to answer the following questions:

- What studios may potentially be a source of employment?

- What is the size of the studio, number of employees?

- What are the studio's areas of specialization?

- What services does the company provide?

This guide is the first step to answering these questions and many others. The guide is designed to be used to quickly reference information on multimedia and animation studios. Please be advised that our objective in creating this guide is to provide you with a starting point. For the most accurate and up-to-date information please contact the studios directly.

Profiled Categories

The studios that are profiled in this book offer services in Computer Graphics, Animation, or Multimedia. The studios are listed alphabetically within three geographic areas in the US: east cost, west cost, central and a general category for Canada. For each profiled studio, the following facts are presented: Area of Specialization; Number of Employees; Description of Studio; Contact Information; Web Address.

East Coast

3D Animation Visual.com

Area(s) of Specialization: Animation and Visual Effects

Number of Employees: 8

The company can provide photo-realistic, computer-generated animation in any format, including AVI, MPEG, Digital Betacam, DVCAM, MiniDV, Betacam SP, Panavision, HDTV, IMAX, and DVD.

3D Animation Visual.com
15212 Dino Dr.
Burtonsville, MD 20866
Phone: 301 476-9470
Alt. Phone: 301 476-9482
Fax: 301 476-9535
URL: http://www.3Danimationvisual.com

A&S Animation

Area(s) of Specialization: Character Animation

Number of Employees: 6+

A&S Animation, Inc. specializes in developing and producing character animation in all forms. Winners of over 36 international animation awards. Producer Mark Simon is also the author of "Producing Independent 2D Animation, Character Animation, and Storyboards: Motion In Art, 2nd Edition."

A&S Animation, Inc.
8137 Lake Crowell Circle
Orlando, FL 32836
Phone: 407 370-2673
Fax: 407 370-2602
Email: mark@storyboards-east.com
URL: http://www.FunnyToons.tv

A.O.K. Publishing Inc.

Area(s) of Specialization: Computer Animation

Number of Employees: 1

A former comic book illustrator and publisher, A.O.K. was one of the first cartoonists to create Webisodes using Flash and currently produce fine animated pieces up to 5 minutes long for almost any use with imaginative art and design, tight production, and clean, well-optimized files.

A.O.K. Publishing Inc.
P.O. Box 346
Croton, NY 10520
Email: anim8@aokpub.com
URL: http://www.aokpub.com

ABC Toon Center

Area(s) of Specialization: Animation, Multimedia

Number of Employees: 6+

An Internet amusement Park full of colorful, musical, and entertaining activities for kids. The site index is presented in six languages and currently receives an average of 1,400 new visitors each day.

ABC Toon Center
Country Downs Circle
Fairport, NY 14450
Email: jackson@frontiernet.net
URL: http://www.abctooncenter.com

Activeworlds.com, Inc.

Area(s) of Specialization: 3D Animation Computer Animation, Virtual Reality

Number of Employees: 23 (+5 consultants)

Activeworlds.com, Inc. provides software products and online services that permit users to enter, move about and interact with others in a computer-generated, three-dimensional virtual environment using the Internet. It hosts hundreds of virtual worlds in three-dimensional environments. In addition, Activeworlds.com develops worlds for other companies granting them licenses for the use of the technology. The company also licenses the technology to clients to create worlds.

Activeworlds.com, Inc.
95 Parker Street
Newburyport, MA 01950
Phone: 978 499-0222
Fax: 978 499-0221
Email: info@activeworlds.com
URL: http://www.activeworlds.com

AFCG, Inc.

Area(s) of Specialization: CGI, Animation, Film/Video Effects

Number of Employees: 2

AFCG has been creating high-end computer animation and effects for the film and commercial production industries since. May 1987. Most work is created using Silicon Graphics workstations running the "Prisms" or "Houdini" software packages from Side Effects Software. The company uses custom-built software tools, as well as the "Amazon" Paint Packages from Interactive Effects and "RasTrack" from Hammerhead Productions. AFCG's most recent work may be viewed in nationally aired television commercials for Campbells Soup, Duracell, Nasdaq, AT&T, Nissan, Dr. Pepper, 7Up, and Motorola.

AFCG Inc.
16 West 22nd Street
New York, N.Y. 10010
Phone: 212 627-8770
Fax: 212 627-8773
Email: fgillis@afcg.com
URL: http://www.afcg.com

Amalgamation House

Area(s) of Specialization: Animation and
Design for Film/Video

Number of Employees: 5+

Amalgamation House Inc. is a multi-story, multi-disciplinary, multi-faceted, multimedia collective serving creative needs within the commercial, corporate, and independent arenas. Through fifteen-odd years, its areas of expertise include cel and high-end computer animation, special effects and graphics for film/video, interactive, & traditional design for print, as well as Web site development.

Amalgamation House
1218-20 Shackamaxon Street
Philadelphia, PA 19125-3914
Phone: 215 427-1954
Fax: 215 426-6372
Email: a-house@pixelmixers.com
URL: http://www.pixelmixers.com

Animagicians

Area(s) of Specialization: CG Effects, Internet/Intranet, Corporate Graphics, Animation, Architecture, Web Graphics

Number of Employees: 500+

AniMagicians is a design firm made up of a staff with freelance backgrounds in 3D animation, graphics, and Web development.

Animagicians
Phone: 617 964-9491
Fax: 617 527-7692
Email: amagic@tiac.net
URL: http://www.quotesnow.com/animagic.htm

Animatics & Storyboards, Inc.

Area(s) of Specialization: Traditional Animation

Number of Employees: 6+

The company produces animation for feature films, commercials, TV shows, industrials, laser shows, kiosks, games, and bar mitzvah. They produce turnkey animation, storyboards, animation, and character design. Clients include These Mouse Guys, Hanna Barbera, Golden Books, Kenner Toys, NASA, P&G, and others. One animator, Jeffrey Varab, has animated for Fox, the Mouse Guys, Amblin, Universal, and another animator Don Bluth has created for Titan A.E., Mulan, Balto, Ferngully, The Tigger Movie, and over a dozen others.

Animatics & Storyboards, Inc.
8137 Lake Crowell Circle
Orlando, FL 32836
Phone: 407 370-BORD (2673)
Fax: 407 370-2602
Email: mark@storyboards-east.com
URL: http://www.storyboards-east.com/anm-fm.html

Animation Toolworks, Inc.

Area(s) of Specialization: Traditional Animation

Number of Employees: 2+

Animation Toolworks have been making frame grabbers for animators since 1996. Animation Toolworks serves professional animators and animation students by providing tools to reduce their cost and reinforce their creativity. Animation Toolworks' first product, the Video LunchBox™, was conceived over lunch in a Portland, Oregon restaurant. The successor to the Video LunchBox, the LunchBox Sync, was introduced in September 2000. The LunchBox Sync retains the lunchbox size and shape combined with the industry's easiest to use interface. It adds support for audio synchronization, editing features, and improves both frame capacity and image quality. The principals of Animation Toolworks are Arthur Babitz and Howard Mozeico. The two worked together several times as engineering managers at Mentor Graphics Corporation, and at Cinemar Corporation, both Portland, Oregon area software companies.

Animation Toolworks, Inc.
18484 S.W. Parrett Mountain Rd.
Sherwood, OR 97140
Phone: 503 625-6438
Fax: 503 925-0221
Email: info@animationtoolworks.com
URL: http://www.animationtool works.com

Animation Technologies

Area(s) of Specialization: 3D Animation, Interactive Programming, Web Design, Consulting

Number of Employees: 25

Animation Technologies is a visual communications company specializing in business-to-business media solutions. The Company uses 3D animation, computer graphics, and interactive media to create visual explanation of complex information. Animation Technologies builds custom, interactive 3D Animation applications for the Internet.

Animation Technologies
60 Canal Street
Boston, MA 02114
Phone: 617 723-6040
Fax: 671 723-6080
Email: info@animationtech.com
URL: http://www.animationtech.com

Animators at Law, Inc.

Area(s) of Specialization: Trial Exhibits/ Animation, Jury Research, Web Design, Marketing Design

Number of Employees: 12

Animators At Law develops strategies and designs for visuals in the courtroom. The company's goal is to create visual presentations that can communicate information faster than the spoken word and that will be retained for longer periods of time. Animators work with the personnel in jury research and trial strategy using a team-based approach to developing demonstrative evidence and trial strategy and create using both artistic design and programming. Animators offers full-service 24 hour support for all work, including trial presentation hardware and on-site

technicians. The company creates teaching tools for the legal community, videos for judicial patent tutorials that distill abstract concepts, CD-ROM books, and interactive programs that explain complex theories, scientific and medical illustration and animation that educate legal teams.

Animators At Law, Inc.
1423 Powhatan Street, Suite 3
Alexandria, Virginia 22314
Phone: 800 337-7697
Fax: 703 548-5450
Email: info@animators.com
URL: http://www.animators.com

Animink Incorporated

Area(s) of Specialization: Animation, Character Animation, CGI, Web design

Number of Employees: 6+

Full animation studio offering Cartoon & Computer Animation, Visual Effects, and Web site Development.

Animink Incorporated
105 E. Birnie St.
Gaffney, SC 29340
Phone: 864 487-8805
Fax: 864 487-8809
Email: inquiry@animink.com
URL: http://www.animink.com

Animusic

Area(s) of Specialization: 3D Animation, Sound

Number of Employees: 6+

ANIMUSIC produces innovative 3D animation and animated music videos with proprietary software.

ANIMUSIC
317 Nye Rd.
Cortland, NY 13045
Phone: 607 756-0190
Fax: 805 241-5505
Email: jeff@animusic.com
URL: http://www.ANIMUSIC.COM

Anivision, Inc.

Area(s) of Specialization: CGI, Animation, Film/Video Production

Number of Employees: 55

Anivision is a full-service animation & video production company. It produces Sales Promotional Tapes, Interactive CD/DVD Authoring, Sales and Management Training Tapes, TV Commercials and Programming, 3D Animation Modeling and Architectural Flythroughs.

AniVision Inc.
228 Holmes Ave. NE
Huntsville, AL 35801

Phone: 800 492-1977
Alt. Phone: 256 382-8000
Fax: 256 382-8002
Email: mitchellb@anivision.com
URL: http://www.anivision.com

Anzovin Studio

Area(s) of Specialization: Animation Production

Number of Employees: 2+

CG Animation studio offering character animation and other services.

Anzovin Studio
534 Main St., Suite C
Amherst, MA 01002
Phone: 413 253-2358
Email: steve@anzovin.com
URL: http://www.anzovin.com

APC Studios

Area(s) of Specialization: CGI, Animation, Film/Video Production

Number of Employees: 9+

APC Studios is a full-service facility that can take a project from a thumbnail sketch to production, through the posting process and finally to the mastering, package design and distribution process.

APC Studios
3838 Oakcliff Industrial
Atlanta, GA 30340
Phone: 770 242-7678
Alt Phone: 770 242-9652
Fax: 770 242-0278
Email: stuff@apcstudios.com
URL: http://www.apcstudios.com

Artbear Pigmation, Inc.

Area(s) of Specialization: Animation
Character Design and Development,
Cel Animation.

Number of Employees: 2+

Artbear Pigmation has been producing
animation, from concept through final
output for the past 27 years. Specializing
in character design, project
development, and animation creating
combinations of live action, 3D
animation, and/or photo collage with
traditional characters. The company
produces shorts on video and film for
the purposes of educational,
instructional videos, or television
commercials.

Artbear Pigmation, Inc.
415 Elm Street
Ithaca, NY 14850
Phone: 607 277-1151
Fax: 607 277-1166
URL: http://www.animationstand.com/
gallery/artbearp/artbearp0.html

Art by Ari

Area(s) of Specialization: Traditional
Animation

Number of Employees: 1+

Professional Artwork and Illustration
for: Children's books; Advertising;
Magazines; Internet/Computer
Graphics.

Art By Ari
133 Murray Hill Blvd.
Murray Hill, NJ 07974
Phone: 908 464-5866
Fax: 908 464-5866
Email: info@artbyari.com
URL: http://www.artbyari.com

Atlanta Video

Area(s) of Specialization: CGI, Film/
Video Production and Post Production,
Animation

Number of Employees: 5+

The Company specializes in graphics,
post production, multimedia, and video
production. The graphics division offers
2D animation and 3D animation and
graphic services, using such software
programs as 3D Animation Studio Max,
Fractal Design Painter, Adobe
Photoshop, After Effects, Autodesk
Animator Studio, Morph, and In Sync

Speed Razor. The post-production area offers various non-linear editing suites. The multimedia area is equipped to do interactive and Web-based projects. Atlanta Video has a large collection of stock footage including Aztec and Mayan sites, peoples, ruins, and art works, all on 16mm film. 3D animation models are also available.

Atlanta Video
368 Moreland Ave.
Atlanta, GA 30307
Phone: 404 523-9660
Fax: 404 523-7795
Email: bill@atlantavideo.com
URL: http://www.atlantavideo.com

Atlantic Motion Pictures

Area(s) of Specialization: Film/Video Production and Effects, Animation

Number of Employees: 8+

Atlantic Motion Pictures is a full-service production company that specializes in visual fx and high end animation for the television, theatrical and the advertising industries. Atlantic began in 1982 as a company specializing in the design and production of film animation and motion graphics, and has expanded its operation to include motion control, stop motion, table top, traditional animation, computer animation, and live action photography, allowing the production of a wide variety of multimedia effects and combinations.

Atlantic Motion Pictures
162 W. 21st St., 4th floor
New York, NY 10011
Phone: 212 924-6170
Fax: 212 989-8736
Email: EFX4TV@AOL.COM
URL: http://www.atlanticmotion.com

Augenblick Studios

Area(s) of Specialization: Traditional Animation

Number of Employees: 6+

Augenblick Studios is a full-service animation facility located in Brooklyn, NY. Opened in 1999 by Aaron Augenblick, the company has produced a wide variety of works for television, film, and the Internet, coupling classic animation techniques with cutting edge technology.

Augenblick Studios, Inc.
45 Main St., #521
Brooklyn, NY 11201
Phone: 718 855-9226
Fax: 718 855-9227
Email: Info@AugenblickStudios.com
URL: http://www.AugenblickStudios.com

Ave.kta Productions

Area(s) of Specialization: Video, 3D Animation, Multimedia, Web site Design

Number of Employees: 7

Ave.kta Productions specializes in using high technology, to assist corporate directors in human resources and marketing. The company has worked with Time Warner, and O'Neil Data Systems and Investor's Business Daily. Ave.kta runs commercials produced on desktop systems on CNN and CNBC featuring Fortune 500 CEO's like MCI President, Gerald Taylor; Publisher, Steve Forbes, and Jack Kemp. Avekta directs the satellite media tours for Steve Forbes and Forbes Magazine. Avekta produced one of the first American made situation comedies for Russia and CIS countries, reaching 150 million viewers.

Ave.kta Productions
145 East 48th St., Suite 17C
New York, NY 10017
Phone: 212 308-8000
Email: sales@Avekta.com
URL: http://www.Avekta.com

Bakedmedia, Inc.

Area(s) of Specialization: Traditional Animation, 3D Animation, CGI

Number of Employees: 30+

Bakedmedia, Inc. is a full-service, affordable 3D animation and graphics studio specializing in informative graphic animation and illustration for video and online markets including medical, pharmaceutical, military, air and space, manufacturing, telecommunications, broadcast, and education.

Bakedmedia, Inc.
9338 S. Whitt Dr.
Manassas Park, VA 20111
Phone: 703 330-4545
Email: billbaker@bakedmedia.com
URL: http://www.bakedmedia.com

Balsmeyer & Everett, Inc.

Area(s) of Specialization: Marketing, CGI, 2D Animation and 3D Animation, Digital Effects, Editing

Number of Employees: 8+

Balsmeyer & Everett, Inc. studio facilities feature the latest in visual effects technology. Digital effects and 3D Animation are created on SGI workstations running Softimage, Cineo, Chalice, and a host of other software packages and are output on a Solitaire Cine III film recorder. Graphics and 2D Animation are created on Macintosh workstations running Adobe After Effects, Premier, Photoshop, etc. Balsmeyer & Everett, Inc. has its own in house film-editing, screening and non-linear video editing facilities. Their 10,000 sq. ft. studio houses a 2000 sq. ft. stage with a Mechanical Concepts/Cooper Controls motion control system. They also provide a variety of portable motion control systems designed by General Lift for location work.

Balsmeyer & Everett, Inc.
161 Ave. of the Americas
New York, NY 10011
Phone: 212 627-3430
Fax: 212 989-6528
Email: info@bigfilmdesign.com
URL: http://www.balsmeyer-everett.com

Betelguese Productions, Inc.

Area(s) of Specialization: Editing, Production, CGI, Animation, Sound Composition

Number of Employees: 100

Betelguese is a full-service facility housing state of the art digital online rooms, multi format online rooms, AVID online/off-line suits, Inferno, Flame, Flinet, Macintosh design suites, interactive design and implementation, digital audio rooms, and tape duplication in every format. Services include digital online programming, multiformat editing, non-linear editing, production services, graphic design, digital compositing and animation, interactive systems, media conversions and transfers, digital audio post, sound composition, and all format duplication.

Betelguese Productions, Inc.
44 E 32ND St.
12 Fl.
New York, NY 10016
Phone: 212 251-8600
Fax: 212 251-8633
Email: info@betelgeuse.com
URL: http://www.Betelgeuse.com

Big Mouth

Area(s) of Specialization: Traditional Animation, Sound, Visual Effects

Number of Employees: 100+

Big Mouth specializes in creating sound and motion: broadcast design, animation, visual effects, original music, sound design, and editorial.

Big Mouth
905 Bernina Ave.
Atlanta, GA 30307
Phone: 404 221.1705
Email: kirstie@bigmouthpost.com
URL: http://www.bigmouthpost.com

Big Tommy

Area(s) of Specialization: Traditional Animation

Number of Employees: 2+

Creator of the animated series "Unga Bunga."

Big Tommy Productions
6083 Flagstone Ct.
Frederick, MD 21701
Phone: 301 698-5370
Fax: 301 698-5370
Email: BigTommyCo@aol.com

Big Sky Editorial

Area(s) of Specialization: Film/Video Production, Editing and Restoration

Number of Employees: 7

Big Sky Editorial focuses on editing and restoration film.

Big Sky Editorial
10 East 40th St.
Suite 1701
New York, NY 10016
Phone: 212 683-4004
Fax: 212 889-6220
Email: cheryl@bigskyedit.com
URL: http://www.bigskyedit.com

BillCo.

Area(s) of Specialization: Traditional Animation, Post Production, 3D Animation

Number of Employees: 2+

Creation and distribution of original 3D Animation concepts. Blending of video with Computer-generated 3D animation.

BillCo.
1625 Ruxton Rd.
Edgewater, MD 21037
Phone: 410 956-3027
Email: MD77610@aol.com

Black Logic

Area(s) of Specialization: 3D Animation, Visual effects

Number of Employees: 40+

Black Logic is a full-service production company whose philosophy is based on creativity and technical excellence. Black Logic offers live action, graphic design, high-end visual effects and computer animation for film and television. Their goal is to rise to every challenge by creating compelling digital imagery that will make their clients' projects truly unique.

Black Logic
216 E 45th Street
New York, NY 10016
Phone: 212 557-4949
Fax: 212 759-2224
Email: bryan@tapehouse.com
URL: http://www.blacklogic.com

Black Moon Digital

Area(s) of Specialization: Traditional
Animation, CGI, Audio/Film/Video
Production

Number of Employees: 30+

Full-service animation company.

Black Moon Digital
153 Lewis St.
Buffalo, NY 14206
Phone: 716 856-9543
Fax: 716 856-9585
Email: blackmoondigital@hotmail.com
URL: http://www.blackmoondigital.com

Blue Rock Editing Co.

Area(s) of Specialization: Advertising
Editing and Post Production

Number of Employees: 55

Blue Rock Editing represents a portion
of the services available under the
Palestrini Post umbrella. The company
provides the advertising community
editing and post production.

The Blue Rock Editing Co.
575 Lexington Ave.
New York, NY 10022
Phone: 212 752-3348
Fax: 212 752-0307
Email: elyse@bluerockny.com
URL: http://www.bluerockny.com

Blue Sky Studios

Area(s) of Specialization: CGI,
Computer Animation

Number of Employees: 150+

Academy Award winning Blue Sky
Studios was founded in 1987 by David
Brown, Alison Brown, Chris Wedge, Carl
Ludwig, Eugene Troubetzkoy, PhD., and
Michael Ferraro with a mission to
pioneer creatively superior photo-
realistic, high-resolution computer-
generated character animation for
commercials, feature films and the
entertainment industry. Blue Sky's most
recent credits include their 1998 Oscar
Award-winning short film "Bunny". The
studio has also completed several
computer-animated characters for the
box-office hit "Star Trek: Insurrection"
(1998 Paramount); the computer-
generated aliens in the Twentieth
Century Fox feature film release "Alien

Resurrection" (1997); numerous characters and special effects for "A Simple Wish" (Bubble Factory/Universal Pictures 1997), and a host of dancing, singing cockroaches for the MTV cult classic "Joe's Apartment" (Geffen Films/ Warner Bros. 1986), and "Fight Club" directed by David Flincher. The studio has also begun working closely with the New York Indie film community completing a number of special effects projects for films such as "Just The Ticket" (1999); "Lulu on the Bridge" (1998), and "Jesus' Son."

Blue Sky Studios
44 South Broadway
White Plains, New York 10601
Phone: 914 259-6500
Fax: 914 259-6499
Email: info@blueskystudios.com
URL: http://www.blueskystudios.com

BNN

Area(s) of Specialization: Film/Video Production

Number of Employees: 40

A Time Warner's New York Cable News service. Established in 1983, BNN has produced for VH1, Disney, The Travel Channel, NBC, the ASPCA and Scholastic. The company is involved in development in Web design and deployment, video journalism, comedy, feature films, and all manner of human expression. BNN is a television production and program development facility located in New York, NY, which has produced program segments for clients including: MTV, CBS, A&E, VH1, Court TV, The Sci-Fi Channel, Lifetime, Fox Television, ABC, NBC, ESPN, The Today Show, MacNeil-Lehrer Newshour, Entertainment Tonight, Travel Channel, and BRAVO.

BNN
253 5th Ave.
New York, NY 10016
Phone: 212 779-0500
Fax: 212 532-5554
Email: Lori.Fechter@CameraPlanet.com
URL: http://www.bnntv.com

Borris FX

Area(s) of Specialization: Computer Animation, 3D Animation Computer Graphics, Desktop, Production

Number of Employees: 51

Founded in 1995 and based in Boston MA, Borris FX creates 3D animation, DVE, titling and compositing plug-in technology serving the video, film and multimedia production markets. Its products offer editors and 2D Animation graphic artists a professional software solution with great creative flexibility. The company maintains partnerships with industry companies such as Avid/Softimage, Adobe, Canopus, Discreet Logic, DPS, FAST, in-sync, Media 100, Panasonic, Sony, and Ulead.

Borris FX
381 Congress St.
Boston, MA 02210
Phone: 617 451-9900
Fax: 617 451-9916
Email: Jobs@borisfx.com
URL: http://www.borisfx.com

B.R.A.T.S

Area(s) of Specialization: Traditional Animation

Number of Employees: 6+

The new weekly syndicated radio program, "B.R.A.T.S." (Blackwell's Radio Animation Talk Show) features professional animators sharing their insight with program host, Joe Blackwell. The focus of "B.R.A.T.S." is to help educate and entertain listeners about the wonderful world of animation. "B.R.A.T.S." spotlights many animation experts who've been anonymous or who've worked behind the scenes. Invited guests include James Parris

(Spiderman), Alonzo Washington (Omega Comics), and many more.

'B.R.A.T.S' (Blackwell's Radio Animation Talk Show)
31-20 103rd St.
East Elmhurst, NY 11369
Phone: 646 489-4134
Email: joe@radioanimation.com
URL: http://www.radioanimation.com

Broadway Video Design

Area(s) of Specialization: CGI, Film/Video Production and Post Production, Interactive Media

Number of Employees: 500

From creative development and production to editing, design, sound and interactive media, Broadway Video offers talent, technology and expertise across all media. Clients include broadcast and cable networks, advertising agencies, dozens of Fortune 500 corporations, independent television producers and major software publishers. Broadway Video is headquartered in the historic Brill Building at 1619 Broadway and is a Partner to the revitalization of Times Square.

Broadway Video Design
1619 Broadway
New York, NY 10019

Phone: 212 333-0500
Alt. Phone: 212 265-7600
Fax: 212 333-0501
Email: info@broadwayvideo.com
URL: http://www.broadwayvideo.com

Bush Entertainment, Inc.

Area(s) of Specialization: Film/Video
Production and Post Production

Number of Employees: 12+

Bush Entertainment is a video and film
Production Company in SW Florida.
They provide services from creative
concept and field crews to post
production editing, design and finishing.
An award-winning staff of producers,
designers and creative professionals
ensure clients projects go smoothly. The
company specializes in 35mm, 16mm
film or BetacamSP production and
camera crews, Bush Entertainment is
located in Fort Myers, Florida, along the
Gulf of Mexico.

Bush Entertainment
11000-2 Metro Parkway
Ft. Myers, Florida 33912
Phone: 941 275-9575
Fax: 941 275-8395
URL: http://www.bushentertainment.com

Buzzco Associates, Inc.

Area(s) of Specialization: Animation

Number of Employees: 5

Buzzco Associates is a traditional
animation house that has created
animation shorts and ID spots for clients
such as Nickelodeon, Burger King and
several others. Since 1987 the company
have created 6 shorts and several
commercial projects.

Buzzco Associates, Inc.
33 Bleecker Street
New York, NY 10012
Phone: 212 473-0808
Fax: 212 473-8891
URL: http://www.buzzco.com
Email: Info@buzzzco.com

BXB, Inc.

Area(s) of Specialization: CGI, Film/
Video, Effects Editing

Number of Employees: 2+

BXB Inc. was created in August 1987 as a
design and special effects editing
company. Its founders, Henry Baker and
Patty Bellucci, started the company as an
instrument through which to conduct
creative work on film/video and effects
editing.

BXB, Inc.
257 West 17 Street
New York City, NY 10011
Phone: 212 924-8654
Email: bxblnc.@aol.com
URL: http://www.bxblnc.com

Camp Chaos Animation Studio

Area(s) of Specialization: Web Cartoons, Animation

Number of Employees: 10

Camp Chaos Entertainment creates cartoons and short films for the Web and, secondarily, for other media using the current production software. The company has been recognized by "Entertainment Weekly," "U.S. News and World Report," "Yahoo! Internet Life," ZDNet, E! Entertainment Television and leading Web sites like The Romp, POP.com, RealNetworks' Real.com, Shockwavecom, AtomFilms.com, ZDNet.com. The company invites customers to license one or more original productions, or commission the creation of original animated productions for Web sites.

Camp Chaos Animation Studio
P.O. Box 2575
West Lawn, PA 19609 2575
Phone: 610 603-0591

Fax:: 425 699-9880
Email: bob@campchaos.com
URL: http://www.campchaos.com

Canine Comics

Area(s) of Specialization: Flash, CGI

Number of Employees: 1+

Producer of the animated serial Dr. Shroud.

Canine Comics
146 A N. Church St.
Doylestown, PA 18901
Phone: 215 340-5941
Email: RobF@caninecomics.com
URL: http://www.drshroud.com

Carl Paolino Studios, Inc.

Area(s) of Specialization: Animation, Video

Number of Employees: 2+

Carl Paolino Studios is a full-service film animation and special effects facility located in midtown Manhattan. With over twenty years of production experience, CPS has been responsible for the animation and special effects of major television, video and live performance projects.

Carl Paolino Studios, Inc.

410 W. 47th St.
New York, NY 10036
Phone: 212 245-3624
Email: contact@paolinostudios.com
URL: http://www.paolinostudios.com

The Cartoon Tycoon

Area(s) of Specialization: Cel Animation

Number of Employees: 2

The Cartoon Tycoon produces traditional and non-traditional cel animation for local, national and international audiences. The company creates TV commercials, show openings, corporate videos, CD-ROMs, series pilots, TV bumpers, or network IDs.

The Cartoon Tycoon
509 North Second Street
Harrisburg, PA 17101
Phone: 717 234-8091
Fax: 717 234-1995
Email: Fred@cartoontycoon.com
URL: http://www.cartoontycoon.com

The CathodeRay Club

Area(s) of Specialization: Animation, Sound, Video

Number of Employees: 10+

A Creative Resource Services company that conceives audio/video graphic and photographic content. Clients are national and international broadcast and cable networks that use the company's ideas, designs, captured images, moving pictures and orchestrated sounds in their program's visual identity and on-air promotion.

The CathodeRay Club
130 West 57th St.
Suite 14C
New York, NY 10019
Phone: 212 245-7073
Fax: 212 262-1761
Email: contact@cathoderayclub.com
URL: http://www.cathoderayclub.com

Cecropia, Inc.

Area(s) of Specialization: Animation,

Number of Employees: 2+

Cecropia, Inc. is a video game development company based just outside of Boston, MA.

Cecropia, Inc.
57 Bedford St., Suite 120
Lexington, MA 02420
Phone: 781 862-6911
Fax: 781 402-2586
Email: jparker@cecropia.com

Central Park Media

Area(s) of Specialization: Traditional Animation

Number of Employees: 10+

A studio that creates documentaries and traditional animation for families.

Central Park Media
250 West 57th St., Suite 317
New York, NY 10107
Phone: 212 977-7456
Fax: 212 977-8709
Email: info@teamcpm.com
URL: http://www.centralparkmedia.com

Century III at Universal Studios

Area(s) of Specialization: CGI, Animation, Film/Video Production and Post Production

Number of Employees: 50+

Century III was established in 1976 for commercial and corporate productions. Century III employs a staff of individuals in project management, location/studio productions, post production, audio design, special effects, computer graphics and animation, engineering design, interactive multimedia development, software development, cost analysis, accounting and marketing. The company has created local, regional, national and international projects for producers, independents, advertising agencies, television stations and broadcast cable networks; as well as government, corporate marketing, communications and training departments.

Century III at Universal Studios
2000 Universal Studios Plaza
Orlando, FL 32819
Phone: 407 354-1000
Fax: 407 352-8662
Email: jkirk@century3.com
URL: http://www.century3.com

Charlex

Area(s) of Specialization: 3D Animation Computer Animation, CGI, Multimedia, Film/Television

Number of Employees: 50

Charlex creates design concepts and layouts for clients such as Ford, Fila, Nissan, Lucent Technologies, Qwest, Ryder Trucks, and Budweiser.

Charlex
2 W. 45th St., 7th Floor
New York, NY 10036
Phone: 212 719-4600
Fax: 212 840-2747

Email: amy@charlex.com
URL: http://www.charlex.com

Children's Television Workshop

Area(s) of Specialization: Film/Video

Number of Employees: 500+

CTW and Sesame Street were created as an "experiment" in 1968, and the show debuted on November 10, 1969. Designed to use the medium of television to reach and teach preschoolers skills that provide a successful transition from home to school. The show includes learning the alphabet, numbers, and pro-social skills.

Children's Television Workshop
One Lincoln Plaza
New York, NY 10023
Phone: 212-595-3456
Fax: 212-875-6088
URL: http://www.ctw.org

Chris Allard Illustration

Area(s) of Specialization: Traditional Animation

Number of Employees: 1+

Chris Allard is an illustrator with 20 years of experience providing storyboards, illustrations, comps and character design for his clients.

Chris Allard Illustration
284 Ash St.
Reading, MA 01867
Phone: 781 944-8584
Email: allardink@aol.com
URL: http://www.allardillustration.com

The Classical Animation Society

Area(s) of Specialization: Traditional Animation

Number of Employees: 6+

The Classical Animation Society is a student organization at the Savannah College of Art and Design and a member organization of ASIFA-Atlanta. CAS is dedicated to the art, craft and industry of animation.

Classical Animation Society
201 W. Oglethorpe Ave.
Savannah, GA 31401
Email: cas_club@hotmail.com
URL: http://
www.geocities.comclassicalanimationsociety

Cineframe Animation

Area(s) of Specialization: 3D Animation Modeling/Animation for Broadcast, Games, Theme Parks, Net, and Film

Number of Employees: 1

Cineframe Animation is David Gallagher's freelance 3D Animation studio located in Utah. He specializes in modeling and animating advanced 3D Animation characters for theme parks, games, advertising, Internet, and film. Cineframe uses Softimage 3D Animation software on an Intergraph TDZ-2000 workstation.

Cineframe Animation
406 Eagle's Ridge Road
Brewster, NY 10509
Phone: 914 937-2196
Email: dAve.@cineframe.com
URL: http://www.cineframe.com

Cineric

Area(s) of Specialization: Film Post Production, Restoration, Digital Film Services

Number of Employees: 20

In New York, Cineric provides titles, optical and Post Production special effects for feature films. The company utilizes both optical printing and digital imaging. They offer scanning, recording, video to film, and specialized image processing services. In optical printing and film restoration, the company creates a 35mm blow-up from a 16mm or Super 16 negative, also providing blow-up/conversions of a wide range of film formats to standard 35mm including Super 8, VistaVision, TechniScope (2-perf), 3-perf, as well as anamorphic conversion from Super 35mm to 35mm 'Scope. The company developed a variety of processes using both photochemical and digital techniques including a new faded color negative restoration process. Cineric has restored over 200 films including "Jason and the Argonauts," "The Birds," "American Graffiti," "A Man for All Seasons," "The Man from Laramie" and "The Caine Mutiny."

Cineric
630 Ninth Ave., 5th Floor
New York, NY 10036
Phone: 212 586-4822
Fax: 212 582-3744
Email: janos@cineric.com
URL: http://www.cineric.com

Cinesite Film, Scanning and Recording

Area(s) of Specialization: CGI, Film/ Video, Digital Imaging and Effects

Number of Employees: 2

Cinesite, a digital effects studio in the world, opened in 1992, as a wholly owned subsidiary of Eastman Kodak Company. With facilities in both Hollywood and Europe. Cinesite is a full-service digital effects company which provides services, in digital compositing, 2D Animation & 3D Animation effects, wire and object removal, film stock repair and restoration, and digital film scanning and recording. Cinesite did visual effects work on such films as "Armagedon," "Dr. Dolittle," "Primary Colors," "The Truman Show," "Lost in Space," "Air Force One," "Sphere," "Event Horizon," "Tomorrow Never Dies," "Jerry Maguire," "Space Jam," and "Smilla's Sense of Snow."

Cinnesite Film, Scanning and Recording
360 W. 31st Street
Suite 710
New York, New York 10001
Phone: 212 631-3414
Fax: 212 631-3436
URL: http://www.cinesite.com

City Lights Media Group

Area(s) of Specialization: CGI, Film/ Video and Motion Picture/Television Production and Post Production

Number of employees: 30+

City Lights Media Group is comprised of four divisions:

City Lights Editorial is the company's Post Production service and facility, which features edit suites containing Avid non-linear editing equipment and software, technical support and a staff of creative editors. City Lights FX is the company's graphics, animation and visual effects division, which features Silicon Graphics and Power Mac workstations, SoftImage and After Effects. City Lights Productions is the company's film and video production unit.

City Lights Media Group
6 East 39th Street
New York, New York 10016
Phone: 212 679-4400
Fax: 212 679-3819
Email: sal@citylightsmedia.com
URL: http://www.citylightsmedia.com

Click 3X

Area(s) of Specialization: Digital Effects, Animation, Broadcast Design

Number of Employees: 31

The Click 3X matrix of design studios offers digital effects, animation, and broadcast design for the commercial, film, and television markets. Click 3X is part of the Illusion Fusion! Group of digital media companies which includes: New York based IF! Interactive and Sound Lounge as well as San Francisco based studio-an integrated digital studio that creates digital content for both the broadcast and Internet markets. Click 3X specializes in visual effects design and supervision, computer animation, character design and compositing. The studios operate multiple Silicon Graphics 3D Animation workstations, Windows NT, Macintosh platforms and an AVID non-linear off-line suite, as well as a Henry suite and Inferno/Flame compositing suites running on Silicon Graphics Onyx II super computers.

Click 3X—New York
16 West 22nd Street
New York, NY 10010
Phone: 212 627-1900
Fax: 212 627-4472
Email: PHILM@CLICK3X.COM
URL: http://www.click3x.com

Click 3X-Atlanta
345 Peachtree Hills Ave.
Atlanta, GA 30305
Phone: 404 237-9333
Fax: 404 237-9393
Email: CONNOR@CLICK3X.COM

CME Digital

Area(s) of Specialization: Traditional Animation, Film, Digital Media

Number of Employees: 6+

CME is a boutique production team of very experienced, highly creative artists, animators, and compositors. CME specializes in rendered animation for video, film and location based entertainment and real time graphics for Web, rich media, and multimedia. The current focus is the short form animated film.

CME Digital
1326 Stetson St.
Orlando, FL 32804
Phone: 321 662-8424
Email: chris@mindgel.com
URL: http://www.mindgel.com

Cole and Company

Area(s) of Specialization: Digital Media Production, Multimedia, Events Management, Sales/Marketing

Number of Employees: 15

Cole & Company specializes in international event management, video production, new product introductions, multimedia and sales and marketing programs. The company provides a full line of digital media production services, and creative services worldwide: video and film production and editing, multimedia, event production and management, public relations, and print support.

Cole and Company
654 Beacon St., Fifth Fl.
Boston, MA 02215
Phone: 617 236-4699
Fax: 617 236-0373
URL: http://www.cole-co.com

Collider, Inc.

Area(s) of Specialization: Computer Graphics, Video, Film, Animation

Number of Employees: 6+

Collider designs a full range of motion graphics, from broadcast and broadband to film and video.

Collider, Inc.
133 W. 19th St., 5th Fl.
New York, NY 10011
Phone: 646 336-9398
Fax: 646 349-4159
Email: mail@collidernyc.com
URL: http://www.collidernyc.com

Continuity Studios

Area(s) of Specialization: 3D Animation, computer assisted animation

Number of Employees: 20+

Continuity has developed various properties, of its own creation and others including Buckly o' Hare, Skeleton Warriors, CyberRad, Ms. Mystic, Nighthawk, etc. for TV and Comics. Neal Adams: the Sketch Book was compiled by Arlen Schumer from Continuity Studios. It spans Adams' comics career, revealing a wealth of unpublished works, Adam's thought process, and storytelling techniques.

Continuity Studios
4710 W. Magnolia Blvd.
Burbank, CA 91505
Phone: 818 980-8852
Fax: 818 980-8974
Continuity Studios
62 W. 45th Street, 10th Floor
New York, NY 10036
Phone: 212 869-4170
Fax: 212 764-6814
Email: nadams@earthlink.net
URL: http://www.nealadams.com

Corey Design Studios, Inc.

Area(s) of Specialization: 2D Animation Character Animation

Number of Employees: 5

The goal of Corey Designs Studio Inc. is to create, communicate, inspire, and entertain viewers with fun interactive animation and graphics. Coreytoons specializes in 2D Animation broadcast animation, Web design, and interactive services. Clients have included Fox Television and Nickelodeon.

Corey Design Studios Inc.
99 Main Street
Nyack, NY 10960
Phone: 914 365-1619
Fax: 914 365-3077
Email: studio@coreytoons.com
URL: http://www.coreytoons.com

Crawford Digital

Area(s) of Specialization: CGI, Multimedia, Animation

Number of Employees: 300+

Crawford Digital designs communications for commercials, documentaries, Web sites, and cable networks.

Crawford Digital
535 Plasamthe Company's Drive
Atlanta, GA 30324
Phone: 404 876-7149
Alt Phone: 800 831-8027
Fax: 404 892-3584

Email: Webmaster@crawford.coms
URL: http://www.crawford.com

Creative Logic Technologies, Inc.

Area(s) of Specialization: Traditional Animation, Video, Film

Number of Employees: 100+

Specializes in Business media productions, video production, Interactive CD/DVD Web site design and maintenance, Software design for school software and accounting.

Creative Logic Technologies, Inc.
2425 Commerce Ave.
Bldg. 2100, Suite 300
Duluth, GA 30096
Phone: 678 417-4057
Fax: 678 417-4041
Email: media@creativelogictech.com
URL: http://Creativelogictech.com

Creative Time

Area(s) of Specialization: Multimedia Production

Number of Employees: 6+

Creative Time produces visual arts exhibitions, theater, performing arts, and music at the foot of the Brooklyn Bridge. Creative Time/DNAid is a series of public art projects that address the implications of today's genetic research on the global futures.

Creative Time
307 7th Ave., Suite 1904
New York, NY 10001
Phone: 212 206-6674
Fax: 212 255-8467
Email: staff@creativetime.org
URL: http://www.creativetime.org

Creek & River

Area(s) of Specialization: Traditional Animation

Number of Employees: 100+

Creek & River matches the abilities and talents of individual freelancers with the creative needs of clients, delivering innovation and productivity in the most efficient and cost-effective manner.

Creek & River
One West St., Suite 100
New York, NY 10004
Phone: 646 274-1424
Email: info@cr-america.com
URL: http://www.cr-america.com

Crush Digital Video

Area(s) of Specialization: Digital Video Disc (DVD) Production and Services

Number of Employees: 15+

Crush Digital Video is a DVD Authoring Studio in New York City. Crush uses digital technology in the fields of entertainment, publishing and business. Crush Digital Video is an independent facility in existence to create DVD products for commercial use.

Crush Digital Video
147 West 25th Street, 4th fl.
New York, NY 10001
Phone: 212 989-6500
Fax: 212 645-9093
URL: http://www.crushdv.com

Curious Pictures

Area(s) of Specialization: CGI, Design, Animation, Television Production, Effects

Number of Employees: 50+

Curious Pictures is an international design and television production company producing comedy, graphically inspired live-action, special effects, graphics and animation of all types. The staff of directors, designers, artists and animators produces TV commercials, on-air graphics/titles and television programming. The company was founded in early 1993 as a division of Harmony Holdings, Inc.; there are branches in New York and San Francisco.

Curious Pictures
440 Lafayette Street
New York, NY 10003
Phone: 212 674-1400
Alt Phone: 212 674-7600
Fax: 212 674-0081
Email: info@curiouspictures.com
URL: http://www.curiouspictures.com

Curious Pictures San Francisco
1360 Mission Street Suite 201
San Francisco, CA 94103
Phone: 415 437-1400
Fax: 415 437-1408

Cutting Vision, Inc.

Area(s) of Specialization: Production and Post Production

Number of Employees: 10

Cutting Vision Inc. creates full resolution editing, graphic design and custom visual effects, as well as sound design with a fully digital record and mix suite. The company redigitizes clients' source material for an exact uncompressed online conform in both NTSC and PAL. The company's Audio Suite works the same way so that edits are instantly read by a 16 track AMS Neve Audiofile for accurate and fast loading to accommodate record and mix sessions.

Cutting Vision, Inc.
665 Broadway Suite 1201
New York, New York 10012
Phone: 212 533-9400
Fax: 212 533-9463
Email: info@cuttingvision.com
URL: http://www.cuttingvision.com

The Darnell Works Agency

Area(s) of Specialization: Sales/ Marketing

Number of Employees: 100+

The Darnell Works Agency launches and supports dynamic ventures worldwide, contacting media and analysts to introduce company executives and their subject-matter expertise for current news stories and to share breaking news, developing custom media distribution lists, authoring, editing and placing byline articles.

The Darnell Works Agency
643 Rocky Creek Rd.
Boone, NC 28607
Phone: 828 264-8898
Fax: 828 264-8813
Email: info@darnellworks.com
URL: http://www.darnellworks.com

Data Motion Arts

Area(s) of Specialization: Animation

Number of Employees: 15

Data Motion Arts has been creating computer animation and imagery for more than a decade. The company lists their specialty as blending emerging technologies with an artistic eye in ways that are humorous, entertaining, and informative.

Data Motion Arts
89 Fifth Ave., Suite 501
New York, NY 10003
Phone: 212 463-7370
Fax: 212 463-7820
Email: dma@dma-animation.com
URL: http://home.dti.net/dma/

Deep Blue Sea

Area(s) of Specialization: Film/Video Visual Effects and Animation

Number of Employees: 15+

Deep Blue Sea is a design, visual effects and animation house servicing national and international networks, advertising agencies and production companies. In addition to 3D animation, 2D animation and compositing, Deep Blue Sea also features a Cel animation department which has created spots for MTV, Pollo Tropical, Banesco Banks of Venezuela in addition to the Florida Lottery, McDonalds, and K-mart.

Deep Blue Sea
2850 Tigertail Ave.
Miami, FL 33133
Phone: 305 857-0943
Fax: 305 856-3692
Email: bstrohmeier@bvinet.com
URL: http://www.deepbluesea.com

Destiny Images

Area(s) of Specialization: Traditional Animation, Film, Video, Post Production

Number of Employees: 30+

Destiny Images creates properties centered around original educational animated series for international broadcast and the direct to video market.

Destiny Images, Inc.
4939 Teays Valley Rd.
Scott Depot, WV 25560
Phone: 304 755-1235
Fax: 304 755-1352
Email: jamie@destinyimages.com
URL: http://www.destinyimages.com

DIEHARD Studio

Area(s) of Specialization: Traditional Animation, Computer Animation, CGI

Number of Employees: 6+

DIEHARD Studio has created characters including Hamster Vice, Kid Caramel: Private Investigator, Black Zero: Mercenary Ant and Falcon Shadow.

Diehard Studio
P.O. Box 145
Glen Ridge, NJ 07028
Phone: 973 672-5897
Fax: 973 672-5897
Email: hunter@diehardstudio.com
URL: http://www.diehardstudio.com

Digital Production Solutions

Area(s) of Specialization: Traditional Animation

Number of Employees: 6+

Digital Production Solutions designs and implements cross-platform solutions in a range of new and traditional media for retail, education, entertainment, and enterprises.

Digital Production Solutions
520 BRd. St.
Newark, NJ 07102
Phone: 973 438-3640
Fax: 973 438-3640
Email: info@DigitalProduction Solutions.com
URL: http://www.digitalproduction solutions.com

Discreet Training Specialist

Area(s) of Specialization: Digital Media, 2D Animation, 3D Animation

Number of Employees: 6+

Provides training consulting for 3D animation, s max, and Autodesk VIZ. Production services available for 2D animation and 3D animation Design.

Design4today
1800 Westover Hills Blvd.
Richmond, VA 23225
Phone: 804 231-9918
Email: design4today@mindspring.com
URL: http://www.design4today.com

Digital Bunker

Area(s) of Specialization: CGI, Multimedia Design

Number of Employees: 2+

A graphic and multimedia design firm located in the Washington, DC area established in January, 1999. Their designers have over six years of designing for the Internet.

Digital Bunker
14001-C Saint Germain Drive #347
Centreville, VA 20121
Phone: 703 578-8581
URL: http://digitalbunker.net/

Digital Gothica

Area(s) of Specialization: Traditional
Animation

Number of Employees: 6+

Animation studio offering a wide range
of services.

Digital Gothica1654 Dahill Rd., Fl. 2
Brooklyn, NY 11223
Phone: 718 375-0816
Email: rocco@digitalgothica.com
URL: http://www.digitalgothica.com

Digital Nightmare Arts

Area(s) of Specialization: Traditional
Animation, 3D Animation, 2D Animation

Number of Employees: 6+

Digital Nightmare Arts creates 3D
animation on DVD or CD in the form of
designs, and interactive games for DVD,
DVD ROM, and CD-ROM.

Digital Nightmare Arts
P.O. Box 19204
Reno, NV 89511

Phone: 775 852-1801
Email: info@dnightmare.com
URL: http://www.dnightmare.com

DMA Animation

Area(s) of Specialization: Traditional
Animation, Web site Design, Television

Number of Employees: 6+

DMA Animation is an award-winning
studio creating animated content for
television, games, film and new media.
DMA offers services in: 2D Animation &
3D Animation Production, Character
Design/Development, Broadcast Design,
FLASH Animation as well as Web site
Design and Development.

DMA Animation
89 Fifth Ave., Suite 501
New York, NY 10003
Phone: 212 463-7370
Fax: 212 463-7820
Email: dma@dma-animation.com
URL: http://www.dma-animation.com

DNA Productions, Inc.

Area(s) of Specialization: Animation,
Production, Television

Number of Employees: 110+

DNA Productions, Inc. is a full-service animation company that has operated in Dallas, Texas since 1987. They serve the entertainment and commercial markets by providing 2D animation and 3D animation character design and animation. In addition, DNA is a creative resource providing script writing, directing and producing for animated series and features. DNA has contributed animation to a wide range of high-profile projects, including **Roseanne's "Saturday Night Special"** (Fox Television), **"The Weird Al Show"** (CBS), **"steve.oedekerk.com"** (NBC) and **"Nanna & Lil' Puss Puss"** (Showtime, Comedy Central, MTV).

DNA Productions, Inc.
2201 W. Royal Lane, Suite 275
Irving, TX 75063
Phone: 214 352-4694
Fax: 214 496-9333
URL: http://www.dnahelix.com

DreamEFFEX

Area(s) of Specialization: Animation, Web site Development, 3D Animation, 2D Animation

Number of Employees: 100+

Atlanta-based, DreamEFFEX studios provide innovative and creative solutions in Web site development, 3D animation, graphic design, and video production for the purpose of education & entertainment.

DreamEFFEX
3855 Drew Campground Rd.
Cumming, GA 30040
Phone: 678 513-2745
Email: info@dreameffex.com
URL: http://www.dreameffex.com

Dynacs Digital Studios

Area(s) of Specialization: Engineering Design and Analysis, Multimedia Digital Services, Marketing

Number of Employees: 15

Dynacs Digital Studios specializes in modeling the motion of flexible craft in space, to designing flight decks for the latest supersonic transports, to developing cryogenic test facilities, to restoring vintage film footage. Dynacs has a number of different locations: Houston, TX; Los Angeles, CA; Seattle, WA; KSC, FL; Cleveland, OH; Albuquerque, NM; Bangalore, India.

Dynacs Engineering Co., Inc.
35111 U.S. Highway 19 N., Suite 300
Palm Harbor, FL 34684
Phone: 727 787-1245
Fax: 727 787-2503
URL: http://www.dynacs.com

Dzignlight Studios

Area(s) of Specialization: Film/Video Digital Effects, CGI, Animation

Number of Employees: 3+

Founded in 1995 in Atlanta, GA, Dzignlight Studios offers digital special effects and computer graphics solutions to film and video professionals.

Dzignlight Studios
621 North Ave. NE #A100
Atlanta, GA 30308
Phone: 404 892-8933
Fax: 404 892-8991
Email: corporate@dzignlight.com
URL: http://www.dzignlight.com

Eagle Films

Area(s) of Specialization: Traditional Animation, Stop-motion, Animation, Film/Video

Number of Employees: 2+

Eagle Films specializes in video production, visual effects, and animation for the corporate-industrial, commercial, entertainment-gaming, and feature film markets. Techniques include: photorealistic computer animation as well as traditional methods such as matte painting, miniatures, stop motion animation, and pyrotechnics.

Eagle Films is owned by Producer/director/writer Philip Cook and is affiliated with professional associates covering film, video, and graphic production.

Eagle Films
2809 Marshall Street
Falls Church, VA 22042-2004
Phone: 703 237-8160
Fax: 703 237-8160
Email: philcook@eaglefilms.com
URL http://www.eaglefilms.com

Emagination-Media

Area(s) of Specialization: Traditional Animation

Number of Employees: 30+

Animation studio offering a wide range of services.

Emagination-Media
225 Andover Way
Nashville, TN 37221
Phone: 615 662-6540
Email: jblockhart@yahoo.com
URL: http://www.emagination-media.com

Empire Video, Inc.

Area(s) of Specialization: DVD and CD-ROM, Audio/Video Editing, Web Site Design

Number of Employees: 6+

Empire Video, Incorporated is a full-service film, video, interactive media, still photography and graphics design and production company. The company was founded on the premise that video provides the most effective means of conveying complex technical concepts or procedures. Initially concentrating on technical training productions shot in video, the company has diversified to include corporate promotional, direct marketing, training and public relations oriented projects, some of which have been shot in 16mm film. Empire continues to produce film and video for the public as well as the private sector. Projects have included programs directly for the office of the Secretary of Defense, and two (2) one hour documentaries for the U. S. Navy (through the Navy League of the United States) and the Arleigh Burke Leadership Foundation.

Empire Video, Inc.
7406 Alban Station Court
Suite A-118
Springfield, VA 22150
Phone: 703 866-1934
Fax: 703 866-1936
Email: EmpireInfo@empirevifdeo.com
URL: http://www.empirevideo.com

Engineered Multimedia, Inc.

Area(s) of Specialization: Interactive Multimedia and Web Development

Number of Employees: 24

Engineered Multimedia Inc. (EMi) develops Web and interactive media and has specialized expertise in science, engineering and instruction design to evaluate and identify clients' needs - and transfer that knowledge into the design, development and deployment of custom interactive solutions that can help solve business-critical problems. EMi's customized solutions for product launch, training, documentation, and sales and marketing share the common goal of maximizing the return on clients' investment by: Increasing revenue opportunities, decreasing the time it takes to reach business objectives, reducing training, sales and marketing costs, and Increasing competitive advantage. The company utilizes technologies such as: streaming content, Flash and 3D Animation, online collaboration, virtual reality, and interactive product simulation.

Engineered Multimedia, Inc.
One Meca Way
Meca Center Building
Norcross, GA 30093
Phone: 770 564-5610

Fax: 770 564-5611
Email: hr@engmm.com
URL: http://www.engmm.com

The Envision Group

Area(s) of Specialization: 3D Animation,
Imaging for Architecture, Broadcast
Television

Number of Employees: 4

The company produces interactive
design with a vision for new multimedia,
serving clients such as Dell, Time
Warner and Picture Television

The Envision Group
19 Stan Hope St.
Suite 3A
Boston, MA 02116
Phone: 617 266-0222
Fax: 617 266-0111
Email: jobs@eginteractive.com
URL: http://www.envision3D
Animation.com

EPI

Area(s) of Specialization: Multimedia
Development/Production/Marketing

Number of Employees: 100+

EPI Communications is a full-service
integrated marketing and graphics firm
specializing in the use of both new and
conventional communications media.
Creative services include the design and
development of Web sites, multimedia
presentations, corporate and training
videos, broadcast spots, print
advertisements, brochures, direct mail,
annual reports, corporate identification,
trade show exhibits and event staging.
Services include high-end prepress,
photographic laboratory, digital output,
exhibit and video production. EPI
Systems also offers digital graphics
systems integration, technical support
and onsite installation.

EPI Communications
8435 Helgerman Court
Gaithersburg, MD 20877
Phone: 301 990-2666
Fax: 301 230-2023
Email: sales@epicolorspace.com
URL: http://www.epi-net.com

Epic Software Group, Inc.

Area(s) of Specialization: Traditional
Animation, 3D Animation, Video

Number of Employees: 12+

The epic software group, Inc. is a 3D
animation and multimedia production
company comprised of over a dozen
talented artists, animators and
multimedia programmers. The business

was founded in 1990 and over the years has created interactive presentations; CD-ROM based electronic catalogs, kiosks, children's books and television commercials.

Epic Software Group, Inc.
710 Sawdust Rd.
The Woodlands, TX 77380
Phone: 281 363-3742
Fax: 281 292-9700
Email: epic@epicsoftware.com
URL: http://www.epicsoftware.com

Epiphany FX

Area(s) of Specialization: Traditional Animation, 2D Animation, 3D Animation

Number of Employees: 6+

Epiphany FX is a 2D Animation/3D Animation Company that works with outside clients to assist them in their animation needs.

Epiphany FX
2922 Mayfair Ave.
Westchester, IL 60154
Phone: 708 562-8049
Fax: 708 562-8049

Ernie Berger Animation

Area(s) of Specialization: Traditional Animation

Number of Employees: 6+

Award-winning computer animation and special effects studio; Telly and Aurora Awards for TV commercials featuring 3D animation characters; computer effects for independently produced movies.

Ernie Berger Animation
P.O. Box 148
Arnold, MD 21012
Phone: 410 757-8377
Email: Studio@ErnieBerger.com
URL: http://www.ErnieBerger.com

Fablevision Animation Studios

Area(s) of Specialization: Animation, Story-based Multimedia, CGI

Number of Employees: 8

FableVision Studios creates positive programming and story-based media for children and adults. Working closely with sister-company Cosmic Blender, a high-end script-to-finish production facility, FableVision creates stories using animation and multimedia.

Fablevision Animation Studios
44 Pleasant St.
Watertown, MA 02472
Phone: 617 926-1231

Alt. Phone: 800 240-3734
Fax: 617 924-3373
Email: Info@FableVision.com
URL: http://www.fablevision.com

Fantasimation Classic Animation

Area(s) of Specialization: 2D Animation

Number of Employees: 7

Fantasimation Animation Studios is a full-service animation production facility specializing in classic style cartoon animation. Located on Long Island, NY, employees write, board, animate, paint and edit productions in house. Fantasimation is a self-contained company that works on Development, Pre-pro, track breakdown, ink and paint, editing, compositing and Web design and Web cartoons.

Fantasimation Classic Animation
3601 Hempstead Turnpike
Levittown, NY 11756
Phone: 516 579-0609
Fax: 516 579-9409
Email: mike@fantasimation.com
URL: http://www.fantasimation.com

Fathom Studios

Area(s) of Specialization: Film, Television, and Computer Animation

Number of Employees: 120

The company creates visual imagery to add a visceral impact to presentations, broadcast spots, television shows, movies, and video games.

Fathom Studios
1800 Peachtree Street NW
Suite 250
Atlanta, GA 30309
Phone: 404 554-4050
Fax: 404 554-4051
Email: hr@fathomstudios.com
URL: http://www.fathomstudios.com

Faux Real, LLC

Area(s) of Specialization: Traditional Animation, Computer Animation

Number of Employees: 6+

Animation studio that creates traditional and computer animation.

Faux Real, LLC
2215 Little Lane
Arden, DE 19810
Phone: 302 529-1516
Fax: 302 529-7913
Email: hkalmus@fauxreal.com
URL: http://www.fauxreal.com

Film/Video Arts

Area(s) of Specialization: Film/Video, Editing, Multimedia Education, Equipment Rental

Number of Employees: 10

Founded in 1968, Film/Video Arts is a nonprofit media arts center in the New York region. Film/Video Arts provides an environment for courses, rent production equipment and edit projects to encourage interaction between producers – whether working on narrative features, documentaries, experimental work, shorts, industrials, cable programs, music videos or student projects.

Film/Video Arts
462 Broadway, Suite #520
New York, NY 10013
Phone: 212 941-8787
Fax: 212 219-8924
Email: info@fva.com
URL: http://www.fva.com

Finish

Area(s) of Specialization: Film/Video Editing, Post Production

Number of Employees: 20

Founded January 1st, 1994, Finish Digital Editing Arena is a full-service post production facility for high end digital editing in Boston along with random access off-line capabilities, plus supervision and coordination of any project including production graphics, audio, and film transfer.

Finish
162 Columbus Ave.
Boston, MA 02116
Phone: 617 292-0082
Fax: 617 292-0083
Email: cheryl.mckeever@finishedit.com
URL: http://www.finishedit.com

Fire Mist Media

Area(s) of Specialization: Logo Animation, 3D Animation Illustration, Simulations, Medical, Animation, Program Openers

Number of Employees: 1

Fire Mist Media, located in Philadelphia, PA, is an animation and graphics company owned by Jeff Brown who has had over 10 years experience in digital animation, photography, theatrical design (lighting and projections) and video. Customers speak directly to the animator. It is a resource for the small to medium sized production company or post house.

Fire Mist Media
Upper Darby, PA

Phone: 800 580-0701
Fax: 610 734-0705
URL: http://www.firemist.com

FlickerLab

Area(s) of Specialization: Traditional
Animation

Number of Employees: 30+

FlickerLab is a full-service animation
studio specializing in content
production for television and film, as
well as a wide range of commercial
work. Recent projects include two pilots
for Cartoon Network, a short cartoon
for Michael Moore's new film, a 40
episode Web series and numerous
national television spots.

FlickerLab
155 W. 20th
Fourth Fl.
New York, NY 10018
Phone: 212 560-9228
Fax: 212 560-9253
Email: info@flickerlab.com
URL: http://www.flickerlab.com

Flying Foto Factory, Inc.

Area(s) of Specialization: Animation,
Digital Production

Number of Employees: under 20

The company specializes in producing
digital 3D animation models,
visualizations and animation production
services, utilizing computer
visualization, animation and digital
production tools for delivering detailed
and accurate digital content for
education, medical and legal
visualizations, entertainment and
marketing applications. Flying Foto
Factory, Inc.

Flying Foto Factory, Inc.
P.O. Box 1166
107 Church Street
Durham, NC 27702
Phone: 919 490-1370
Alt. Phone: 800 682-3411
Email: kathyb@flyingfoto.com
URL: http://www.flyingfoto.com

Forged Images

Area(s) of Specialization: Traditional
Animation

Number of Employees: 6+

Forged Images produces high quality
educational and entertainment
programming for home, classroom, and
broadcast. Although primarily engaged
in their own productions, their studio
offers clients a full range of services for
broadcast, video, or multimedia. They
produce TV commercials, corporate/

industrial videos, training videos, educational programs, and documentaries.

Forged Images Productions
6 Davis Place
Bar Harbor, ME 04609
Phone: 207 288-5156
Email: info@forgedimages.com
URL: http://www.forgedimages.com

Front St.

Area(s) of Specialization: Audio, Video, Animation, Multimedia

Number of Employees: 6+

A multimedia/post production studio owned by Shin Kurokawa, a co-founder of an anime company, with hundreds of video, film, audio and music credits going back to the 80's. Specialties include VFX and DVD, audio/video remastering, restoration, rotoscoping, animation touch-ups/clean-up, matte creation, image processing, etc.

Front St.
Wilimington, NC 28401
Email: info@maximumoutputdesigns.com
URL: http://www.maximumoutput designs.com

4-Front Video Design, Inc.

Area(s) of Specialization: CGI, Multimedia Design

Number of Employees: 8

At 4-Front Design, Inc. prides itself in having a staff of artists and designers who are not only artistically talented, but can interpret concepts, find solutions and execute designs in a timely and cost efficient manner. Their ultimate goal to not only create outstanding designs that are visually appealing and communicate the goals of their clients, but do so in an environment that is friendly and supportive

4-Front Video Design, Inc.
1500 Broadway, 5th Floor
New York, NY 10036
Phone: 212 944-7055
Fax: 212 944-7193
URL: http://www.4-frontdesign.com

The Frank Barnhill Company

Area(s) of Specialization: Animation

Number of Employees: 3+

Creators of Dr. Huggie Bear, animated character serving medical professionals working with children.

The Frank Barnhill Company, LLC
1231 N. Limestone St.
Gaffney, SC 29342
Phone: 864 487-4911
Email: frank@drhuggiebear.com
URL: http://drhuggiebear.com

Frank Beach and Associates, Inc.

Area(s) of Specialization: Multimedia Production and Consultant

Number of Employees: 8+

Beach Associates is a communications and media production and consultation business headquartered in Arlington, Virginia, with an extension office in Lexington, Kentucky, and associates located throughout the United States.

Frank Beach and Associates, Inc.
2601-A Wilson Blvd.
Arlington, VA 22201
Phone: 703 812-8813
Fax: 703 812-9710
Alt Phone: 800-598-6567
Email: projects@beachassociates.com
URL: http://www.beachassociates.com

Fugu Labs

Area(s) of Specialization: Animation, Sound, CGI, Post Production

Number of Employees: 6+

High quality animation solutions that cover a wide range of project complexity and need. Character design. Storyboarding, background design and production. Sound and music creation.

Fugu Labs
P.O. Box 920102
Needham, MA 02492
Phone: 781 449-3954
Email: info@fugulabs.com
URL: http://www.fugulabs.com

Funline Animation

Area(s) of Specialization: Traditional Animation

Number of Employees: 6+

Funline Animation is a full animation studio based in New York City. They offer traditional cel animation, Web development, Flash animation and character design. The studio has been established since 1996 and is the joint endeavor of Helena Uszac, Krzysztof Giersz, Tonya Smay and Michael Perkins.

Funline Animation
636 Broadway, Suite 1009
New York, NY 10012
Phone: 212 375-1295
Fax: 212 477-0226

Email: funlineny@aol.com
URL: http://www.funlineanimation.com

Funny Garbage

Area(s) of Specialization: Print and Interactive Multimedia Design and Production

Number of Employees: 100

Funny Garbage is a full-service design and production company that has created Web sites, CD-ROMs, title graphics and print campaigns for clients ranging from The Cartoon Network, Compaq Computers, and Nike to Luaka Bop, The American Museum of Moving Image and ID Magazine. Funny Garbage creative directors began their artistic life as graffiti writers, painting on NYC subway cars and abandoned lots. Girardi became the creative director at the Voyager Company, a producer of CD-ROMs and laser discs.

Funny Garbage
73 Spring St.
Suite 605
New York, NY 10012
Phone: 212 343-2534
Fax: 212 343-3645
Email: newbusiness@funnygarbage.com
URL: http://www.funnygarbage.com

Garth Gardner Company, Inc.

Area(s) of Specialization: 2D Animation and 3D Animation Production, Publishing, Video Production, Consulting

Garth Gardner Company develops, publishes, and sells multimedia products in print and electronic media for the educational and professional markets worldwide. In addition, the company also provides services in the form of production and consultation in the areas of computer graphics, animation and multimedia. The company's clients include: Universal Records, Air Jamaica, Florida A&M University, Fashion Institute of Technology.

Garth Gardner Company, Inc.
5107 13th St NW
Washington, D.C. 20011
Phone: 202 541-9700
Fax: 202 541-9750
URL: http://www.gogardner.com

Gearboxx

Area(s) of Specialization: Web Design with Animation

Number of Employees: 20

Gearboxx provides Web and CD-based designs. The company provides services in Web site revision, multimedia authoring, script programming, or video and audio production for corporations, nonprofit organizations, government agencies and educational institutions.

Gearboxx
100 Executive Drive, Suite 200-G
Dulles, VA 20166
Phone: 703 904-9880
Fax: 703 783-0071
Email: support@gearboxx.com
URL: http://www.gearboxx.com

Giant Studios

Areas of Specialization: Motion Capture Production, Animation

Number of Employees: 25+

Giant Studios is the representative for Biomechanics Inc.'s Motion Reality 3D Animation motion capture production system for the entertainment marketplace. The Motion Reality proprietary tracking and analysis algorithms and suite of software allow 3D Animation professionals from around the world.

Giant Studios, Inc.
2160 Hills Ave.
Suite A
Atlanta, GA 30318
Phone: 404 367-1999
Fax: 404 367-8485

Email: rand@giantstudios.com
URL: http://www.giantstudios.com

Glasgow Media

Area(s) of Specialization: Animation, Video, 3D Animation, Web site Design

Number of Employees: 100+

Glasgow Media is a creative communications company that offers graphic design and Web development.

Glasgow Media
448 Hartwood Rd.
Fredericksburg, VA 22406
Phone: 540 286-2539
Fax: 540 286-0136
Email: dale@glasgowmedia.com
URL: http://www.glasgowmedia.com

G3 Enterprise

Area(s) of Specialization: Animation, Multimedia

Number of Employees: 10+

G3 Enterprise is full-service multimedia company located in Charlotte North Carolina. Specialties include: 2D Animation/3D Animation, Broadcast and Graphic Design, Post Production, Interactive Multimedia, Web Production, CD/DVD Authoring.

G3 Enterprise, Inc.
7520 E. Independence Blvd., Suite 400
Charlotte, NC 28227
Phone: 704 567-3060
Fax: 704 568-0199
Email: jgaris@g3enterprise.com
URL: http://www.g3enterprise.com

Gold Skeleton

Area(s) of Specialization: Animation, Multimedia

Gold Skeleton is a hub for organizing Chicago-based freelance animators into ready-made crews on a per-job basis.

Gold Skeleton Pictures
1231 Douglas Ave.
Flossmoor, IL 60422
Phone: 708 647-6079
Fax: 708 647-6097
Email: info@goldskeleton.com
URL: http://goldskeleton.com

GTV

Area(s) of Specialization: Multimedia Design, Production, Post Production, Marketing

Number of Employees: 7

GTV's office in Midtown Manhattan provides in-house capabilities for clients from conceptual design to a finished campaign. Services and equipment available at GTV include computer animation, D1, Beta SP, and Digital Beta editing, a blue screen insert studio stage with motion control animation stand, paintbox, cameras and lighting, as well as location shooting and art direction.

GTV
1697 Broadway # 404
New York, NY 10019
Phone: 212 262-2620
Fax: 212 262-4709
Email: sales@gtvnyc.com
URL: http://www.gtvnyc.com

Henninger Video

Area(s) of Specialization: CGI, Film/ Video, Sound, Multimedia

Number of Employees: 120

Begun in 1983, Henninger Video now houses Henninger Digital Audio, Henninger Design and Effects, Henninger Digital Captioning, and Henninger Studio Production Services. Henninger Video provides digital online editing (D2 and Digital Betacam), random access non-linear editing, digital audio mixing and design, graphic design and animation, Ultimatte 6 studio production capabilities, tape-to-tape color correction, and all digital closed captioning. Henninger Video serves networks, producers, and companies such as The Discovery Channel, Fox Television's America' Most Wanted, CBS News "60 Minutes," Gannett Company, and Guggenheim Productions.

Henninger Video
2601-A Wilson Blvd.
Arlington, Virginia 22201
Phone: 888 243-3444
Fax: 703 243-5697
URL: http://www.henninger.com

Hi-Wire

Area(s) of Specialization: Animation, CGI, Multimedia, Post Production

Number of Employees: 10+

Minneapolis-based HI-WIRE offers full-service content creation and postproduction services. The company's creative capabilities include editorial, film, video and audio, 3D animation and graphic design. One of the first companies in the country to offer HDTV services, Hi-Wire is dedicated to staying on the leading edge of technology.

Hi-Wire
555 Nicollet Mall, Suite 391
Minneapolis, MN 55402
Phone: 612 252-3900
Fax: 612 252-3939
Email: info@hi-wire.com
URL: http://www.hi-wire.com

Home Run Pictures

Area(s) of Specialization: Film/Video Production, CGI, Animation

Number of Employees: 5+

Home Run Pictures is involved in the production of computer generated imagery, creating animation for television programming, commercials, corporate video, special wide screen presentations, and interactive applications. The company utilizes computer based tools via a network of SGI workstations.

Home Run Pictures
100 First Ave., Suite 450
Pittsburgh, PA 15222
Phone: 412 391-8200
Fax: 412 391-1772
Email: infield@hrpictures.com
URL: http://www.hrpictures.com

House of Bliss

Area(s) of Specialization: Traditional Animation, Television, Video, Web site Design

Number of Employees: 4

House of Bliss is a complete creative studio. Blue does it all - from concept, design, scripting and storyboarding to graphics and animation for TV, film, video and the Web.

House of Bliss
4400 Bowser Ave. #101
Dallas, TX 75219
Phone: 214 219-0214
Email: blue@houseofbliss.com
URL: http://www.houseofbliss.com

The ID League

Area(s) of Specialization: Animation, Web site Design

Number of Employees: 6+

Full-service studio offering a wide range of creative services.

The ID League
17 Wedgewood Rd.
Natick, MA 01760
Phone: 508 651-0516
Email: csb@idleague.com
URL: http://www.idleague.com

Ill Clan Productions

Area(s) of Specialization: Animation, CGI, 3D Animation

Number of Employees: 6+

Studio that creates animation using real-time 3D animation rendering engines used in today's high-profile computer games.

Ill Clan Productions
236 Leondard St., #2
Brooklyn, NY 11211
Phone: 347 277-1920
Email: illbixby@illclan.com
URL: http://www.illclan.com

Image Group Design

Area(s) of Specialization: Post Production

Number of Employees: 500+

The Image Groups' visual effects division Image Design creates visual effects for cable and broadcast television, motion pictures and corporate communications. Image Design utilizes technical tools such as Discreet Logic Flames and Inferno; Quantel Hal, Harry and paintbox; Alias on Silicon Graphic and Apple work stations.

Image Group Design
401 5th Ave.
New York, NY 10016
Phone: 212 401-4981
Fax: 212 355-0523
Email: kennethb@neplnc.com
URL: http://www.image-group.com

Impact Studios

Area(s) of Specialization: Production, Business Communication, Multimedia

Number of Employees: 3

Impact Studios is a full-service business communications company.

Impact Studios
22 Elizabeth St.
Norwalk, CT 06854
Phone: 203 852-6550
Fax: 203 852-6553
Email: info@impactstudiostv.com
URL: http://www.impactstudiostv.com

Improv Technologies

Area(s) of Specialization: Multimedia Software Development and Distribution

Number of Employees: 40

Improv Technologies makes software to simplify digital content creation and distribution from high-end 3D animation and video game development to Internet production. They produce proprietary and patent-pending technologies to change how disparate forms of digital media and related applications integrate.

Improv Technologies
23 East 31st Street

14th Floor Penthouse
New York, NY 10016
Phone: 212 725-4590
Fax: 212 725-4390
Email: info@improv-tech.com
URL: http://www.improv-tech.com

The Ink Tank

Area(s) of Specialization: Animation, CGI, Film/Video

Number of Employees: 10-12

Founded in 1977, Ink Tank has worked 20 years in studio filmmaking. The company specializes in full-service animation, 2D animation, 3D animation, character animation, and commercial work. The company's primary markets are commercials, television, and feature films.

The Ink Tank
2 W. 47th St., 14th Floor
New York, NY 10036
Phone: 212 869-1630
Fax: 212 764-4169
Email: inktank@inktank.net
URL: http://www.inktank.net

Insight Research Group

Area(s) of Specialization: Animation, Sales/Marketing, Post Production, Web site Design

Number of Employees: 6+

This company's research helps clients gain a fresh perspective in developing media programs, new technology, consumer products, and marketing and branding strategies.

Insight Research Group
462 Broadway, Suite 510
New York, NY 10013
Phone: 212 343-9894
Fax: 212 343-9895
URL: http://www.insightresearch.biz

Interface Media Group

Area(s) of Specialization: CGI, Animation, Film/Video/Internet Production

Number of Employees: 52

Interface Media Group film, video and Internet related production services for professional communicators in the Washington, DC area since 1977. The company services include studio production and teleconferencing, graphic design, production of computer animation and visual effects, resolution, independent digital compositing, non-linear and tape based editing, film to tape transfer and tape to tape color correction, audio production and sound design, satellite and fiber optic transmission, duplication, distribution and world standards conversion, Internet related services and the development of specialized software products.

Interface Media Group
1233 20th Street, NW
Washington, DC 20036
Phone: 202 861-0500
Fax: 202 296-4492
Email: info@mail.interfacevideo.com
URL: http://www.interfacevideo.com

Intoons

Area(s) of Specialization: Performance Animation

Number of Employees: 30

InToons Performance Animation is a computer generated, interactive character animation system for design of a custom character, mascot or logo. IEG supplies equipment and personnel from a single monitor kiosk to a large video wall presentation. InToons promotes identity and corporate messages by allowing audiences to talk to and interact with the familiar character or logo at Trade Shows, Concerts, Stadiums or Business Meetings.

Intoons
371 Little Falls Rd.
Cedar Grove, NJ 07009-1250
Phone: 973 857-7242

Alt Phone: 888 446-8666
Fax: 973 857-8867
Email: intoons@plsstaging.com
URL: http://www.intoons.com

Interactive Alchemy

Area(s) of Specialization: Animation

Number of Employees: 6+

Interactive Alchemy Is a front-end Design & Consulting group, specializing in 3D animation and interactive Media. Animation services include custom Maya Solutions through MEL scripting, and Maya API consulting.

Interactive Alchemy, LLC
159 Rick Rd.
Milford, NJ 08848
Phone: 908 996-6278
Fax: 908 996-6405
Email: ialchemy@mac.com
URL: http://homepage.mac.comiAlchemy

Island Animation

Area(s) of Specialization: Animation, 2D Animation, 3D Animation, Post Production

Number of Employees: 6+

Island Animation is a 2D animation/3D animation production which specializes in character design, project development and production for TV, commercials, Web and interactive projects. Island Animation also offers online training in animation, character design and layout.

Island Animation
P.O. Box 9941
Savannah, GA 31412
Phone: 912 897-4557
Email: lanimate@hotmail.com
URL: http://www.awn.comtooninstitute

Italica Comics

Area(s) of Specialization: Traditional Animation

Number of Employees: 6+

A small animation studio offering a wide range of services.

Italica Comics
6 Coborca Way
Toms River, NJ 08757
Phone: 732 349-0244
Email: italicacomics@netzero.net
URL: http://www.italicacomics.com

The Jim Henson Company

Area(s) of Specialization: Multimedia, Film/Video Production, Publisher

Number of Employees: 600+

The Jim Henson Company is a private, independent multimedia production company; a top character licensors in the industry; and home to Jim Henson Television, Jim Henson Pictures and Jim Henson's Creature Shop; and a leading of children's books. The Creature Shop has received two Academy Awards, including one in 1996 for Best Visual Effects for the hit film, Babe, and the other in 1992 for the Henson Performance Control System.

The Jim Henson Company
117 East 69th Street
New York, NY 10021.
Phone: 212 794-2400 (NY)
Alt. Phone: 323 802-1500 (CA)
Fax: 212 570-1147
Email: fanmail@henson.com
URL: http://www.henson.com

John Lemmon Films

Area(s) of Specialization: Clay and Cel Animation

Number of Employees: 2

John Lemmons Films produces clay animation television commercials for clients across the U.S. including Pacific Bell, Dairy Queen, Farmhouse Foods, Cedar Point Amusement Park, the Coleman Company, IGA Supermarkets and Tandy corporation. The company recently completed interactive CD-ROM uses cel animation with clay backgrounds, and the studio has produced the package artwork for Interplay's hit videogame "Clay-Fighter."

John Lemmon Films
4921 Albemarle Rd. Suite 111
Charlotte, NC 28205
Phone: 704 532-1944
Fax: 704 566-1984
Email: jlemmon@jlf.com
URL: http://www.jlf.com

Judson Rosebush Company

Area(s) of Specialization: Multimedia Concept-Production, Programming/ Design

Number of employees: 5

The Judson Rosebush Company specializes in concept development, project planning and management, content creation, art direction, sound design, precise interactive navigation, software architecture and programming, and testing and mastering. The company's programmers, artists and designers work in multiple programming languages, major multimedia authoring tools, still and video imaging, and desktop publishing. Delivery methods include CD-ROM, World Wide Web and floppy disk.

Judson Rosebush Company
154 West 57th Street, Studio 826
New York, NY 10019
Phone: 212-581-3000
Fax: 212 757-8283
Email: info@rosebush.com
URL: http://www.rosebush.com

K Design

Area(s) of Specialization: Traditional
Animation

Number of Employees: 6+

K Design, is an award-winning digital
design studio specializing in the creation
of motion graphics, animation, digital
video and interactive software.

K Design
2150 Joshua's Path, Suite 10
Hauppauge, NY 11788
Phone: 631 232-3768
Fax: 631 232-3769
Email: info@kdesign.tv
URL: http://www.kdesign.tv

Kleiser-Walczak Construction Co.

Area(s) of Specialization: Film/
Commercial Animation, Effects,
Interactive Media

Number of Employees: 50+

Kleiser-Walczak Construction Co.
produces of computer generated
animation and visual effects for feature
films, special venue attractions,
commercials and interactive media. The
company has production studios in
Hollywood, Manhattan, and
Massachusetts (at MASS MoCA - the
Museum of Contemporary Art located
in the Northern Berkshires).

Kleiser-Walczak Construction Co./
Massachusetts
87 Marshall St., Bldng. 1.
North Adams, MA 01247
Phone: 413 664-7441
Fax: 413 664-7442
Email: marie@kwcc.com
URL: http://www.kwcc.com

Kleiser-Walczak Construction Co./New
York
23 W. 18th. St.
New York, NY 10011
Phone: 212 255-3866
Fax: 212 929-6747
URL: http://www.kwcc.com

Kosarin Productions, Inc.

Area(s) of Specialization: Traditional
Animation

Number of Employees: 6+

Animated TV series production, direction, script and development consultation, specializing in international co-productions. Pre-production services, including X-sheet animation direction, track reading, lip-sync timing. Full-service animation production of shorts, spots, interstitials.

Kosarin Productions, Inc.
316 12 St.
Park Slope, NY 11215
Email: kosarinprodsInc.@aol.com

Kristin Harris Design, Inc.

Area(s) of Specialization: Traditional Animation

Number of Employees: 6+

Kristin Harris Design, Inc. specializes in character design and animation for young children. Kristin Harris, Creative Director and Animator, has developed a style of 2D Animation that Incorporates a wonderful sense of color and clean bold style that speaks to children, but is appreciated by all.

Kristin Harris Design, Inc.
3035 Hazelton St.
Falls Church, VA 22044
Phone: 703 536-9594
Fax: 703 241-7463
Email: Kristin@kristinharrisdesign.com
URL: http://www.kristinharrisdesign.com

L.A. Bruell

Area(s) of Specialization: Video, Animation, Web Design.

Number of Employees: 5

L.A.Bruell is a full-service multimedia productions facility offering 3D Animation and 2D Animation computer animation, and world wide Web design. L.A. Bruell's animation and musical scores have appeared on television productions, movie trailers, interactive games, online services, technical and medical productions, and how-to videos. The company's roster of clients includes: McGraw-Hill, Nynex, PBS, The Cartoon Network, Ex-machina, Inc. Sudler & Hennesey and Intramed (Divisions of Young and Rubicam), The Big Apple Circus and The N.Y.C Police Department L.A.

L.A. Bruell
157 West 57th. St.
Suite 500
New York, NY 10019
Phone: 212 956-0800
Fax: 212 956-3807
URL: http://www.labruell.com

Loop Filmworks

Area(s) of Specialization: Cel Animation, Pixelation, Stop Motion, Live Action, DVD, Web Site Design

Number of Employees: 15+

LOOP Filmworks is involved in cel animation, stop motion, pixilation, live action, DVD and Web site design; they have been in existence 10 years.

Loop Filmworks, Inc.
45 Washington Street
Suite 602
Brooklyn, NY 11201
Phone: 718 522-LOOP (5667)
Fax: 718 522-5668
URL: http://www.loopfilmworks.com

Lovett Productions, Inc.

Area(s) of Specialization: Film/Video Production, Editing, CGI, Sound

Number of Employees: 10+

Located in the heart of New York's SoHo district, Lovett Productions is a fully equipped production and editing facility. The offices are equipped with Avid Media Composer 400 and 4000's, 3/4" and Beta dubbing machines, and computer graphics equipment and production office space. The company was founded in 1989 by Joseph F. Lovett, a 10-year veteran and producer at ABC News' 20/20.

Lovett Productions, Inc.
155 Sixth Ave. 10th Floor
New York, NY 10013-1507

Phone: 212-242-8999
Fax: 212-242-7347
Email: info@lovettproductions.com
URL: http://www.lovettproductions.com

Macquarium, Inc.

Area(s) of Specialization: Internal/External Communication Development and Management, Broadcast, Interactive Media, E-Commerce

Number of Employees: 120

Macquarium Intelligent Communications works in communications issues such as development and management of internal and external communications initiatives. The results are expressed through broadcast, interactive media, and Web-centric applications such as intranet, extranet, and e-commerce enterprise solutions.

Macquarium, Inc.
1800 Peachtree St. NW
Suite 250 Atlanta, GA 30309-2517
Phone: 404 554-4000
Fax: 404 554-4001
Email: info@macquarium.com
URL: http://www.macquarium.com

Magick Lantern

Area(s) of Specialization: Post Production, Editing, Design, CGI and Animation

Number of Employees: 20

Magick Lantern creates in the areas of post production, editing, design, CGI and animation.

Magick Lantern
750 Ralph McGill Blvd.
Atlanta, GA 30312
Phone: 404 688-3348
Fax: 404 584-5247
Email: post@magicklantern.com
URL: http://www.magicklantern.com

Magnetic Image Video

Area(s) of Specialization: Video Post Production, Editing, Internet Television

Number of Employees: 10

Magnetic Image Video is a post production facility, located in lower Manhattan. Established in 1989 to serve the broadcast television community with analog linear, digital linear and non-linear editing. The company also services the international community with Internet television.

Magnetic Image Video
119 Fifth Ave.
Fourth Floor
New York, NY 10003
Phone: 212 598-3000
Fax: 212 228-3664
Email: contact@magneticimage.com
URL: http://www.magneticimage.com

MBC Teleproductions

Area(s) of Specialization: Video, 3D Animation

Number of Employees: 5+

MBC Teleproductions is a full-service production house, capable of creating video and film from the 30 second commercial to the live sporting event. included in the spectrum is industrial, promotional, and educational video, long and short format broadcast production, 2D and 3D Animation graphics, animation, and multimedia design.

MBC Teleproductions
3000 East Rock Rd.
Allentown, PA 18103
Phone: 800 232-3024
Fax: 610 797-6922
Email: info@mbctv.com
URL: http://www.mbctv.com

M&M Creative Services

Area(s) of Specialization: CGI, Web Design, Advertising

Number of Employees: 22

M&M offers services in Graphic Design, Web Design and Advertising.

M&M Creative Services
P.O. Box 2457
Tallahassee, FL 32316
Phone: 888 224-1169
Fax: 850 656-9146
Email: mark@thinkcreative.com
URL: http://www.mmdg.com

Manhattan Transfer

Area(s) of Specialization: Commercial/ Television Post Production, Visual Effects and Design

Number of Employees: 150

Manhattan Transfer creates visual effects, design, telecine grading, and editorial work for television commercial clients and episodic series. Additionally Manhattan provides feature film dailies service. The company works on projects ranging from complete channel redesigns to visual effects for high-end commercials. The artists, designers, and animators at Manhattan Transfer work with Discreet's flame, inferno, and fire, Quantel's Henry, HAL and Paintbox, and CG software such as SoftImage | 3D Animation, Alias Maya, 3D Animation Studio Max, Renderman, and a host of proprietary software tools created by in-house programmers.

Manhattan Transfer
545 Fifth Ave.
New York, NY 10017
Phone: 212 687-4000
Fax: 212 687-2719
URL: http://www.mte.com

Marvel Entertainment Group, Inc.

Area(s) of Specialization: Animation, Comic Books

Number of Employees: 100+

Marvel Entertainment Group is a comic book company and the creators of Marvel Comics. Creators of X Men, Spider Man, and the Ave.ngers.

Marvel Enterprises, Inc. a character-based entertainment company with operations in five divisions: licensing, toys-via its Toy Biz division, comic book and trade publishing, entertainment and the Internet. Through the ownership of over 3,500 proprietary characters, Marvel licenses its characters in a wide range of consumer products, services and media such as feature films, television, the Internet, apparel, video games, collectibles, snack foods and promotions.

Marvel Entertainment Group, Inc.
387 Park Ave. South
New York, NY 10016
Phone: 212 696-0808
Email: pgitter@marvel.com
URL: http://www.marvel.com

Mechanism Digital

Area(s) of Specialization: Film/ Television Digital Effects and Animation, Interactive Media

Number of Employees: 4+

Mechanism Digital Inc. is a New York City based production studio creating high-end digital effects and animation for film, television, and interactive media. The company's creative team specializes in 3D Animation character animation, morphing, visualization, effects, and blue screen techniques. Actively involved in the 3D Animation computer art industry, Mechanism is a charter member of ECDC (East Coast Digital Consortium) and the company principal Lucien Harriot serves on the Board of Directors for New York City ACM SIGGRAPH.

Mechanism Digital
514 W 24th Street, 3rd Floor
New York, NY 10011
Phone: 646 230-0239
Fax: 646 336-8395
Email: Gabe@MechanismDigital.com
URL: http://www.mechanismdigital.com

Media Blasters

Area(s) of Specialization: Animation, 3D Animation, 2D Animation

Number of Employees: 30+

Full-service animation studio.

Media Blasters
265 W. 40th St., Suite 700
New York, NY 10018
Phone: 212 532-1688
Fax: 212 532-3388
Email: jsirabella@media-blasters.com
URL: http://www.media-blasters.com

Media Education Foundation

Area(s) of Specialization: Film/Video Research and Production for Education

Number of Employees: 8

MEF is involved in media research and production of resources to aid educators and others in fostering analytical media literacy, which is essential to a democracy in a diverse and complex society. MEF has produced some 15 videos on issues of media representation and gender, race, violence, and other concerns. It was founded in 1991 by Professor Sut Jhally with the video, Dreamworlds: Desire, Sex, and Power in Music Video.

Media Education Foundation
26 Center Street
Northampton, MA 01060
Phone: 800-897-0089
Fax: 413 586-8389
URL: http://www.mediaed.org/

Metastream (View Point)

Area(s) of Specialization: Production/ Development 3D Animation Streaming (MTS), 3D Animation Modeling.

Number of Employees: 100 at Headquater

Metastream is a provider of Internet visualization technology and 3D Animation rendering services for online retailers. The company provides a cohesive association of technology, tools, and partners that enable e-tailers to create photorealistic 3D Animation product presentation and sales Web sites. Metastream develops a streaming 3D Animation file format called MTS, and sells annual licenses to broadcast in this format to e-commerce sites. In addition, Metastream provides services for creating the 3D Animation content and integrating it into a customer's site. In November 2000 Metastream acquired view point and changed the company name to View Point.

Metastream
498 Seventh Ave., Suite 1810
New York, NY
Phone: 212 201-0800
Fax: 212 201-0801
Email: info@viewpoint.com
URL: http://www.metastream.com

MetriGnome Visual

Area(s) of Specialization: Traditional Animation

Number of Employees: 6+

Professional 2D Animation and 3D Animation digital animation group specializing in "Digital Puppetry." Quick turnaround and competitive pricing on animated television spots, short films, Web animation, and episodic television.

MetriGnome Visual
112 Poole Ct.
Knightdale, NC 27545
Phone: 919 3686612
Email: info@metrignome.net
URL: http://www.metrignome.net

Mindvisions (3D Animation Studios)

Area(s) of Specialization: Web Design, Electronic Presentations, Interactive CDs, Online Marketing

Number of Employees: 6

3D Animation Studios is now Mindvisions, working in multimedia development with in-house design, technical, and promotions.

Mindvisions
18859 Emerald City Highway
Destin, FL 32541
Phone: 800 334-9427
Alt Phone: 850 837-6166
Fax: 850 837-0254
Email: service@MindVisions.com
URL: http://www.mindvisions.com

MindWorks Multimedia

Area(s) of Specialization: Video/CD-ROM/DVD/Web-Based Production, Post Production

Number of Employees: 60

MindWorks Multimedia's teams produce communications applications for training, marketing, product information, corporate overview, and television commercials. The company covers network sports shows, bilingual training and human resource programs, plus marketing and commercial productions for industries such as textiles, pharmaceuticals, automotive, finance, and many more. The company has video production facilities including non-linear edit suites (Avid and Edit systems), linear BetaSP, graphics design suite, 20x20 studio, and complete BetaSP field camera packages.

MindWorks Multimedia
P.O. Box 1058
Siler City, NC 27344
Phone: 919 806-0411
Fax: 919 806-0779
Email: growland@mwmm.com
URL: http://www.mwmm.com

Mitch Butler Company, Inc.

Area(s) of Specialization: CGI, Animation, Video Production, Web Design

Number of Employees: 33

Mitch Butler Company, Inc. is a 3D Animation computer animation firm. The services provided include: complete 3D Animation and 2D Animation, video production and Web design. Clients include corporations such as Viewpoint Datalabs, Hewlett-Packard, Micron Technology, as well as advertising agencies like Elgin Syferd Drake, WRC Advertising and The Johnson Company. For 3D Animation modeling and animation The company uses Newtek's Lightwave 3D Animation for Windows NT. The company also uses a network of Pentium and Pentium II systems, including one Intergraph Pentium II 300Mhz with an Intense 3D Animation Pro 2200 display card, and utilizing Speed Razor for video editing and DPS Perception for video output.

Mitch Butler Company, Inc.
23 East 31st Street, 14th floor
New York, NY 10016
Phone: 212 725-4590
Fax: 212 725-4390
Email: mitch@mitchbutler.com
URL: http://www.mitchbutler.com/

Motion Image

Area(s) of Specialization: Film/Video Production, CGI, Multimedia, Sound, Animation

Number of Employees: 6

Motion Image is a Film and Video Production Company creating visual media for broadcast, corporate, and multimedia. The company's services include production and support for film, video, graphics, 2D animation/3D animation, and audio design. The company provides production, design and compression services for multimedia projects.

Motion Image
2140 S Dixie Hwy, Suite 306
Coconut Grove, FL 33133
Phone: 305 859-2000
Fax: 305 859-2412
Email: info@motionimage.com
URL: http://www.motionimage.com

Moviemice

Area(s) of Specialization: Traditional Animation, Television, Video

Number of Employees: 3+

High quality 2D animation and design for over 30 years with the animation on hundreds of commercials, short films, TV shows and features

Moviemice
645 Brinton's Bridge Rd.
West Chester, PA 19382
Phone: 610 793-9587
Email: moviemice@aol.com

Multimedia Productions

Area(s) of Specialization: Web design

Number of Employees: 1+

Multimedia Productions creates Web design and links on the Internet.

Multimedia Productions
50 West Main Street
Merrimac, MA 01860
Phone: 508 346-0641
URL: http://world.std.com/~ldjackso/
Email: ldjackso@world.std.com

MuseArts

Area(s) of Specialization: Animation, Web site Design

Number of Employees: 6+

MuseArts is an award-winning Web development team specializing in animation, interactivity, databases, and Web design.

MuseArts, Inc.
41 Cedar St.
Brattleboro, VT 05301
Phone: 802 254-0129
Email: info@musearts.com
URL: http://www.musearts.com

Nick Digital

Area(s) of Specialization: Traditional Animation, CGI, Visual Effects

Number of Employees: 6+

Nick Digital is a full-service production facility offering innovative CGI design, animation and visual effects for all of MTV Networks' channels as well as other companies. They handle all stages of production - from initial design to the execution of pre-designed work - creating distinctive, tailored work that complements each client's brand. Offices in Burbank and New York.

Nick Digital
1515 Broadway – 10th Fl.
New York, NY 10036
Phone: 212 846-6156
Fax: 212 846-1711
Email: nickdigital@nick.com
URL: http://www.nickdigitallabs.com

Nick Ericson Studio

Area(s) of Specialization: Special Effects/ Animation Production

Number of Employees: 5+

NES is a full-service animation and Post Production studio, located in the Flatiron District of Manhattan, creating high-quality special effects for commercial, broadcast and film productions. The company's styles range from highly stylized 2D animation-design to photo-realistic 3D animation.

Nick Ericson Studio
127 West 25th Street
New York, NY 10001
Phone: 212 337-0089
Fax: 212 337-0169
URL: http://www.nickstudio.com

Oculus

Area(s) of Specialization: Film Post Production, Design and Effects, CGI

Number of Employees: 100+

Oculus services the New York Film community. Oculus offers services from simple scene retouching to complicated visual effects. The Oculus team creates of natural and unnatural phenomenon, digital compositing, non-linear editing, audio sweetening and mixing, title design, rig removal and visual effects supervision.

Oculus
220 East 42nd Street
New York, NY. 10017
Phone: 212 393-2255
Fax: 212 818-0655
URL: http://www.oculus.com/

Olive Jar Studios, Inc.

Areas of Specialization: Film Stop-motion Animation and Traditional Cell Animation

Number of Employees: 60

Founded in 1984, Olive Jar Studios, Inc. is a design and film production studio specializing in animation techniques that include mixed-media, stop-motion, CG, cel, drawn, and live action/special effects.

Olive Jar Studios, Inc.
35 Soldiers Field Place
Boston, MA 02135
Phone: 617 783-9500
Fax: 617 783-9544
URL: http://www.olivejar.com

O'Plenty Animation Studios

Area(s) of Specialization: Traditional Animation, CGI

Number of Employees: 5

O'Plenty Animation is an independent animation studio in Long Branch. The studio's founder and executive producer, Chris Larson has been a part of projects such as "Ren & Stimpy," MTV' S "Liquid Television" and Weird Al Yankovic's Grammy nominated Jurassic Park Video. O'Plenty Animation specializes in traditional character animation. The studio was founded in 1995 and produced a Merrill Lynch training film that combined hand drawn cel animation, CGI and live action. The artists that contribute to O'Plenty have worked on Disney's "Aladdin," "The Prince & The Pauper," "Pocahontas," "Fantasia Continued," "Fa Mulan," "Hercules" And "Runaway Brain" as well as Turner's "Cats Don't Dance" and "Iron Giant."

O'Plenty Animation Studios
&605 Second Ave.
West End, NJ 07740
Phone: 732 714-7517
Fax: 732 714-7516
Email: oplenty@oplenty.com
URL: http:.'.'www.oplenty.com

Ovation Media Group

Area(s) of Specialization: Animation, Web site Design, Post Production, Film, Video

Number of Employees: 6+

Ovation Media Group is a creative design firm providing entertainment and business communication through interactive media and creative design. Services include animation, 3D Animation modeling, content writing, presentations, interactive multimedia, Web development, creative outsourcing, and creative/strategic consulting.

Ovation Media Group
11323 Georgetown Circle
Tampa, FL 33635
Phone: 813 891-6749

Email: info@ovationmediagroup.com
URL: http://www.ovationmediagroup.com

Oxygen Media, Inc.

Area(s) of Specialization: Television

Number of Employees: 300+

Studio offering Animation Production, Television Studio, Short Films, Television Series.

Oxygen Media, Inc.
75 Ninth Ave.
New York, NY 10011
URL: http://www.oxygen.com

Perspective Studios

Area(s) of Specialization: Traditional Animation

Number of Employees: 6+

Perspective Studios provides high-end motion capture and animation solutions to the entertainment industry.

Perspective Studios
3200 Expressway Dr. South
Islandia, NY 11749
Phone: 631 232-1499
Fax: 631 232-2655
Email: consulting@perspective
studios.com
URL: http://www.perspectivestudios.com

Palace Production Center

Area(s) of Specialization: Film/Video, Sound, CGI, Animation

Number of Employees: 25-50

PPC houses television, film, and multimedia creative artists. The company works in network specials as well as home video series. The New Media Group creates content for the World Wide Web while the Riverside Stage Company produces readings of new American plays featuring some of the new and established playwrights on the Broadway scene today.

Palace Production Center
29 N. Main St.
South Norwalk, CT 06854
Phone: 203 853-1740
Fax: 203 855-9608
URL: http://www.palacedigital.com

The Pixel Factory, Inc.

Area(s) of Specialization: Computer Graphics, Animation, and Design Development and Production

Number of Employees: 8-20

The Pixel Factory creates computer graphics, animation, and design. The company offers a range of creative services to coordinate productions from start to finish.

The Pixel Factory, Inc.
P.O. Box 618413
Orlando, FL 32861-8413
Phone: 407 839-1222
Fax: 407 839-1235
Email: info@pixfactory.com
URL: http://www.pixfactory.com

Pixel Liberation Front, Inc.

Area(s) of Specialization: Digital Production, Animation, CGI, Visual Effects

Number of Employees: 8

PLF is a visual effects company, pre-visualization and 3D animation integration in addition to 3D animation and virtual environments creation. With offices in both New York and Los Angeles Pixel Liberation Front is a coast to coast full-service digital production house.

Pixel Liberation Front, Inc.
New York
150 W. 28 St. #1003
New York, NY 10001
Phone: 212 239-1455
Fax: 212 239-3201
Pixel Liberation Front, Inc.
Los Angeles
1316 Abbot Kinney Blvd.

Venice, CA 90291
Phone: 310 396-9854
Fax: 310 396-9874
Email: plf@thefront.com
URL: http://www.thefront.com

Pixel Soup

Area(s) of Specialization: Design for Television/Video/CD-ROM/Internet

Number of Employees: 2

Pixel Soup is a design firm specializing in designing logos and complete identity packages, or creating a complete news, kids or promotion package unique to the company's station. The staff is comprised of designers, producers, photographers, editors, 3D animation animators and model makers. The staff designs, produces and composites much of the work at Pixel Soup on high-end desktop animation systems.

Pixel Soup, Inc.
28 South Main Street
Sharon, MA 02067
Phone: 781 784-5540
Fax: 781 784-0565
Email: stuart@pixelsoup.com
URL: http://www.pixelsoup.com

Planet Three Animation Studio

Area(s) of Specialization: 3D Animation, Visual Effects for Video/Film

Number of Employees: 5

Planet Three Animation Studio, started by Joe F. Jarman, offers animation and visual effects for the film and broadcast industries. Tools include a network of: Silicon Graphics (SGI) workstations, Alias|Wavefront Maya with Maya F/X, Power Animator with Advanced Animation and Power Modeling modules. Clients include: Lucasfilm, Ltd., Seasonal Films, Renaissance Pictures, Wilmington Regional Film Commission, DuPont Films (List of Credits). From creating completely synthetic characters and seamlessly integrating them into an environment, to creating photorealistic pyrotechnic and visual effects, the studio solves visual problems for directors and producers.

Planet Three Animation Studio
1223 North 23rd Street
Wilmington, NC 28405
Phone: 910 343-3720
Fax: 910 343-3722
Email: jarman@planet3animation.com
URL: http://www.planet3animation.com

R/GA's new media producer at the studio's recording facilities. Courtesy of Garth Gardner Photo Archive.

Paper 2 Pixel Creative Group, Inc.

Area(s) of Specialization: Animation, Graphic Design, 3D Animation, Website Design

Number of Employees: 25+

Paper 2 Pixel Creative Group, Inc. is a unique design company that blends world-class creativity and strategic problem solving into a group of services. Primary service areas Include Design (Environmental Design, Graphic Design, 3D Animation Modeling, Web Design, Product Design, Branding & Identity, etc.), Multimedia (Animation, Interactive Media, Web Development, Video Production, etc.), Consulting (Creative Ideation Workshops, Strategic Consulting, Project Management, etc.), and Web Hosting.

Paper 2 Pixel Creative Group, Inc.
8009 Birman St.
Maitland, FL 32751
Phone: 321 356-4815
Email: info@p2pcg.com
URL: http://www.paper2pixel.com

PaperForge

Area(s) of Specialization: Animation

Number of Employees: 6+

PaperForge is a design and animation service for corporate clients. PaperForge specializes in character design, presentations, corporate cartoons, print, and 2D animation GIF and Flash animation.

PaperForge
54 Heatherdell Rd.
Ardsley, NY 10502
Phone: 914 693-2356
Email: pfontaine2@hotmail.com
URL: http://
paperforge.homestead.comhomepage.html

Post Modern Editorial, Inc.

Area(s) of Specialization: Film/Video Editing, Post Production

Number of Employees: 10

Since 1989, Post Modern owner has utilized AVID for non-linear editing.

Post Modern Editorial, Inc.
4450 Peachtree Lakes Dr., Suite 100
Duluth, GA 30096
Phone: 678 405-0066
Fax: 678 405-0070

Email: info@post-modern.com
URL: http://www.post-modern.com

Primal Screen

Area(s) of Specialization: Animation, Sound, Television

Number of Employees: 6+

Primal Screen creates animation, sound, and broadcast design.

Primal Screen
550 Ralph McGill Blvd.
Atlanta, GA 30312
Phone: 404 874-7200
Fax: 404 874-7224
Email: scream@primalscreen.com
URL: http://www.primalscreen.com

Rab-Byte Computer Graphics, Inc.

Area(s) of Specialization: 3D Animation and Computer Graphics

Number of Employees: 3

Rab-Byte Computer Graphics Inc. has a complete paint and animation facility that produces 3D animation photo-realistic animation. The company has two full-service graphic libraries.

Rab-Byte Computer Graphics, Inc.
452 Wilson Ave.
Lindenwold, NJ 08021
Phone: 800 229-0184
Fax: 856 627-6492
Email: info@rab-byte.com
URL: http://www.rab-byte.com

Razorfish

Area(s) of Specialization: Web Site
Design, Interface Design

Number of Employees: 1,600
(worldwide)

Razorfish plans, designs and builds
products and services for Web site
design and interface design. Services
include: Post Production, Editing,
Design, CGI and Animation.

Razorfish-New York
32 Mercer Street
New York, NY 10013
Phone: 212 966-5960
Alt. Phone: 800 950-IDEA
Fax: 212 966-6915
Email: careers@sbigroup.com
URL: http://www.razorfish.com

Razorfish-Boston
101 Main Street
Cambridge, MA 02142
Phone: 617 250-2500
Fax: 617 250-2501

The Reel Score

Area(s) of Specialization: Animation,
CGI, Video, Television

Number of Employees: 10+

Original music composition for Film
and Video with the addition of sound,
efx, and foley for Flash and QuickTime
animation.

The Reel Score
63 S. Huntington Ave.
Jamaica Plain, MA 02130
Phone: 617 738-8835
Email: info@thereelscore.com
URL: http://www.thereelscore.com

Red Car

Area(s) of Specialization: CGI,
Commercial Production and Post
Production

Number of Employees: 30

The staff at Redcar New York consists of
graphics artists, sound designers, and
type stylists. The company's clientele
includes: Wieden & Kennedy, Leo
Burnett (leoburnett.com), Young &
Rubicam (yandr.com), and Nike.

Red Car-New York
196 Mercer St.
Penthouse

New York, NY 10012
Phone: 212 982-5555
Fax: 212 982-7179
Email: jenniferl@redcar.com
URL: http://www.redcar.com

Registered Films

Area(s) of Specialization: Film/Video
Production, Sound, Animation

Number of Employees: 4+

Registered Films is a film and television production company in New York City offering film and video production. The company has a 15,000 sq. ft. studio, equipped with 2 film stages, 2 online non-linear video editing suites, full broadcast graphics, a voice-over booth and a Protools audio sweetening and mixing room. Digital is the post production division of (r) Films offering online and off-line digital editing, effects, compositing, 2D animation and 3D animation. Plus staff and freelance artists, animators, and editors. Registered Films produces television commercials, television programs, documentaries and corporate video projects as well as offering international production services.

Registered Films
214 W 29th Street
New York, NY 10001

Phone: 212 714-0111
Email: mbrassert@registeredfilms.com
URL: http://www.registeredfilms.com

Replica Technology

Area(s) of Specialization: 3D Animation
Modeling, CD-ROM Production

Number of Employees: 1

Based in North Collins, New York, REPLICA Technology is a 3D animation content developer of high quality 3D animation objects and CD-ROM collections. 3D animation collections are used with consumer photo-imaging and business productivity software packages. Collections are also used with commercial 3D animation modeling, rendering and animation software. Each CD-ROM includes hundreds of models, scenes, textures and pre-rendered browser images of many models.

Replica Technology
4650 Langford Rd.
North Collins, NY 14111
Phone: 716-337-0621
Fax: 716-337-0701
Email: sales@replica3D Animation.com
URL: http://www.replica3D
Animation.com

R/GA Digital Studio

Area(s) of Specialization: Interactive Design, Digital Production

Number of Employees: 160

R/GA Digital studios consist of two major departments-R/GA Interactive and R/Greenberg Associates. Established in 1993, R/GA Interactive is a strategic design agency that creates Web sites, kiosks, CD-ROM and games for companies. With over 20 years experience R/Greenberg Associates is an Academy Award-winning digital production company that creates visual effects, 3D Animation graphics, design and motion graphics.

R/GA Interactive
350 West 39th Street
New York, NY 10018
Phone: 212 946-4000
Fax: 212 946-4010
Email: heidi@rga.com
URL: http://www.rga.com

Right Purdy Pictures

Area(s) of Specialization: Traditional Animation

Number of Employees: 6+

Starting with film and stop motion animation, Right Purdy pictures has done commercials, industrial and educational films, with short subject animation shown on MTV, HBO and Public Television.

Right Purdy Pictures
221-13th St. Northwest
Cedar Rapids, IA 52405
Phone: 319 366-4784
Email: rightpurdy@earthlink.net

Rhinoceros Visual Effects

Area(s) of Specialization: 3D Animation

Number of Employees: 60

Rhinoceros Visual Effects and Design is a MultiVideo Group/Gravity company. The MultiVideo Group, Ltd. owned and associated companies include New York-based Rhinoceros Editorial and Post, Cool Beans Digital Audio, Wall to Wall Films and WAX Music and Sound Design. Associated international companies include Gravity Effects in Tel Aviv, and Digital Renaissance in Oberhausen, Germany.

Rhinoceros Visual Effects
Multi Video Group Ltd.
50 E 42nd Street
New York, NY 10017
Phone: 212 697-4466
Fax: 212 972-0702
URL: http://www.rhinofx.com/

Rhinodesign

Area(s) of Specialization: Computer graphics and design

Number of Employees: 25+

Rhinodesign develops Internet strategies. The company offers media services including new media production, graphic design, Web hosting, on-site training, and maintenance, as well as full-service integrated marketing.

Rhinodesign
1439 Park Hill Lane
Escondido, CA 92025
Phone: 760 604-6453
Email: info@rhinodesign.com
URL: http://www.rhinodesign.com

Royal Vision Productions

Area(s) of Specialization: 3D Animation Computer Animation

Number of Employees: 2

Royal Vision Productions, located in South Florida, has been in business since August 1998 and has designed work for different organizations, including churches, schools, educational supply companies, Web entrepreneurs and biomedical engineering companies. The company designs graphics for Web pages, specializes in graphic mediums such as logo design, print, photo retouching, and multimedia.

Royal Vision Productions
12850 S.R. 84 #8-25
Davie, FL 33325
Phone: 954 916-1980
URL: http://www.rvproductions.com

Service Group, Inc.

Area(s) of Specialization: Web Site Design and Implementation, Digital Prints, Animation, CT Legislation

Number of Employees: 6

Service Group, Inc. offers complete design and implementation of Web sites from basic home page creation to complete multimedia sites.

Service Group, Inc.
P.O. Box 799
Glastonbury, CT 06033
Phone: 800 432-9706
Fax: 800 432-9706
URL: http://www.servgrp.com

Sixus1 Media Solutions

Area(s) of Specialization: Animation, Video, Film, CGI

Number of Employees: 100+

Full-service studio.

Sixus1 Media Solutions
10515 McPherson St., Suite D
Indianapolis, IN 46280
Phone: 317 574-8805
Email: lgarner@sixus1.com
URL: http://www.sixus1.com

Sonalysts Studios, Inc.

Area(s) of Specialization: Interactive
Multimedia, Operations Research,
Software Development, Program
Management, System Engineering

Number of Employees: 450+

Sonalysts Incorporated, is a
multidisciplinary, employee-owned
corporation, involved in interactive
multimedia, operations research,
software development, program
management and system engineering.

Sonalysts Studios, Inc.
215 Parkway North
P.O. Box 280
Waterford, CT 06385
Phone: 800.526.8091
Fax: 860 447-0669
Email: Recruiting@Sonalysts.com
URL: http://www.sonalysts.com

Sound Company of New York, Inc.

Area(s) of Specialization: Traditional
Animation

Sound Company of New York, Inc.
150 W. 56th St., Suite 3807
New York, NY 10019
Phone: 212 459-0655
Fax: 212 459-0655

Source W Media

Area(s) of Specialization: CGI, Electronic
Media, Production, Printing

Number of Employees: 100

Source W Media has 110-year history as
Westinghouse's source for graphic
design, electronic media, production and
printing. Source W is an integrator of
communications technology, content,
and design.

Source W Media
New Media Division
11 Stanwix Street
Pittsburgh, PA 15222
Phone: 877 268-9224
Alt Phone: 412 624-3600 or 412 829-
6300
Fax: 412 829-6321
URL: http://www.source-w.com

Spicer Productions

Area(s) of Specialization: Film/Video Production and Post Production, Interactive Multimedia, Animation, CGI

Number of Employees: 40

Spicer Productions is a film and video communications company in Baltimore, Maryland, providing creative and production services which include a large studio, digital post production, graphics, 3D animation, multimedia, digital audio, duplication and Web design.

Spicer Productions
1708 Whitehead Rd.
Baltimore, MD 21207
Phone: 410 298-1200
Fax: 410 298-5151
Email: bill@spicerpro.com
URL: http://www.spicerpro.com

Spot

Area(s) of Specialization: Film/Video

Number of Employees: 10

Spot works in film and video. Clients include ad agencies Hill Holliday, Arnold, Ingalls, HMME, Clark Goward, and Mullen. They follow spots from Carl's and Larry's Avid cuts through film to tape, online and mix.

Spot
45 Newbury Street
Suite 444
Boston, MA 02115
Phone: 617 267-9565
Fax: 617 267-4703
Email: Larry@spoteditorial.com
URL: http://www.editatspot.com

ST45

Area(s) of Specialization: Traditional Animation, Film, Post Production

Number of Employees: 3+

A small independent studio, ST45 specializes in modeling, rigging and animating 3D animation characters for stills video and film.

ST45
1433 S. 1600 East
Preston, ID 83263
Phone: 208 852-0650
Email: artists@st45.com
URL: http://www.st45.com

Stone Soup

Area(s) of Specialization: Traditional Animation

Number of Employees: 6+

Stone Soup is Located in Houston, Texas and has been in operation since 1992.

Stone Soup produces cel animation, 2D animation & 3D animation, for the Broadcast, Advertising and Corporate Communications Industries internationally. Equipped with the latest in digital tools, Stone Soup provides film & video output as well digital content for Web and electronic distribution.

Stone Soup
2640 Fountain View Dr., Suite #127
Houston, TX 77057
Phone: 713 278-0342
Fax: 713 278-0074
Email: ssoup@ssoup.net
URL: http://ssoup.net

Studio X

Area(s) of Specialization: Animation, 3D Animation, Television

Number of Employees: 6+

Studio X is a small 3D animation modeling and animation house that has created content for broadcast, games and architectural clientele throughout the U.S.

Studio X
1 Lakewood Dr.
Norwalk, CT 06851
Phone: 203 846-8682
Fax: 203 846-8728
Email: xalex@optonline.net
URL: http://www.studio-x.com

Successful Images

Area(s) of Specialization: Educational and Commercial Film/Video/CD Production

Number of Employees: 7+

Successful Images employees include directors, writers, cinematographers, editors and digital artists. The company is involved in developing training videos, educational CD's, Marketing presentation, special interest films and commercials.

Successful Images
111 S.W. 6th. Street
Fort Lauderdale, FL 33301
Phone: 954 467-7200
Fax: 954 467-5411
Email: ruchel@successfulimages.com
URL: http://www.successfulimages.com

Summer Kitchen Studio

Area(s) of Specialization: Animation

Number of Employees: 2+

Summer Kitchen Studio is an animation production company specializing in hand-rendered techniques including clay-on-glass, a technique that has the quality of molten stained glass, or an animated fingerpainting; stop-motion; cut-outs; xerography; and an array of other styles. The studio's work has been featured in festivals and on television worldwide. The company has been commissioned by ITVS (the Independent Television Service) to create five new animated interstitial spots for kids to be broadcast nationally on PBS children's programming.

Summer Kitchen Studio
44 Bollinger Rd.
Elverson, PA 19520
Phone: 610 286-7818
Email: summerkitchen@netreach.net
URL: http://www.netreach.net/
~summerkitchen/

Sunbow Entertainment

Area(s) of Specialization: Children's Television Production, Animation

Number of Employees: 25

Sunbow Entertainment is a production company that makes animated children's television. The New York office consists of the management team and Los Angeles office is where actual animation production is done. Sunbow Entertainment develops an idea, produces it to sell, and distributes it all over the world, then markets it and merchandises it. They are a division of Sony.

Sunbow Entertainment
100 Fifth Ave., 3rd Floor
New York, NY 10011
Phone: 212 886-4900
Fax: 212 366-4242
URL: http://www.sonymusic.com

Sunburst Technology

Area(s) of Specialization: Digital Educational Software Production and Publication

Number of Employees: 150

Sunburst Technology is a division of Houghton Mifflin Company engaged in creating and publishing teaching materials. About half of the company's products are computer-based programs for grades K-12 that include, among others, problem solving, early learning, tools, language arts, and mathematics. The remaining half of the products are video programs for grades K-12 that include conflict resolution, self esteem, drug education, sex education, and success skills.

Sunburst Technology
101 Castleton Street
Pleasantville, NY 10570
Phone: 914 747-3310
Fax: 914 747-4109
Email: service@nysunburst.com
URL: http://www.sunburst.com

Susan Brand Studio, Inc.

Area(s) of Specialization: CGI, Interactive Media Design, Animation

Number of Employees: 3+

With ten years experience in traditional animation and special effects, Susan Brand formed Susan Brand Studio, Inc. in 1995 to produce design and animation for children's software. In 2000, the studio moved to Maplewood, New Jersey and offers consulting services for Web-based projects.

Susan Brand Studio
82 Courter Ave.
Maplewood, NJ 07040
Phone: 973 275-9244
Fax: 973 275-4710
Email: info@susanbrand.com
URL: http://www.susanbrand.com

Tbdesign

Area(s) of Specialization: Traditional Animation, Production, 2D Animation, 3D Animation

Number of Employees: 6+

Animation studio that provides custom, on-site 3D animation which focuses on modeling, materials, and lighting production techniques.

Tbdesign
207 Sagamore Ave.
Portsmouth, NH 03801
Phone: 603 431-4334
Email: tedb@tbmax.com
URL: http://www.tbmax.com

Teleduction, Inc.

Area(s) of Specialization: Broadcast and Educational Film/Video Production and Distribution

Number of Employees: 8+ (freelance)

Teleduction, an independent production company based in Wilmington, Delaware, has produced and distributed programs to broadcast and educational audiences. Teleduction titles range in content from issue-oriented public affairs programs and cultural/historical documentaries to narrative children's programming. The company is also producing independent programs for national audiences on PBS, Nickelodeon, A&E, The History Channel and BRAVO.

Teleduction, Inc.
305 A Street
Wilmington, DE 19801
Phone: 302 429-0303
Fax: 302 429-7534
Email: info@teleduction.com
URL: http://www.teleduction.com

Terminal Side F/X Studios

Area(s) of Specialization: Animation

Number of Employees: 5

Terminal Side F/X Studios is a freelance Computer Animation provider.

Terminal Side F/X Studios
6507 The Lakes Drive
Raleigh, NC 27609
Phone: 919 676-6959
Email: mike.cosner@tsfx.com
URL: http://www.tsfx.com

Texturelighting

Area(s) of Specialization: Animation

Number of Employees: 6+

Creative Visualization and 3D Animation for Broadcast, Medical, Scientific, Games, Architectural, and Legal projects.

Texturelighting
255 Harvard Rd.
Stow, MA 01775
Phone: 978 823-0934
Email: Robert@texturelighting.com
URL: http://www.texturelighting.com

THTFCT

Area(s) of Specialization: Traditional Animation

Number of Employees: 1+

THTFCT is a one man shop that pulls in a variety of other freelancers as necessary to complete a project (often through my affiliation with Brand Central Station http://URL: http://www.brandcentralstation.com).

THTFCT
416 Pine St.
Burlington, VT 05401
Phone: 802 658-4267
Email: info@THTFCT.com
URL: http://www.THTFCT.com

Two Animators

Area(s) of Specialization: Traditional Animation, 3D Animation, Television, Graphic Design

Number of Employees: 2+

Two Animators is a professional animation and design company that specializes in Traditional and Flash animation. They create highly imaginative state-of-the-art animations, for use on Web sites, in video games, and on television.

Two Animators
P.O. Box 3174
Mercerville, NJ 08610
Phone: 609 581-6670
Email: cartoons@twoanimators.com
URL: http://www.twoanimators.com

Trace Digital Animation

Area(s) of Specialization: Traditional
Animation, Film, Video, Web site Design

Number of Employees: 6+

Full-service studio offering a full range
of creative services.

Trace Digital Animation
107 Inglewood Ct.
Charlottesville, VA 22901
Phone: 434 984-4239
Fax: 434 984-5490
Email: art@traceholo.com
URL: http://www.traceholo.com

Tribune Broadcasting

Area(s) of Specialization: Multimedia,
CGI

Number of Employees: 40,000+

A division of Tribune Media Services,
Tribune Broadcasting provides
information and entertainment products
to newspapers and electronic media.

TMS syndicates and licenses comics,
features and opinion columns, television
listings, Internet, online and wire
services, and advertising networks.

Tribune Creative Services Group
435 North Michigan Ave.
Chicago, IL 60611
Phone: 312 222-9100
Fax: 312 527-1118
Email: chennessey@tribune.com
URL: http://www.tribune.com

TZ-NY

Area(s) of Specialization: CGI,
Interactive Multimedia, Marketing

Number of Employees: 250

TZ works in the development of
network, cable and interactive marketing
and communications.

TZ-NY
460 West 42nd Street
New York, NY 10036
Phone: 212 564-8888
Fax: 212 967-0691
URL: http://www.telezign.com

Unbound Studios

Area(s) of Specialization: Multimedia,
CGI

Number of Employees:

Unbound works with film and television production combined with game and Web design, Flash animation and programming capabilities.

Unbound Studios
242 W. 27th Street, 3rd Floor
New York, NY 10001
Phone: 212 414-9866
Fax: 212 412-9068
Email: info@unboundstudios.com
URL: http://www.unboundstudios.com

Universal Studios

Area(s) of Specialization: Multimedia

Number of Employees: 1,000+

Universal Studios is a diversified entertainment company in motion pictures, recreation, television and home-based entertainment. Universal Studios owns Universal Music Group. Core businesses are Universal Pictures, Universal Studios Recreation Group, Universal Television and Networks Group, Universal Studios Consumer Products Group and Spencer Gifts, DAPY, GLOW!. In addition, the Corporate division has a number of other opportunities including: Universal Studios Online, Universal Studios Information Technology (IT) and Universal Studios Operations Group.

Universal City Florida
1000 Universal Studios Plaza
Orlando, Florida 32819-7610
Phone: 407 363-8080
Fax: 407 224-7987
URL: http://www.universalstudios.com

Unreel Pictures, Inc.

Area(s) of Specialization: Traditional Animation, Film, Television

Number of Employees: 10+

Animation studio that provides the following services: TV & Film Production Budgeting, 3D Animation Previsualization, On Set Real-time Composting Metadata & Post Production Supervision, Real-time, 3D Animation On-Air Graphics Systems, Integration, Camera Tracking Solutions, Retroreflective, Keying Studio Build Out.

Unreel Pictures Inc.
1375 Boardman St.
Great Barrington, MA 01230
Phone: 413 644-0256
Fax: 413 644-0257
Email: paul@unreel.com
URL: http://www.unreel.com

Vapor Post

Area(s) of Specialization: Film/Video Production and Post Production: Sound, Editing, Animation, Effects

Number of Employees: 8+

Vapor Post offers clients high quality video production. All field footage is recorded directly to Digital Betacam. The footage is then edited on digital non-linear workstations for a pure Digital Betacam product. Vapor Post offers everything, from a team of professionals, to a top of the line "post Boutique." In addition to a post production facility, Vapor Post offers a ProTools 24 Audio Suite and has both high quality 3D animation and digital effects.

Vapor Post
71 NW 29th Street
Miami, FL 33127
Phone: 305 438-9333
Fax: 305 438-2888
Email: info@vaporpost.com
URL: http://www.vaporpost.com

Vegamation

Area(s) of Specialization: Traditional Animation

Number of Employees: 6+

Vegamation is a Graphic Design, Illustration, Web Design and 3D Animation Modeling business.

Vegamation
194 Sixth St.
Harrison, NJ 07029
Phone: 973 204-1324
Email: shaotemp@earthlink.net
URL: http://www.vegamation.com

Venture Productions

Area(s) of Specialization: Film/Video Production and Post Production

Number of Employees: 45+

Venture Productions is a Florida-based company started in 1979. Since its inception, Venture has expanded from sole-proprietor field production company to one of the largest full-service production companies in the southeast, with a full-time stag of over 45 employees.

Venture Productions
2095 N. Andrews Ave.
Pompano Beach, FL 33069
Phone: 954 971-4100
Fax: 954 971-4090
URL: http://www.ventureproductions.com

Video Solutions

Area(s) of Specialization: Video/Film Design, Production, Marketing, and Distribution

Number of Employees: 3+

Established in 1991, Video Solutions was created to provide companies, trade associations, non-profit organizations and individuals with video production services. Headquartered in the Washington, DC Area, Video Solutions focuses on three primary communications areas: 1. Promotional & Marketing Programs including Membership, Recruiting, Fundraisers and Public Relations programs, Direct Mail, Video Brochures, Trade Show Demos, and Broadcast & Cable TV Commercials. 2. Events and Presentations such as public speakers and presentations, video news releases, and private functions. 3. Instructional and Training Videos consisting of On-the-Job Training and Professional Development, Instructional "how to" Programs, and Issue Awareness and Public Relations pieces.

Video Solutions
P.O. Box 25484
Alexandria, VA 22313
Phone: 703 683-5305
Fax: 703 683-5307

Email: staff@thevideosolution.com
URL: http://www.thevideosolution.com

Video Tape Associates

Area(s) of Specialization: CGI, Video Production and Post Production, Multimedia

Number of Employees: 50

Headquartered in Atlanta, VTA serves clients from advertising agencies, production companies, television stations, networks, and corporations. The Atlanta facility is a video post production center.

Video Tape Associates
1575 Sheridan Rd. NE
Atlanta, GA 30324
Phone: 404 634-6181
Alt Phone: 800 554-8573
Fax: 404 320-9704
Email: glenn.martin@vta.com
URL: http://www.vta.com

ViewPoint Studios

Area(s) of Specialization: Corporate Identity, Promotion, Program Graphics, Visual Effects, Animation

Number of Employees: 23

ViewPoint's team of art directors and compositing artists integrates graphics and animation with live action material to produce seamless visual effects, using technology like Flame, Hal Express, Abekas and Pluto. The animation studio also uses Maya and Alias PowerAnimator to create imagery.

ViewPoint Studios
140 Gould Street
Needham, MA 02494
Phone: 781 449-5858
Fax: 781 449-7272
Email: jobs@viewpointcreative.com
URL: http://www.viewpointstudios.com

VFX Studio

Area(s) of Specialization: Traditional Animation

Number of Employees: 6+

Luminetik 3D Animation and VFX Studio is a New York based animation studio right in the heart of Gotham city. Luminetik's clients include feature film, commercial, broadcast, and long form feature & television clients. Luminetik's partners have worked in some of the top studios on the west coast and New York and bring their expertise to Luminetik's Proprietary Pipeline. As the audience for 3D animation and Visual Effects changes, Luminetik is constantly adapting to the marketplace with cutting edge technologies.

VFX Studio
535 W. 34th St.
New York, NY 10001
Phone: 646 792-2565
Fax: 646 792-2566
Email: Luminetik@Luminetik.com
URL: http://www.Luminetik.com

Wave Works Digital Media

Area(s) of Specialization: Television/ Commercial Sound, Video Effects, Animation

Number of Employees: 25

A new media company creating sound tracks for television and radio commercial spots. The company is also equipped to do post production video effects and 3D animation computer animation.

Wave Works
1100 N. Glebe Rd. 100
Arlington, VA 22201
Phone: 703 527-1100
Fax: 703 527-1308

Wave Works
1301 Beverly Road
McLean, VA 22101
Phone: 703 506-1600
Fax: 703 506-0223

Email: jbloch@waveworks.net
URL: http://www.waveworks.net

WDDG

Area(s) of Specialization: Web Design and Development

Number of Employees: 15

WDDG is a full-service Web architecture and design group. The company is focused on designing Web sites utilizing technology such as Flash 4, dynamic systems and innovative strategy.

WDDG
511 Canal Street, 4th Floor
New York, NY 10013
Phone: 212 219-9222
Fax: 212 219-3426
Email: jeffrey@wddg.com
URL: http://www.wddg.com

The Weber Group

Area(s) of Specialization: Communication Multimedia

Number of Employees: 100+

The Weber Group is public relations firm specializing in immediate, interactive and information-driven new media. The Weber Group works in Marketing PR, Brand and Reputation Management, Global Public Relations Management, Public Affairs, Investor Relations, and Media and Presentation Training.

The Weber Group
Worldwide Headquarters
101 Main Street
Cambridge, MA 02142
Phone: 617 661-7900
Fax: 617 661-0024
The Weber Group/Greater Washington, DC Area
2300 Clarendon Blvd.
Arlington, VA 22201
Phone: 703 351-5620
Fax: 703 351-5616
Email: iiswish@microsoft.com
URL: http://www.Webergroup.com

Wachtenheim/Marianetti

Area(s) of Specialization: Traditional Animation, 2D Animation

Number of Employees: 6+

Animation studio that creates all types of 2D animation traditional animation.

Wachtenheim/Marianetti, LLC
341 Grand Blvd.
Scarsdale, NY 10583
Phone: 914 725-6835
Fax: 914 725-6835
Email: david@WManimation.com
URL: http://www.WManimation.com

Wild Hare Studios

Area(s) of Specialization: Traditional Animation

Number of Employees: 6+

Wild Hare Studios is a full-service television, Internet and film animation production house comprised of award winning animation directors who have produced commercial animation for broadcast, television series, and original show development. Wild Hare's complete line of innovative animation services includes traditional cel animation, illustration, conceptual sketches, character design, plotting and scripting, storyboards, digital ink and paint, sound design, computer compositing, Web design and special effects.

Wild Hare Studios
763 Trabert Ave., Suite D
Atlanta, GA 30318
Phone: 404 352-3673
Fax: 404 352-3768
Email: harry@wildharestudios.com
URL: http://www.wildharestudios.com

Women Make Movies, Inc.

Area(s) of Specialization: Film/Video, Film Distribution

Number of Employees: 15

Women Make Movies is a multicultural, multiracial, non-profit media arts organization which facilitates the production, promotion, distribution and exhibition of independent films and videotapes by and about women. Women Make Movies was established in 1972 to address the under representation and misrepresentation of women in the media industry. The organization provides services to both users and makers of film and video programs, with a special emphasis on supporting work by women of color. Women Make Movies facilitates the development of feminist media through Distribution Services and a Production Assistance Program.

Women Make Movies, Inc.
462 Broadway, Suite 500WS
New York, NY 10013
Phone: 212 925-0606
Fax: 212 925-2052
Email: info@wmm.com
URL: http://www.wmm.com

Wreckless Abandon

Area(s) of Specialization: Commercial and Entertainment Animation

Number of Employees: 20+

Wreckless Abandon Studios is a production company that specializes in clay animation, stop-motion production and 3D animation computer animation for the commercial and entertainment industries. The company produces non-violent family and children's programming and provides complete services including development, creative, production, effects and post production.

Wreckless Abandon
17 Connecticut South Dr.
East Granby, CT 06026
Phone: 860 844-7090
Fax: 860 844-7095
Email: info@wrecklessabandon.com
URL: http://www.wrecklessabandon.com

Zander's Animation Parlour

Area(s) of Specialization: Animation, Commercial Campaigns

Number of Employees: 2+

Zander's Animation Parlour is a commercial animation production company producing commercial campaigns. The company's client list includes Kraft, Fisher Price, 7UP, Burger King, Parker Bros., Chase Visa, HBO, Hasbro, Club Med and Cinemax and over fifty animated commercials for AT&T's ongoing " True Voices" 1996 television campaign. ZAP is recognized for 2D animation, classical animation techniques, live action productions and special effects projects. ZAP has produced music videos for EMI Records and Def Jam Records. Zander produced "Gnomes," a 60 minute CBS TV special, as well as an AIDS Awareness PSA campaign for the AD Council featuring Melissa Etheridge.

Zander's Animation Parlour
118 E. 25th. St., Tenth Fl.
New York, NY 10010
Phone: 212 477-3900
Fax: 212 674-7171
Email: info@zanderproductions.com
URL: http://www.zandersanimation.com

Zero Degrees Kelvin

Area(s) of Specialization: Computer Animation, Design

Number of Employees: 2+

ZDK has created logos and commercials for such clients as Arm and Hammer, Johnson and Johnson and several other corporations. The company uses advanced 3D animation computer graphics software programs to design and create animation.

Zero Degrees Kelvin
304 Hudson St.
New York, ny 10013
Phone: 718 222-5047
Fax: 212 791-2599

Email: WebRequest@jdhci.com
URL: http://www.zerodegreeskelvin.com/

ZFx, Inc.

Area(s) of Specialization: 3D Animation for Web Sites

Number of Employees: 13

ZFx is a technology company creating 3D animation for Web site. ZFx developed the OZX software, enabling the development and deployment of custom complex interactive Web sites and Internet-based applications.

ZFx, Inc.
999 Executive Park Blvd
Suite 301
Kingsport, TN 37660
Phone: 1-866-640-0500
Fax: 423 392-1758
Email: contacts@zfx.com
URL: http://www.zfx.com

ZKAD Productions

Area(s) of Specialization: 2D Animation and 3D Animation

Number of Employees: 12

ZKAD Productions is a U.S. based company utilizing technology and custom hardware and software to create 3D animation and music. The company works with broadcasters such as: the BBC, Channel 4 UK, PBS, ABC, NBC, CBS and the FOX owned BSkyB network.

ZKAD Productions
43 North Court
North East, MD 21901
Phone: 410 287-7483
Fax: 410 287-4391
Email: vynny@zkad.com
URL: http://www.zkad.com

Zooma Zooma

Area(s) of Specialization: Commercials, Music Videos, Short Films

Number of Employees: 7+

A bi-coastal production company specializing in commercials, music videos and short films. Established 8 years ago, Zooma Zooma is a production company for young filmmakers to showcase talent.

Zooma Zooma
11 Mercer Street, 3rd floor
New York, NY 10013
Phone: 212 941-7680
Fax: 212 941-8179
Email: lori@zoomazooma.com
URL: http://www.zoomazooma.com

Central U.S.

2112 F/X

Area(s) of Specialization: Traditional Animation, Digital Video, 3D Animation

Number of Employees: 6+

3D Animation for Web, CD, and DVD delivery. Specializing in 3D animation, Flash character animation, and digital video.

2112 F/X
2801 Denton Tap Rd.
Lewisville, TX 75067
URL: http://www.2112fx.com

Adtech Animation and Graphic Design

Area(s) of Specialization: Integrated Design for Electronic Media (Web, Video, Film, Multimedia)

Number of Employees: 2

Adtech is a communications electronic media. Technical capabilities include: particle systems and generation, image morphing, blob metamorphosis, natural phenomenon such as fog & water, lattice deformations, magnets, collisions, ray tracing with reflection, refraction and shadows, rotoscoping, bump mapping, texture mapping, environmental mapping, object metamorphosis, inverse kinematics, programmable painterly effects, glass and chrome effects, gleams, glows, multiple digital overlays, airbrush effects, embossing, blends, tints, translucency, non-linear transformations, multiple object deformations, and fractals. Adtech is an SGI based studio working with a variety of 3D Animation and 2D Animation systems including Synergy Custom 3D Animation Software, Houdini 3D Animation Procedural Animation software.

Adtech Animation and Graphic Design
8220 Commonwealth Drive, Suite 201
Eden Prairie, MN 55344.
Phone: 612 944-6347
Fax: 612 944-5643
Email: sales@adtechInc.com
URL: http://www.adtechInc.com

AniMagic Productions

Area(s) of Specialization: Traditional Animation

Number of Employees: 6+

AniMagic Productions, LLC was founded in 1997 to provide superior digital graphics to the architectural, commercial and virtual set markets. In a short time, the firm has evolved into a leading visualization technology provider with a national client base and award-winning portfolio.

AniMagic
1307 Washington Ave., Suite 604
St. Louis, MO 63103
Phone: 877 408-6738
Fax: 314 436-0343
Email: info@aniprod.com
URL: http://www.aniprod.com

Animation Closet, LLC (The)

Area(s) of Specialization: Traditional Animation

Number of Employees: 6+

Animation studio offering a wide range of services.

Animation Closet, LLC (The)
1304 Westmeadow Dr.
Beaumont, TX 77706
Phone: 409 866-2031
Email: gjball@animationcloset.com
URL: http://www.animationcloset.com

ArmAve.rse Armatures

Area(s) of Specialization: Traditional Animation

Number of Employees: 6+

ArmAve.rse Armatures provides stop-motion animation supplies to professional and student animators worldwide. A variety of adaptable, interchangeable pieces and kits combine to form affordable ball-and-socket armatures for any creature or object imaginable.

ArmAve.rse Armatures
906 East Walnut St.
Lebanon, IN 46052
Phone: 765 483-6455
Email: info@armAve.rse.com
URL: http://www.armAve.rse.com

TGWB, Inc.

Area(s) of Specialization: Computer Animation and Visualization

Number of Employees: 3

TGWB, INC. creates presentation graphics, photo-realistic animated walkthroughs, multimedia simulations, and other visual aids to visualize the three-dimensional qualities of client's projects.

TGWB, Inc.
8325 Forestview Ct.
Frankfort, IL 60423
Phone: 815 685-5755

Email: animation@tgwb.com
URL: http://www.tgwb.com

Astropolitan Pictures, Inc.

Area(s) of Specialization: Digital Effects, 3D Animation, Graphics, and Editing

Number of Employees: 5+

Astropolitan is a Chicago-based film and television production and Post Production company that offers a range of services from digital effects and 3D animation, computer animation to online editing and original music. Their award-winning staff has created visuals for projects with Sony Electronics, Coca-Cola, Motorola, MTV and Paramount Pictures.

Astropolitan Pictures, Inc.
P.O. Box 13128
Chicago, IL 60613
Phone: 773 935-7960
Fax: 773 935-7970
Email: info@astropolitan.com
URL: http://www.astropolitan.com

Atlantis Studio of Designs

Area(s) of Specialization: Animation

Number of Employees: 3+

Small privately owned company on the Gulf Coast, specializing in 2D animation, classical animation, visual development, and non traditional (clay, stop motion) animated shorts.

Atlantis Studio of Designs
3501 Smith Rd.
Nashville, IN 47448
Phone: 812 988-6165
Fax: 812 988-0881
Email: mystudio57@yahoo.com

Atomic Imaging

Area(s) of Specialization: Film/Video Production, Digital Imaging, Multimedia, CGI

Number of Employees: 12+

Atomic Imaging started in 1985 as a film and video production house in Chicago. With facilities in Chicago, Las Vegas and Barcelona, Atomic Imaging is international and full-service. The company works on feature films, national television programs and commercials, major live events, interactive multimedia, Web pages, computer graphics and animation.

Atomic Imaging World Headquarters
1501 N. Magnolia Ave.
Chicago, IL 60622
Phone: 312 649-1800
Fax: 312 642-7441

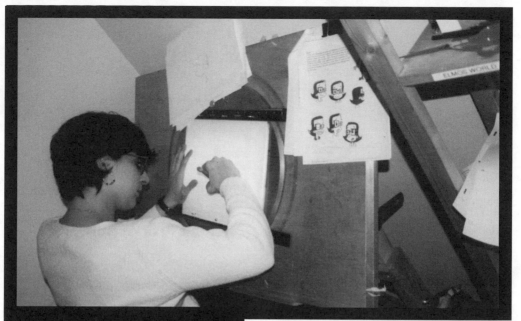

Cel animator at Curious Pictures in NY on the production of HBO's "A Little Curious". Courtesy of Garth Gardner Photo Archive.

Inking a scene at Curious Pictures for HBO's "A Little Curious". Courtesy of Garth Gardner Photo Archive.

Email: aigar@atomicimaging.com
URL: http://www.atomicimaging.com

Balance Studios

Area(s) of Specialization: Traditional Animation, Multimedia, 2D Animation, 3D Animation

Number of Employees: 6+

Balance Studios is comprised of young, aggressive creatives specializing in animation, visual fx, broadcast and interactive development. This fusion of creativity and technology excels from concept to completion in the following specialties: 3D animation and 2D animation, digital effects, Web development, CD and DVD interactive multimedia, software development, and broadcast production.

Balance Studios, Inc.
333 1/2 N. Broadway St.
Green Bay, WI 54303
Phone: 920 433-9770
Fax: 920 433-9780
Email: jobs@balancestudios.com
URL: http://www.balancestudios.com

Bazillion Pictures

Area(s) of Specialization: Animation, 3D Animation, 2D Animation, Digital Media

Number of Employees: 100+

Full-service studio.

Bazillion Pictures
118 S.W. Blvd., Suite 201
Kansas City, MO 64108
Phone: 816 474-7427
Fax: 816 842-7179
Email: bazpics@swbell.net
URL: http://www.bazillionpictures.com

Big Idea Production

Area(s) of Specialization: Children's Multimedia

Number of Employees: 168

Big Idea works in home video, music and books.

Big Idea Productions
P.O. Box 189
Lombard, IL 60148
Phone: 630 652-6000
Fax: 630 652-6001
Email: hr@bigidea.com
URL: http://www.bigidea.com

Bix Pix

Area(s) of Specialization: Traditional Animation

Number of Employees: 6+

Chicago-Based Bix Pix Entertainment is a full-service clay animation studio where original work for television and independent clients is created from conception to completion.

Bix Pix Entertainment
1917 W. Belmont Ave.
Chicago, IL 60657
Phone: 773 248.5430
Fax: 773 248.5480
Email: info@bixpix.com
URL: http://www.bixpix.com

Blak Boxx

Area(s) of Specialization: Animation, 3D Animation, Film, Audio

Number of Employees: 25+

Blak Boxx Computer Graphics is a full-service creative studio offering a range of services.

Blak Boxx Computer Graphics Company
100 N. High St., Suite B
Dublin, OH 43017
Phone: 614 210-5000
Fax: 614 210-5001
Email: info@blakboxx.com
URL: http://www.blakboxx.com/

Boxershorts Cartoons

Area(s) of Specialization: Animation, 3D Animation, 2D Animation

Number of Employees: 15+

BoxerStudios began as Boxershorts Cartoons in early 1998 as an answer to founder Chris Moujaes' dream to create the world's newest and best loved cartoon & comic characters and stories. BoxerStudios produces original, high-end cartoon and comic entertainment, targeting kids and teens 11-15, and is distributed on the company's SquirrelWorks Network joint venture.

Boxershorts Cartoons
BoxerStudios.com
10301 Ranch Rd. 2222, Suite 1426
Austin, TX 78730
Phone: 512 502-1644
Fax: 253 498-8818
Email: hello@boxerstudios.com
URL: http://www.boxerstudios.com

Broadview Media

Area(s) of Specialization: Film/Video, Web Design, Satellite Feeds, Virtual Tours, Television Production

Number of Employees: 50+

With offices in Minneapolis and Chicago, Broadview Media creates content for television, radio, and the Internet. The company serves broadcast and cable networks, ad agencies, corporate clients, Web developers and consumers. The company shoots, edits, adds visual effects and provides sound design, original music, and mix. The shows are viewed each week on The Discovery Channel, Home & Garden Television (HGTV), the Learning Channel, and others. The company's commercials can be seen on national TV and often during the Super Bowl.

Broadview Media, Chicago
142 E. ON Street
Chicago, IL 60611
Phone: 312 337-6000
Fax: 312 337-0500

Broadview Media, Minneapolis
4455 West 77th Street
Edina, MN 55435
Phone: 952 835-4455
Fax: 952 835-0971
URL: http://www.broadviewmedia.com/flash.html

Calabash Animation, Inc.

Area(s) of Specialization: Film and Commercial Animation

Number of Employees: 13+

Calabash Animation is a traditional character animation house specializing in cel, computer, clay, cut-paper, sand animation and more. Calabash produced some of the animation seen in the Warner Bros. feature, "Space Jam." The company has animated TV specials for CBS-owned and operated stations, 10-minute films for Encyclopedia Britannica and many TV commercials. Calabash has the USAnimation/Toon Boom software and Alias/Wavefront on a network of SGI computers.

Calabash Animation, Inc.
657 W. Ohio St.
Chicago, IL 60610-3916
Phone: 312 243-3433
Fax: 312 243-6227
Email: Info@calabashanimation.com
URL: http://www.calabashanimation.com

Capstone Multimedia, Inc.

Area(s) of Specialization: Animated-Interactive Multimedia Presentations

Number of Employees: 2

Capstone Multimedia, Inc. is a small, Minnesota-based corporation focusing on specific digital-presentation needs and requirements. The illustrates, animates, films, records, writes, edits, authors, and programs multimedia to create a comprehensive, audience-focused, multimedia-presentation solution.

Capstone Multimedia, Inc.
1324 Highway 47
Ogilvie, MN 56358-3536

Phone: 320 272-4225
Fax: 320 272-4635
URL: http://www.at-capstone.com

Charlie Uniform Tango

Area(s) of Specialization: Digital Effects,
Editing, Post Production

Number of Employees: 15

A full-service animation studio offering
a wide range of services.

Charlie Uniform Tango
3232 McKinney Ave., Suite 231
Dallas, TX 75204
Phone: 214 922-9222
Fax: 214 922-9227
Email: lola@charlietango.com
URL: http://www.charlietango.com

Character Builders, Inc.

Area(s) of Specialization: Animation for
Feature Films (CGI), Television, and
Commercials

Number of Employees: 15-20

Character Builders is a full-service
studio specializing in high-quality
traditional animation for feature films,
television and commercials, providing
services such as: animation,
storyboarding, sequence direction,
design and animation assist, as well as
project development and direction. The
company's credits include: Space Jam,
The Swan Princess, Bebe's Kids, Betty
Boop, A Goffy Movie, The Ren and
Stimpy Show, The Quest for Camelot
and others.

Character Builders
1476 Manning Pkwy
Powell, OH 43065
Phone: 614 885-2211
Fax: 614 885-3873
Email: info@cbuilders.com
URL: http://www.cbuilders.com

Credic Hohnstadt Illustration

Area(s) of Specialization: Traditional
Animation

Number of Employees: 1+

Freelance animation in Flash. Also
character design, concept art and
storyboards.

Cedric Hohnstadt Illustration
820 24th Ave. South, #11
Moorhead, MN 56560
Phone: 218 233-7351
Fax: 218 236-6448
Email: info@cedricstudio.com
URL: http://www.cedricstudio.com

The Creegan Company

Area(s) of Specialization: Animation, Costume Characters, Audio

Number of Employees: 20

The Creegan Company creates animated settings for Christmas, Halloween and Easter as well as other seasonal special events. Some of the company's clientele has included: Disney World, Sea World, Hershey's Chocolate World, shop designs for casinos like Excalibur and the new Venetian in Las Vegas. The company, whose specialty is animation and costumes, has a staff that produces animation not only mechanically powered and controlled but can also animate displays and characters that are computer controlled and pneumatically driven. The staff works in mechanical, carpentry, costuming and artistic finishing.

The Creegan Company
508 Washington Street.
Stubenville, OH 43952
Phone: 740 283-3708
Fax: 740 283-4117
URL: http://www.creegans.com/

Da Vinci Motion Graphics, LLC

Area(s) of Specialization: 3D Animation Stills and Animation

Number of Employees: 6

Da Vinci Motion Graphics provides computer-rendered 3D animation, still images and animation to the advertising, video-production, engineering, architectural, and legal communities.

Da Vinci Motion Graphics
7012 NW 63rd Street, Suite 201
Bethany, OK 73008
Phone: 405 972-2262
Fax: 405 971-1723
Email: info@dVMG.com
URL: http://www.dvmg.com

Digital DK Studios

Area(s) of Specialization: Web Site Design and Development

Number of Employees: 6+

Digital DK provides consultation for many digital and graphic design projects, particularly in Web site design and development.

Digital DK Studios
9350 South Western St.
Oklahoma City, OK 73159

Phone: 405 413-5588
Fax: 405 703-8069
Email: info@digitaldk.com
URL: http://www.digitaldk.com

DNA Productions, Inc.

Area(s) of Specialization: 2D Animation
and 3D Animation Characters, Special
Effects, Computer Graphics

Number of Employees: 100

DNA Productions, Inc. is a full-service
animation company that has operated in
Dallas, Texas since 1987, serving the
entertainment and commercial markets
by providing 2D animation and 3D
animation character design and
animation. In addition, DNA is a
creative resource providing script
writing, directing and producing for
animated series and features. DNA has
contributed animation to a range of
projects, including Roseanne's "Saturday
Night Special" (Fox Television), "The
Weird Al Show" (CBS),
"steve.oedekerk.com" (NBC) and
"Nanna & Lil' Puss Puss" (Showtime,
Comedy Central, MTV).

DNA Productions, Inc.
2201 West Royal Lane, Suite 275
Irving, TX 75063
Phone: 214 352-4694
Fax: 214 496-9333

Email: dnainfo@dnahelix.com
URL: http://www.dnahelix.com

Dreamscape Design, Inc.

Area(s) of Specialization: Digital Video,
Web Services, 3D Animation Graphics
and Animation

Number of Employees: 10

Formerly known as Admakers
Multimedia, Dreamscape Design Inc. has
been providing proactive hi-tech
marketing solutions since 1981. In
addition to their 3D animation graphics
and hi-tech programming, they have the
ability to consult with their clients on a
variety of marketing and networking
solutions.

Dreamscape Design, Inc.
Corporate Headquarters
1 Henson Place, Suite A
Champaign, IL 61821
Phone: 217 359-8484
Fax: 217 239-5858
Email: info@dreamscapedesign.com
URL: http://www.dreamscapedesign.com

Dream Magic Animation Studios

Area(s) of Specialization: Animation, 3D
Animation, Digital Media

Number of Employees: 6+

Dream Magic Animation Studios, located in Bryan Texas, specializes in 3D animation and special-effects; they also have a commercial division.

Dream Magic Animation Studios
2904 Old Hearne Rd.
Bryan, TX 77803
Phone: 979 778-9519
Fax: 775 402-0703
Email: dreammagicstudio@cs.com

EDR Media

Area(s) of Specialization: Film and Video Production and Post Production

Number of Employees: 10+

EDR is a group of technology professionals who design and implement integrated hardware and software systems.

EDR Media
23330 Commerce Park Rd.
Cleveland, Ohio 44122
Phone: 216 292-7300
Fax: 216 292-0545
Email: vrettas@edr.com
URL: http://www.edr.com

Fearless Eye, Inc.

Area(s) of Specialization: Animation, Visual Effects for Film/Video/Multimedia

Number of Employees: 5

Fearless Eye was founded in 1992 to produce high resolution animation and digital graphics for the commercial, film, entertainment and multimedia industries. Projects range from creating articulated character animation to virtual environments. Core services include: 2D animation and 3D animation, visual effects for television and film, simulations & reconstructions, and multimedia CD-ROM's and Web page design. Other production capabilities include: character animation, digital compositing, rotoscoping, blue screen, simulations, custom modeling and non-linear film and video production.

Fearless Eye, Inc.
308 W 8th 208
Kansas City, MO 64105
Phone: 816 221-1047
Alt Phone: 800 729-6939
Fax: 816 221-2775
Email: cody@fearlesseye.com
URL: http://www.fearlesseye.com

Fischer Edit

Area(s) of Specialization: Post
Production, Advertising

Number of Employees: 15

Fischer Edit is a full-service, creative post
production facility specializing in film-
originated television commercials.
Founded in 1991, Fischer Edit works in
non-linear off-line editing, special effects
work, and finishing.

Fischer Edit
801 Nicollet Mall, Suite 300W
Minneapolis, MN 55402
Phone: 612 332-4914
Fax: 612 332-4910
Email: bill@fischeredit.com
URL: http://www.fischeredit.com

Gathering of Developers, Inc.

Area(s) of Specialization: Computer and
Video Game Publisher

Number of Employees: 20-30

Gathering of Developers, a Texas-based
computer and video game publishing
company, was founded in January 1998
to service independent game developers.

Gathering of Developers, Inc.
2700 Fairmount St.
Dallas, TX 75201

Phone: 214 880-0001
Alt Phone: 887 463-4263
Fax: 214 871-7934
URL: http://www.godgames.com

GenneX Health Technologies

Area(s) of Specialization: Multimedia and
Web Development

Number of Employees: 10

Gennex Healthcare Technologies offers
the full range of Internet services to
health and medical organizations.
Incorporated in 1994, Gennex is
involved in Internet and health
information.

GenneX Health Technologies
2201 W. Campbell Park Dr. #226
Chicago, IL 60612
Phone: 312 226-6750
Fax: 312 226-6755
URL: http://www.gennexhealth.com
Email: gennex@gennexhealth.com.

Ghost Productions, Inc.

Area(s) of Specialization: Animation,
Post Production, Effects Design

Number of Employees: 10+

Artists at Ghost Productions Inc. create
storyboards and animatics then shoot,
edit, animate and create all the necessary

effects to complete their clients commercial litigation. With animation they explain the insides and workings of an unsafe product and replay an accident multiple times with unlimited camera angles. Tissue, bone and instruments, animation can be used to explain surgical procedures, implants and educate patients. Web Casting: Add Flash, Shockwave, Fireworks, Quicktime movies and animation to clients' Web sites for added appeal. They optimize and compress video and animation to playback efficiently on virtually any server. Interactive DVD, CD-ROM, and HTML can be scripted with completely interactive interfaces.

Ghost Productions, Inc.
2233 Hamline Ave. N
Roseville, MN 55113
Phone: 651 633-1163
Email: nic@ghostproductions.com
URL: http://www.ghostproductions.com

Gourmet Images

Area(s) of Specialization: Media Production

Number of Employees: 3

Gourmet Images is a high-end visual media shop to handle projects from Inception to duplication, or handle any of the elements in between such as corporate informational or motivational videos, music videos, broadcast television programs and commercials, CD-ROM authoring or Web page design. The staff consists of writers, producers, directors, DP's, sound recordists, editors, graphic designers and animators.

Gourmet Images
144 N. 38th Ave.
Omaha, NE 68131-2302
Phone: 402 558-4985
Fax: 402 556-3646
Email: staff@gourmet-images.com
URL: http://www.gourmet-images.com

Grace & Wild Digital Studios

Area(s) of Specialization: Teleproduction for Commercial, Broadcast, and Communication Markets

Number of Employees: 215

Grace & Wild Digital Studios specializes in high-level, creative teleproduction services for the commercial, broadcast and corporate communications markets. Located in Studio Center, Grace & Wild Digital Studios offer clients a range of services, including: Video Camera packages, Three Sound Stages, Teleconferencing and Two-Way Fiber Optic Feeds, Satellite Uplinks and Downlinks, Advanced Film Transfer and

Color Enhancement Capabilities, Extensive Graphics and Animation Capabilities, including Computer, Cel and Clay Animation, Component Digital Online Editing, Multi-format Online Editing, Avid Off-line and Online Non-linear Editing, and Video Duplication and Standards Conversion.

Grace & Wild Digital Studios
23689 Industrial Park Drive
Farmington Hills, MI 48335
Phone: 800 471-6010
Fax: 248 473-8300
Email: sales1@gwstudio.com
URL: http://www.gwstudio.com

Green Rabbit Design Studio, Inc.

Area(s) of Specialization: 2D Animation and 3D Animation, Traditional Animation, Digital Effects

Number of Employees: 6

Green Rabbit has been producing animation for the past 5 years. Green Rabbit produces 2D animation and 3D animation, traditional (character) cel animation and special effects for video. Production equipment includes Quantel's Hal express (with transform fx) as well as Silicon graphics, Alias Power Animator, Softimage, Liberty and Elastic Reality. Additionally, the company utilizes several Macintosh workstations with Photoshop, Adobe Illustrator, QuarkXpress and Animation Stand. Clients include Small But Mighty Films, Riester Corporation and Regional Public Transit Authority's Clean Air Campaign.

Green Rabbit Design Studio, Inc.
7229 E. First.Ave., Suite C
Scottsdale, AZ 85251
Phone: 602 425-9003
Alt Phone: 800 804-2005
Email: jenelle@greenrabbit.com
URL: http://www.greenrabbit.com

HDMG Digital Post & Effects

Area(s) of Specialization: Post Production, Digital Effects

Number of Employees: 12+

HDMG offers direct operator contact in post production and digital effects.

HDMG Digital Post & Effects
6573 City West Parkway
Minneapolis, MN
Phone: 612 943-1711
Fax: 612 943-1957
URL: http://www.hdmg.com

Hellman Associates, Inc.

Area(s) of Specialization: Design, Illustration, Animation, Marketing

Number of Employees: 100

Hellman Associates, Inc., was founded in 1967 as a design house and expanded to incorporate illustration and animation. The organization is a full-service marketing and advertising agency serving national and international clients. Locations include: Waterloo, Des Moines, Dubuque, and Newton, Iowa; and Minneapolis, Minnesota. Hellman Associates, Inc., employs individuals in the areas of marketing, creative, and support services.

Hellman Associates, Inc.
1225 W. Fourth St.
Waterloo, Iowa 50702
Phone: 319 234-7055
Fax: 319 234-2089
Email: info@hellman.com
URL: http://www.hellman.com

Human Code, Inc.

Area(s) of Specialization: Digital Content, Animation, Audio, Film/Video

Number of Employees: 300+

Human Codes Inc. have been providing custom e-commerce, smart toys, learning systems and online marketing communications for the entertainment industry, educators, and entrepreneurs since 1993. The company works in the Internet, computer, broadband, iTV and wireless media.

Human Code (Austin Studios)
319 Congress Ave.
Suite 100
Austin, Texas 78701
Phone: 512 477-5455
Fax: 512 477-5456
Email: info@sapient.com
URL: http://www.humancode.com

Imageworks Computer Graphics Imaging, Inc.

Area(s) of Specialization: Graphics, Computer Animation, Interactive Multimedia, Web Site Design

Number of Employees: 50

Imageworks Computer Graphics Imaging Inc. was established in 1995 in Austin, Texas, and specializes in Web site design and technology solutions. Imageworks offers clients complete project development capability in Web site design and development, interactive multimedia authoring, and graphic art design.

Imageworks Computer Graphics Imaging, Inc.
P.O. Box 80083
Austin, Texas 78708-0083
Phone: 512 832-8664
URL: http://www.imageworkscgi.com

Innervision Productions, Inc.

Area(s) of Specialization: 2D Animation and 3D Animation Graphics, Video and Audio, Web Design and Interactive CD-ROM Design

Number of Employees: 32

Innervision Productions, Inc. creates some of the best 2D animation and 3D animation graphics in addition to traditional video, audio and Multimedia.

Innervision Productions, Inc.
11783 Borman Dr.
St. Louis, MO 63146
Phone: 314 569-2500
Fax: 314 569-3534

Intelecon

Area(s) of Specialization: Digital Editing, 2D Animation and 3D Animation, Specializing in presentations for trade shows and other events

Number of Employees: 85

Intelecon Services Inc., headquartered in Dallas, provides of business communications technology and producer services, audio-visual rentals, sales, installations and staging services. The company offers turnkey solutions for productions, concerts, corporate events, tradeshows and multimedia. Services include Stereoscopic 3D animation, 2D animation and 3D animation, online and off-line non-linear non-compressed digital editing, special effects, 3D animation visualizations, audio, lighting, rigging, video walls, large screen and panoramic projection.

Intelecon
8818 John W. Carpenter Fwy.
Dallas, TX 75247
Phone: 214 571-0622
Alt Phone: 800 466-9125
Fax: 214 571-0100
URL: http://www.intelecon.com

Janimation, Inc.

Area(s) of Specialization: 3D Animation, Design, Visual Effects

Number of Employees: 9

Janimation offers full production services and effects supervision from pre-production through finishing. Janimation's network of Silicon

Graphics, Intergraph NT workstations, and Power Macs connects the animators, designers and compositors. Graphics cards provide animators with instant feedback, which enable further experimentation, softer shadows and motion blur.

Janimation, Inc.
840 Exposition Ave.
Dallas, TX 75226
Phone: 214 823-7760
Fax: 214 823-7761
Email: fran@janimation.com
URL: http://www.janimation.com

J.K. Benton Design Studio, Inc.

Area(s) of Specialization: Traditional Animation

Number of Employees: 1+

Jim Benton specializes in the creation of properties for entertainment projects as well as merchandise. Skills include creation, development, character design, scripts and boarding.

J.K. Benton Design Studio, Inc.
3170 Middlebury
Bloomfield, MI 48301
Phone: 248 644-5875
Fax: 248 540-8002
Email: jkbenton@aol.com
URL: http://www.jimbenton.com

Juntunen Media Group

Area(s) of Specialization: Post Production, DVD Authoring, Graphics, Special Effects

Number of Employees: 45

Juntunen Media Group is an integrated media development firm located in Minneapolis, working in media, Internet, video and print.

Juntunen Media Group
708 N. First St.
Minneapolis, MN 55401
Phone: 612 341-3348
Alt Phone: 800 535-4366
Fax: 612 341-0242
Email: contactus@juntunen.com
URL: http://www.juntunen.com

Kaleidoscope Animation, Inc.

Area(s) of Specialization: 3D Animation Modeling and Animation, Training, Professional Support

Number of Employees: 35

Kaleidoscope Animations works in high-end 3D animation applications and modeling tools. The company provides storyboards to the final render.

Kaleidoscope Animation, Inc.
23625 Commerce Park Rd., Suite 130

Cleveland, OH 44122
Phone: 216 360-0630
Fax: 216 360-9109
Email: id@kascope.com
URL: http://www.kascope.com

KUNGFUKOI

Area(s) of Specialization: Traditional Animation

Number of Employees: 1+

KUNGFUKOI consists of the freelance entity of Jeffrey Dates. KUNGFUKOI has recently just wrapped up production on "Day Off The Dead," an animated short film outlining what the dead do, exactly, on their day off.

KUNGFUKOI
6015 Oram #F
Dallas, TX 75206
Phone: 214 821-9241
Email: jdates@reelf.com
URL: http://www.reelfx.comjdates

Lamb and Company

Area(s) of Specialization: 2D Animation and 3D Animation, Computer Animation, CGI, Traditional Cel Animation

Number of Employees: 10

Based in Minneapolis, Minnesota, Lamb & Company has created imagery for television, film, video, games, rides, and forensic presentations. Lamb & Company combines techniques such as 2D animation and 3D animation computer animation with cel animation and live action.

Lamb and Company
1942 Humboldt Ave.
Minneapolis, MN 55403
Phone: 612 377-5980
Fax: 612 377-5979
Email: larry@lambcom.com
URL: http://www.lamb.com

Laredo Productions, Inc.

Area(s) of Specialization: Film/Video, Multimedia

Number of Employees: 25+

Laredo can post for digital broadcast television, as well as the 4:3 digital and analog formats and 16:9 widescreen DTV. In addition to high-end video post, the company accommodates complete off-line post production for film projects, providing frame-accurate EDLs for negative cutters and optical houses.

Laredo Productions, Inc.
7349 Via Paseo Del Sur, #157
Scottsdale, AZ 85258

Phone: 480 947-5255
Fax: 480 947-5285
Email: flypack@laredoproductions.com
URL: http://www.laredoproductions.com

Leaping Lizards, Ltd.

Area(s) of Specialization: Digital Film and Video, Interactive CD-ROM and DVD authoring, Web Design

Number of Employees: 2 (plus freelancing)

Leaping Lizards, Ltd. is a Design, Effects and Animation Studio, located in Southfield, Michigan, working with advertising, marketing and corporate communications companies. Leaping Lizards' staff creates graphics, animation, & interactive content for Digital Video & Film, Interactive CD/DVD, Internet and Print. Leaping Lizards offers a proprietary state-of-the art Digital Graphics System which features networking of Quantel Paintbox, Accom DDR, Power PC Macintoshes, NT and Silicon Graphic work stations. The company specializes in cross-platform motion graphics for high-end video, interactive and Web design.

Leaping Lizards, Ltd.
29829 Greenfield Rd., Suite 103
Southfield, MI 48076
Phone: 248 423-9311

Fax: 248 423-7945
Email: deni@leapinglizards.com
URL: http://www.leapinglizards.com

LiveWire Marketing, Inc.

Area(s) of Specialization: CGI, Multimedia

Number of Employees: 18

Livewire Marketing Inc. offers comprehensive marketing services for helping clients develop, implement, and manage Web marketing strategies.

LiveWire Marketing, Inc.
4814 Washington Blvd, Suite 300
St Louis, MO 63108
Phone: 314 361-8500
Fax: 314 361-0500
Email: info@lwm.com
URL: http://www.lwm.com

Manga Entertainment, Inc.

Area(s) of Specialization: Animation, Film, Video, Digital Media

Number of Employees: 25+

Manga Entertainment Inc. is a film company specializing in the production, distribution and marketing of Japanese animation for theatrical, television broadcast, DVD and home video release worldwide. The company is headquartered in Chicago with additional offices in New York, London and Tokyo. Manga is the Japanese animation division of Palm Pictures, an audio-visual entertainment company started in 1998 by Chris Blackwell, founder of Island Records. Over the past seven years, the Manga U.S. division has aggressively developed the American market for Japanese animation with huge success, releasing over 200 titles on VHS and DVD into U.S. retail and rental stores. In addition, the company has been instrumental in making *anime* one of the most popular and growing trends of the new millennium.

Manga Entertainment, Inc.
727 N. Hudson St., Suite 100
Chicago, IL 60610
Phone: 312 751-0020
Fax: 312 751-2483
URL: http://www.manga.com

Match Frame Post Production

Area(s) of Specialization: Graphics, Telecine, Post Production, Interactive DVD Authoring

Number of Employees: 35+

Match Frame is a digital production company. The company has capabilities in Telecine, Graphics, Post Production and Interactive.

Match Frame Post Production
8531 Fairhaven
San Antonio, TX 78229
Phone: 210 614-5678
Alt Phone: 800 929-2790
Fax: 210 616-0299
Email: ken@matchframe.com
URL: http://www.matchframe.com

Maximillion Zillion Animation

Area(s) of Specialization: Long Form Cel Animation, Concept/Scripting and Video Production

Number of Employees: 3

Maximillion Zillion Animation has been providing cel animation since 1990. Hand drawn frames and custom character creations along with concept, scripting, and production are all available as a turnkey package. Storyboards are supplied to establish a concrete visual preview, or animation can be drawn from storyboards and characters.

Maximillion Zillion Animation
502 State St
Saint Louis, MS 39520
Phone: 228 463-0615
Fax: 228 463-0616

Email: information@mzanimation.com
URL: http://www.mzanimation.com

Midway Games Inc.

Area(s) of Specialization: Video Game
Design and Development

Number of Employees: 300+

Midway Games Inc. develops and
manufactures coin-operated arcade and
home video game entertainment
products. Midway publishes video games
for Nintendo, Sega, Sony and personal
computer platforms. The Midway and
Atari brands have generated games such
as Pong, Defender, Missile Command,
Pac-Man, Centipede, NBA Jam, Cruis'n
USA, and Mortal Kombat. Midway is
based in Chicago, Illinois. Midway
Home Entertainment has offices in
Corsicana, Texas and San Diego,
California. Atari Games is based in
Milpitas, California.

Midway Games Inc.
3401 N. California Ave.
Chicago, IL 60618
Phone: 773 961-2222
Fax: 773 961-2376
Email: Webmaster@midway.com
URL: http://www.midway.com

Mirage Digital

Area(s) of Specialization: Virtual
Modeling, 3D Animation Design, Sound

Number of Employees: 4

Mirage Digital is a creative/technical
design and implementation service
company for broadcast, entertainment,
corporate and live shows. Housed in the
Great Scott Studio center, a commercial
post production facility in Phoenix, AZ.
The company provides the video and
show market with virtual set, 3D
animation high resolution video and
surround sound technology.

Mirage Digital
Great Scott Studio Center
834 North 7th. Ave.
Phoenix, AZ 85007
Phone: 602 254-1600
Fax: 602 495-9949
Email: jfassett@miragedigital.com
URL: http://www.miragedigital.com

Mutant Baby Productions

Area(s) of Specialization: Animation,
Video

Number of Employees: 2+

Mutant Baby Productions produces
animations for recording artists (music
videos).

Mutant Baby Productions
6430 S. Stony Island, #2011
Chicago, IL 60637
Phone: 773 324-0521
Email: smithdamion@hotmail.com

Network Century / Cinema Video

Area(s) of Specialization: Network Services, Programming, Web Development, Production, Post Production, Duplication

Number of Employees: 45

Network Century has acquired Cinema Video, a film and video production house. The company works in multimedia and video broadcast.

Network Century
211 E. Grand Ave.
Chicago, IL 60611
Phone: 312 644-1650
Fax: 312 644-2096
Email: sales@networkcentury.com
URL: http://www.networkcentury.com

Nvision, Inc.

Area(s) of Specialization: E-Commerce Solutions

Number of Employees: 300+

NVision, Inc. provides 3D animation products and services for animation, visual effects, game development, reverse engineering, rapid prototyping, and inspection/gaging. NVision has proprietary and patented tools and works with clients such as Digital Domain, Dream Quest, Disney, Interplay, Hughes Christensen, and Northrop-Grumman.

Nvision, Inc.
1409 N. Cedar Crest Blvd., PMB 117
Allentown, PA 18104
Phone: 610 366-2111
Fax: 610 391-1880
Email: info@nvision.com
URL: http://www.nvision.com

Omni Studio, Inc.

Area(s) of Specialization: Graphic Design, Illustration, Animation, Multimedia

Number of Employees: 7

Omni Studio, Inc. offers Graphic Design, Illustration, Animation, and production art. The company's clients include industries in the areas of sports and leisure, electronics, computer technology, wood products, health care, food products and travel.

Omni Studio, Inc.
603 West Franklin Street
Boise, Idaho 83702
Phone: 208 344-1332
Fax: 208 344-1878
Email: omnimail@gotoomni.com
URL: http://www.gotoomni.com

Oops Animation, Inc.

Area(s) of Specialization: 2D Animation
and 3D Animation, Graphics

Number of Employees: 8

Oops Animation Inc. located in
Minnesota has a 3D animation, graphics
and special effects facility. Software
programs include: Maya,
PowerAnimator, Alias, Softimage, 3D
Animation Studio Max, Flint, Composer
and Adobe After Effects. For visual
marketing objectives comprehension,
Oops Animation offers 3D Animation
and special effects for television
commercials, sales messages or the
improvement of technical training.

Oops Animation, Inc.
600 Washington Ave. North, Suite B103
Minneapolis, MN 55401
Phone: 612 340-9598
Fax: 612 340-9601
Email: oops@oopsanimation.com
URL: http://www.oopsanimation.com

Paradigm Productions

Area(s) of Specialization: 3D Animation,
Computer Graphics, Multimedia

Number of Employees: 2

Paradigm Productions, LLC of
Memphis, Tennessee, was founded in
March of 1992 to provide 3D animation
and computer graphics services. The
company also produces medical
visualization, exhibit design, television,
video production, legal reenactments,
and interactive multimedia.

Paradigm Productions
1661 International Place, Suite 210
Memphis, TN 38120
Phone: 901 685-7703
Fax: 901 261-4746
Email: info@2D Animationimes.com
URL: http://www.2D Animationimes.com

Picturestart

Area(s) of Specialization: 3D Animation
Design and Animation for Video/Film

Number of Employees: 1+

Picturestart works in the areas of
animation, compositing, design and
editorial projects.

Picturestart
17819 DAve.nport Road, Suite 110

Dallas, TX 75252
Phone: 972 490-6351
Fax: 972 490-6352
Email: jharris@picturestart.com
URL: http://www.picturestart.com

Pixel Farm

Area(s) of Specialization: Graphic Design/Special Effects, Advertising

Number of Employees: 15

Pixel Farm specializes in special effects, compositing, graphic design, and film transfer, for broadcast and corporate pieces. Clients include Harley Davidson, ABC, Best Buy, K Mart, Target, VH-1, Ocean Spray, and Hostess.

Pixel Farm
251 First Ave. North, Suite 600
Minneapolis, MN 55401
Phone: 612 339-7644
Fax: 612 339-7551
Email: amanda@pixelfarm.com
URL: http://www.pixelfarm.com

PLW Productions, LLP

Area(s) of Specialization: Traditional Animation, Video, Television

Number of Employees: 6+

PLW Productions, LLP provides quality clay animation production services. It also engages in original animated content creation for Direct to Video and Television markets.

PLW Productions, LLP
RR 1 Box 30
Fisher, MN 56723
Phone: 218 281-6109
Fax: 218 281-6109
Email: plwproductions@yahoo.com
URL: http://
www.talesofthegallantknight.com

PopTop Software, Inc.

Area(s) of Specialization: Computer Strategy Game Development and Production

Number of Employees: 20+

PopTop Software Inc. is a developer of computer strategy games. In 1998, PopTop released Railroad Tycoon II, and several follow-ups and ports have followed in the last 2 years. PopTop is currently primarily focused on the game Tropico.

PopTop Software Inc.
1714 Gilsinn
Fenton, MO 63026
Phone: 214 303-1202
Email: www@www.poptop.com
URL: http://www.poptop.com

Red Car

Area(s) of Specialization: Film/Video

Number of Employees: 24+

Red Car Dallas consists of graphics artists, sound designers, type stylists, and special effects personnel, working in film and video. Clients include: Wieden & Kennedy, Leo Burnett (leoburnett.com), and Young & Rubicam (yandr.com).

Red Car-Dallas
2626 Cole Ave.
Dallas, TX 75204
Phone: 214 954-1996
Fax: 214 954-4499
Email: carriec@redcar.com
URL: http://www.redcar.com

Red Car-Chicago
455 e. Illinois
Suite 370
Chicago, IL 60611
Phone: 312 645-1888
Fax: 312 645-1866
Email: vivianc@redcar.com
URL: http://www.redcar.com

Reel FX Creative Solutions

Area(s) of Specialization: Animation, CGI, Multimedia, Film/Video

Number of Employees: 20+

Reel FX Creative Studios produces, concepts, creates, animates, composites, edits, sound designs and mixes for TV, HDTV, and Film.

Reel FX Creative Solutions
2211 N. Lamar, Suite 100
Dallas, TX 75202
Phone: 214 979-0961
Alt Phone: 214 632-2188
Fax: 214 979-0963
Email: chuck@reelfx.com
URL: http://www.reelfx.com

Reelworks Animation Studio

Area(s) of Specialization: 2D Animation

Number of Employees: 10+

Reelworks Animation Studio, Inc. is a full-service traditional animation studio specializing in the commercial production of character animation, moving illustration and animation combined with live action. Reelworks Animation studio has been creating character-driven animated spots since 1979, using a painterly hand-done style. The studio has created spots for clients like Coca Cola, Time Magazine, and Hershey's and has received awards such as the Clio, Mobius, and The Show.

Reelworks Animation Studio
2836 Lyndale Ave. South, Suite 4
Minneapolis, MN 55454

Phone: 612 333-5063
Fax: 612 871-9336
Email: joe@reelworks.com
URL: http://www.reelworks.com

Right Stuf International

Area(s) of Specialization: Traditional
Animation, Video, Television

Number of Employees: 30+

Right Stuf International is an Anime
publisher in the as well as an online
Anime superstore. The company has 3
main publishing labels: Right Stuf which
publishes family oriented materials like
classic 1960s shows such as Astro Boy,
Gigantor, and Kimba as well as new
anime like Irresponsible Captain Tylor
and His and Her Circumstances; Critical
Mass which handles more adult oriented
materials such as Cool Devices, Imma
Youjo and the Vanilla Series; and
AnimeTrax - a joint venture with ADV
Films to publish original Japanese anime
music in the U.S.

Right Stuf International (The)
P.O. Box 71309
Des Moines, IA 50325
Phone: 800 338-6827
Fax: 515 252-0555
Email: info@rightstuf.com
URL: http://www.rightstuf.com

Rw Productions

Area(s) of Specialization: Animation,
Web site Design, Post Production

Number of Employees: 10+

Rw Productions provides services along
the entire production timeline, including
planning, PM, location shooting,
editing, animation/FX, duplication and
delivery. They also provide new media
support for interactive CD and DVD,
Web content and other communication
channels.

Rw Productions
15630 Michigan Ave.
Dearborn, MI 48126
Phone: 313 945-9292
Fax: 313 945-9295
Email: mmiller@rwpmi.com
URL: http://www.rwpmi.com

SEMAFX

Area(s) of Specialization: Traditional
Animation

SEMAFX (Southeast Michigan
Animation and Special Effects) Network,
a group of talented animators and
dynamic artists who form a powerful
network of resources for the video, film
and Web markets.

SEMAFX Network
1404 Yorkshire
Grosse Pointe Park, MI 48230
Phone: 313 884-2277
Email: scott@semafx.com
URL: http://www.semafx.com

Spyglass, Inc.

Area(s) of Specialization: Providing Web
Software and Services

Number of Employees: 200+

Spyglass is a provider of strategic
Internet consulting, software and
professional services for content
providers, service operators and device
manufacturers the Internet. Spyglass
Professional Services provides consulting
for defining, developing and delivering
complete, end-to-end projects.

Spyglass, Inc.
1240 E. Diehl Rd.
Naperville, IL 60563
Phone: 630 505-1010
Fax: 630 505-4944
URL: http://www.spyglass.com

Strictly FX

Area(s) of Specialization: Laser
Production

Number of Employees: 15+

Strictly FX is a company that designs,
implements, and produces live special
effects. Its commitment is to
transparently design and perform shows
for an event, completely in-house.

Strictly FX
1230 Jarvis
Elk Grove Village, IL 60007
Phone: 847 290-0272
Fax: 847 290-0273
Email: mark@strictlyfx.com
URL: http://www.strictlyfx.com

Sunstorm Interactive

Area(s) of Specialization: Animation,
Multimedia, Digital Media

Number of Employees: 10+

Sunstorm Interactive is an
entertainment software development
company.

Sunstorm Interactive
120 E. Market St., Suite 1100
Indianapolis, IN 46204
Email: heather@sunstorm.net
URL: http://www.sunstorm.net

Taylor Entertainment Group

Area(s) of Specialization: Animation,
Video, 3D Animation

Number of Employees: 6+

Specializes in 3D Animation and video for flash emails, Web sites, and business presentation.

Taylor Entertainment Group, LLC
P.O. Box 251
No. Easton, MA 02356
Email: rtaylorjr@attbi.com
URL: http://www.woastudio.com

Technisonic Studios

Area(s) of Specialization: Film/Video, CGI, Multimedia, Animation, Sound

Number of Employees: 25

Technisonic Studios develops high-concept audio and visual media for television, radio, the Internet, film, corporate videos, DVD, CD-ROM and kiosks for clients across the United States and in Europe. The company's staff includes sound designers, graphic artists, editors, cinematographers, animators, producers, computer programmers, engineers and support staff.

Technisonic Studios
500 S. Ewing
Suite G
St. Louis, MO 63103
Phone: 314 533-1777
Fax: 314 533-6527

Email: info@technisonic.com
URL: http://www.technisonic.com

There TV

Area(s) of Specialization: Film/video

Number of Employees: 10

There TV consists of broadcast designers, animation directors and digital artists working in film and video.

There TV
1351 West Grand Ave.
Chicago, IL 60622
Phone: 312 421-0400
Fax: 312 421-1915
Email: tom@theretv.com
URL: http://www.theretv.com

Trinity Animation & Visual Effects

Area(s) of Specialization: Animation and Visual Effects

Number of Employees: 3

Trinity offers a variety of services relating to modifying captured images, creating new 3D Animation environments and characters, and combining live action with computer-generated imagery. Trinity has created animation and visual effects for national audiences, including broadcast television and major motion pictures. The company has experience with motion morphs, painterly effects, wire-removal and combining separately filmed pyrotechnics with live action. It can put live action into a 3D Animation rendered scene, or mix 3D Animation animated characters with live action.

Trinity Animation & Visual Effects
676 SE Bayberry Lane, Suite 103B
Lee's Summit, MO 64063-4389
Phone: 800 548-1578
Fax: 816 525-1594
Email: info@trinity3D Animation.com
URL: http://www.trinity3D Animation.com

TUV Productions RRR by ABC of Film

Area(s) of Specialization: Animation, Film/Video, Multimedia, CGI

Number of Employees: 5+

A motion-picture-making-company working in the world of cinematography, animation and movie-making, computer-graphics Web design and media.

TUV Productions RRR by ABC of Film
4410 Clayburn Dr.
Indianapolis, IN 46268
Phone: 317 872-FILM
Fax: 317 872-3456

URL: http://www.geocities.com/codeman14150/

Udream2

Area(s) of Specialization: Animation

Number of Employees: 10+

Full-service creative studio.

Udream2
1561 Saddlebrook Lane D1
Westlake, OH 44145
Phone: 440 808-1353
Email: kolesar@udream2.com
URL: http://www.udream2.com

United Developers

Area(s) of Specialization: Traditional Animation

Number of Employees: 6+

United Developers provides an administration, business and management infrastructure for game development and game publishing.

United Developers
2019 N. Lamar St., Suite 240
Dallas, TX 75202-1704
Phone: 214 855-5955
Fax: 214 855-5980
Email: info@ud.com
URL: http://www.udgames.com

Vidox Image and Data

Area(s) of Specialization: Commercial Films/Videos, Interactive Multimedia

Number of Employees: 10

Vidox Image & Data has been creating high quality commercials, documentaries and industrial videos since 1982. They specialize in communicating through on-screen presentation and their computer and video skills converge when producing for interactive formats such as live presentation, electronic product kiosks, and World Wide Web pages.

Vidox Image and Data
1223 St. John Street
Lafayette, LA 70506
Phone: 337 237-1700
Fax: 337 237-1712
Email: Chris@vidox.com
URL: http://www.vidox.com

Virtual Pictures Company

Area(s) of Specialization: Graphic Design, 3D Animation, Design

Number of Employees: 5+

VPC designs and authors high-quality CD-ROM titles, Web sites, 3D animation and motion graphics for the corporate, broadcast, and motion picture industries. The company also composes musical composition for client's projects.

Virtual Pictures Company
1438 W. Broadway Rd., Suite B-210
Tempe, AZ 85282
Phone: 480 894-0607
URL: http://www.virtualpictures.com
Email: vpc@virtualpicture.com

Visioneerz Studios

Area(s) of Specialization: Animation

Number of Employees: 10+

A full-service group that includes: Animation Production, Comic Book Publishers, Multimedia/Interactive Development, Post Production Services, Pre-Production Services, Visual Effects Production, Web Animation Production2D Animation/Traditional, 2D Animation Computer Animation, Digital/Visual Effects, Flash/Internet Animation, Animated Characters, Commercials, Multimedia/New Media, Music Videos, Short Films, Television Specials, Title Sequences.

Visioneerz Studios
175 Pinetree Ct.
Howell, NJ 07731
Phone: 732 625-3076
Email: adamwho@yahoo.com
URL: http://www.visioneerz.com

VirtualONE, Inc.

Area(s) of Specialization: 3D Animation, Animation

Number of Employees: 1+

Richard has been working with 3D animation studio since the original DOS version. Before moving back to Chicago in 1998, he worked as the lead animation instructor at the Art Institute in Ft Lauderdale and started the SE Florida 3D Animation Studio Users group.

VirtualONE, Inc.
6719 Fieldstone Dr.
Burr Ridge, IL 60527
Phone: 630 561-8987
Email: c3Danimationgrafx@hotmail.com
URL: http://www.virtualone.net

Visuality LLC

Area(s) of Specialization: Web design, Storyboards, Scripts, Interactive Media Production

Number of Employees: 5

Visuality functions as a full-service preproduction, post production, and interactive design (Web sites CD-ROM). Visually provides preproduction services such as script writing, storyboards, concept development, casting, and production services such as location shooting, lighting, green screen and audio, and post production services such as off-line non-linear editing, online editing, 3D animation computer graphics and media design. In addition it provides interactive services such as Web design and CD-ROM development.

Visuality LLC
5980 Executive Dr., Suite A
Madison, WI 53719
Phone: 608 271-3305
Fax: 608 271-3328
Email: jay@visuality.com
URL: http://www.visuality.com

VT/TV Graphics and Post

Area(s) of Specialization: Post Production

Number of Employees: 16

VT/TV provides visual effects, editing, 3D animation, turnkey production and/or complete project management.

VT/TV Graphics and Post
2401 West Bellfort
Houston, Texas 77054
Phone: 713 877-1877
Fax: 713 877-8002
Email: info@vt2.com
URL: http://www.vt-tv.com

VQE, Inc.

Area(s) of Specialization: Traditional Animation

Number of Employees: 2+

VQE, Inc. is an animated production start-up with plans of marketing a G-rated cartoon based around 3rd graders.

Vision Quest Entertainment, Inc.
2415 Lakeshore Ct.
Lebanon, IN 46052
Phone: 765 482-2857
Fax: 765 482-2857
Email: tomadams@in-motion.net

Wandering Pilot Pictures

Area(s) of Specialization: Animation, Film, Television

Number of Employees: 6+

Wandering Pilot Pictures produces short films for release in Film, Television, Video/DVD, and the Web. Freelance services include: Character Design and Development, Layout, Storyboards, Flash based animation, Concept art, Graphic Design, Illustration and Comic Book Art.

Wandering Pilot Pictures
2284 E. Cork St., #3A
Kalamazoo, MI 49001

Phone: 616 342-2596
Email: mpaulik@iserv.net
URL: http://www.wanderingpilot.com

Webpromotions, Inc.

Area(s) of Specialization: Web Site Design and Development, Corporate Identity, Logos, Illustration, Animation for Broadcast

Number of Employees: 6

Webpromotion's goal is to help clients convey an image through the design of Web sites, logos, ad banners, catchy graphics and animations. Webpromotion's animation projects for video have been used in broadcast television, at national conventions and in corporate video productions.

Webpromotions, Inc.
7740 29th Ave.
Kenosha, Wisconsin 53143
Phone: 262 605-1201
Fax: 262-605-1281
Email: info@Webpromotion.com
URL: http://www.Webpromotion.com

WelbornWorks

Area(s) of Specialization: Animation, 2D Animation, 3D Animation

Number of Employees: 3+

WelbornWorks began as Welborn Illustration, and quickly joined the 3D animation world. Bryan S. Welborn owner and creative director has taken his 2D animation skills in fine art and commercial illustration into texturing and environment creation for 3D animation and game level development.

Welborn Works
P.O. Box 2038
Kountze, TX 77625
Phone: 409 246-3195
Email: bryan@welbornworks.com
URL: http://www.welbornworks.com

Winner Communications, Inc.

Area(s) of Specialization: Television Broadcast

Number of Employees: 100

Founded in 1981, Winner Communications originally produced syndicated Quarter horse racing telecasts. Today, Winner produces a variety of programming for ESPN, ESPN2, and numerous local and regional television outlets. Winner production personnel have contributed to telecasts of major events as the Olympic Games, the Breeders' Cup, Major League Soccer's championship game (MLS Cup), and Thoroughbred racing's Triple Crown. Winner Communications is a full-service television production and multimedia company.

Winner Communications Inc.
6120 South Yale
Tulsa, OK 74136
Phone: 918 496-1900
Fax: 918 494-3786
Email: jwilburn@winnercomm.com
URL: http://www.winnercomm.com

Yagers Animation

Area(s) of Specialization: Traditional Animation

Number of Employees: 1+

Small animation studio.

Yagers Animation
237 N. College Ave.
Salina, KS 67401
Phone: 785 827-6632
Email: gman0708@aol.com

Zandoria Studios

Area(s) of Specialization: Traditional Animation, CGI, Film, Television

Number of Employees: 6+

Zandoria Studios provides character design and animation for film, TV, and games. From conceptual artwork and design, to photo-realistic CG models and finished animation.

Zandoria Studios
7203 Sylvia Trail
Chattanooga, TN 37421
Phone: 423 899-5408
Email: info@zandoria.com
URL: http://www.zandoria.com

Zero Gravity Production & Design

Area(s) of Specialization: Traditional Animation

Number of Employees: 6+

Small animation studio offering a wide range of services.

Zero Gravity Production & Design
P.O. Box 9
Big Bass Lake
Gouldsboro, PA 18424
Phone: 570 842-9234
Fax: 570 842-5252
Email: info@zgpd.com
URL: http://www.zgpd.com

West Coast

3D Animation Bob Productions

Area(s) of Specialization: Animation, CGI, Digital Media

Number of Employees: 30+

3D Animation Bob Productions is an award-winning CG animation studio specializing in character and visual effects design, animation, and story development. 3D Animation Bob's clients are served through an in-house art and development department, experienced production staff, advanced network and systems capabilities, and a creative, well-trained and service-oriented artistic team.

3D Animation Bob Productions
3519 W. Pacific Ave.
Burbank, CA 91505
Phone: 818 559-9700
Fax: 818 559-9768
Email: info@3Danimationbob.com
URL: http://www.3Danimation bob.com

3D Animation labs

Area(s) of Specialization: Animation, Graphic Design

Number of Employees: 6+

3D Animation labs, a wholly-owned subsidiary of Creative Technology Ltd., supplies graphics accelerator solutions to a broad range of professionals.

3D Animation labs, Ltd.
1901 McCarthy Blvd.
Milpitas, CA 95035
Phone: 408 428-6600
Fax: 408 432-6701
Email: sales@3Danimation labs.com
URL: http://www.3Danimation labs.com

3D Animation MIRAGE

Area(s) of Specialization: Traditional Animation, 3D Animation

Number of Employees: 6+

3D Animation MIRAGE is an innovative 3D Animation consulting company based in New York that offers 3D animation training and internships in a fast-paced production environment.

3D Animation MIRAGE
3 E. 28th St., 12th Fl.
New York, NY 10016
Phone: 212 967-7777
Fax: 212 967-7971

Email: info@3Danimation mirage.com
URL: http://www.3Danimation
mirage.com

310 Studios

Area(s) of Specialization: Animation,
Post Production

Number of Employees: 6+

310 Studios is a full-service post
production/Vfx house.

310 Studios
17458 Gilmore St.
Van Nuys, CA 91406
Phone: 310 859-5500
Fax: 310 859-5530
Email: info@310studios.com
URL: http://www.310studios.com

3birds

Area(s) of Specialization: Animation

Number of Employees: 10+

A full-service animation studio.

3birds
1431 Lemontree Ct.
La Habra, CA 90631
Phone: 562 694-8346
Fax: 562 691-1115
Email: samuelchi@3birds.com
URL: http://www.3birds.com

3D Animation Central

Area(s) of Specialization: Animation, 3D
Animation

Number of Employees: 6+

3D Animation Central is a full-service
animation studio specializing in 3D
animation character animation for
broadcast and games.

3D Animation Central
2705 N.E. 35th Place
Portland, OR 97212
Phone: 503 284-0484
Fax: 503 284-0484
Email: jason@3D Animation central.com
URL: http://www.3D Animation
central.com

3D Animation X COURSEWARE

Area(s) of Specialization: Animation,
Sales/Marketing

Number of Employees: 6+

3D Animation X COURSEWARE
evolved from 3D Animation Exchange,
founded in 1996 as a professional
training facility. 3D Animation X
Courseware distributes the same
professional quality, "learn-at-your-
own-pace" LightWave curricula and

courseware developed by 3D Animation Exchange for its onsite/online training.

3D Animation X Courseware
27734 Ave. Scott, Suite 190
Valencia, CA 91355
Phone: 661 702-9240
Fax: 661 702-9239
Email: info@fi3D Animation.com
URL: http://www.fi3D Animation.com

525 Studios

Area(s) of Specialization: Digital Effects Design and Post Production Services

Number of Employees: 40

525 Studios provides high-end Digital Effects Design and Post Production Services. Clients include agencies and directors involved in advertising, music, television, feature films, and new media. The company's services include: pre-production planning/ visual effects design, on-location supervision / shoot consultation, telecine transfers in NTSC/ PAL, HD and 2K, 2D animation & 3D animation effects and compositing, and editing.

525 Studios
1632 5th St.
Santa Monica, CA 90401
Phone: 310 525-1234
Fax: 310 525-2501
URL: http://www.525studios.com

8fish

Area(s) of Specialization: Animation, Television

Number of Employees: 10+

8fish focuses on 2D animation and 3D animation effects and animatics with emphasis on illustration for use in television commercials and corporate videos.

8fish
12193 S. Joseph View Lane
Draper, UT 84020
Phone: 801 572-0522
Fax: 801 572-1346
Email: info@8fish.com
URL: http://www.8fish.com

Academy of Television Arts & Sciences

Area(s) of Specialization: Film/Video, Multimedia

Number of Employees: 50+

Academy of Television Arts & Sciences
5220 Lankershim Blvd.
North Hollywood, CA 91601-3109
Phone: 818 754-2830
Fax: 818 761-2827
URL: http://www.emmys.org

Aces Research, Inc.

Area(s) of Specialization: Multimedia, CGI, Software Development

Number of Employees: 5

Aces Research, Inc. (Aces), founded in 1993, designs, develops, and markets Windows and Macintosh multimedia software for consumers, educators, librarians, and distributors worldwide. Aces has in-house development staff of product managers, programmers, graphic designers, interface specialists, curriculum design specialists, and authoring experts.

Aces Research, Inc.
Mission Blvd., #175
Fremont, CA 94539
Phone: 510 683-8855
Fax: 510 683-8875
Email: jobs@acesxprt.com
URL: http://www.acesxprt.com

Acme Filmworks Animation

Area(s) of Specialization: Animation, CGI, Multimedia

Number of Employees: 25

Acme Filmworks is an animation production house located in Hollywood, California. Acme offers animation styles and techniques including Stop Motion, Typography, Photo Collage, Design, Traditional Character Animation and Computer Graphics. Acme has produced commercials, identifiers, title sequences and short subjects for a host of corporations and organizations such as AT&T, Nabisco, Starbucks, NBC, Levi's, Weight Watchers, Nike, Coca-Cola, Toyota, Reebok, Amnesty International, Walt Disney, and Universal Pictures.

Acme Filmworks Animation
6525 Sunset Blvd. #10
Hollywood, CA 90028
Phone: 323 464-7805
Fax: 323 464-6614
Email: acmeinfo@acmefilmworks.com
URL: http://www.acmefilmworks.com

A.D.2, Inc.

Area(s) of Specialization: CGI, Multimedia

Number of Employees: 12

A.D.2, Inc. has been developing and producing marketing materials since 1980 and digital products for more than fourteen years. Clients include: Amblin Entertainment, Columbia/TriStar Pictures and Hilton Hotels, among others.

A.D.2, Inc.
2118 Wilshire Blvd., Suite 205
Santa Monica, CA 90403

Phone: 310 394-8379
Fax: 310 451-0966
Email: jobs@ad2.com
URL: http://www.ad2.com

Adobe Systems, Inc.

Area(s) of Specialization: CGI, Multimedia

Number of Employees: 1400

Adobe Systems Incorporated helped launch the desktop publishing revolution in 1982 and continues to work in graphics, publishing, and electronic document delivery. Many of the images on the Web today were created or modified with one or more of Adobe's products, such as Adobe Photoshop®, Adobe Illustrator®, Adobe Acrobat®, Adobe GoLive™, Adobe InDesign™, Adobe FrameMaker®, Adobe PageMaker®, Adobe Premiere®, and Adobe After Effects®.

Adobe Systems Inc./ San Jose
345 Park Ave.
San Jose, CA 95110-2704
Phone: 408 536-6000
Fax: 408 537-6000
URL: http://www.adobe.com

Adobe Systems Inc./ Seattle
801 N. 34th. St.
Seattle, WA 98103

Phone: 206 675-7000
Fax: 206 675-6809
URL: http://www.adobe.com

Advantage Audio

Area(s) of Specialization: Audio for Animation and Film Effects

Number of Employees: 10+

Advantage Audio is a full-service audio production and post, featuring animation sound and effects creation.

Advantage Audio
1026 Hollywood Wy.
Burbank, CA 91505
Phone: 818 566-8555
Fax: 818 566-8963
Email: bill@advantageaudio.com
URL: http://www.advantageaudio.com

Aftershock Digital

Area(s) of Specialization: Video Editing

Number of Employees: 1+

Founded in 1994 by editor Fritz Feick, Aftershock provides Post Production, editorial, visual effects, sound design, and graphic design to the advertising, film and television industries.

Aftershock Digital
8222 Melrose Ave., Suite 304

Los Angeles, CA 90046
Phone: 800 230-2290
Alt Phone: 323 658-5700
Fax: 323 658-5200
Email: edit@aftershockdigital.com
URL: http://www.aftershockdigital.com

A.I. Effects, Inc.

Area(s) of Specialization: Motion Picture Visual Effects

Number of Employees: 4

A.I. Effects Inc. creates visual effects for film, television, commercials, special projects, and computer graphics and interactively. The company's projects include works on such projects as HBO's From the Earth to the Moon, True Lies, Terminator II, Near Dark, Fright Night II, Super Mario Bros., The Abyss, Coneheads, Star Trek-The Next Generation, Dracula, and The Last Action Hero. AI is also involved in stereoscopic imaging.

A.I. Effects, Inc.
7114 Laurel Canyon Blvd., Suite A
North Hollywood, CA 91605
Phone: 818 764-2063
Fax: 818 764-2065
URL: http://www.aifx.com

Alias-Wavefront

Area(s) of Specialization: 2D Animation, 3D Animation, Graphics, Software Development

Number of Employees: 500+

Alias-Wavefront develops software for the film and video, games and interactive media, industrial design and visualization markets. Based in Toronto, Alias|Wavefront is a wholly owned, independent software subsidiary of Silicon Graphics, Inc.

Alias-Wavefront
Santa Barbara
614 Chapala Street
Santa Barbara, CA 93101
Phone: 416 362-9181
Alt. Phone: 800 447-2542
Fax: 416 369-6140
URL: http://www.aw.sgi.com

All Video Production

Area(s) of Specialization: 3D Animation, Digital Video Editing, Post Production, Audio, CD-ROM and DVD Authoring

Number of Employees: 2+

All Video Production, Inc. provides concept to completion video production including marketing, tradeshow, public relations, advertising, cinematic, video news releases, product information, training, and project documentation. The company uses digital video field gathering equipment; online non-linear postproduction equipment and offer broadcast quality, high definition 3D animation. The post production facilities offer online editing with digital special effect compositing, audio sweetening, narration, and a CD production music library. Other services include: script and storyboard generation, talent search, location scouting, high end "rush" and "dailies" editing, world standards conversion, studio production, aerial videography, digital cinematic production, digital still photography, and 3D animation animated cinematic compositing.

All Video Production
5311 Western Ave., Suite C
Boulder, CO 80301
Phone: 303 939-8515
Fax: 303 939-8516
Email: allvideodan@aol.com
URL: http://www.allvideoproduction.com

American Production Services

Area(s) of Specialization: CGI, Multimedia, Animation, Film/Video, Sound

Number of Employees: 80-90

In existence for 20 years, American Production Services offers digital video and audio editing and distribution services, including HDTV production. The company operates the APS High Definition Center, offering complete HDTV production services. American Production Services also help publish a magazine focused on the high definition HDTV production.

American Production Services
2247 15th. Ave. West
Seattle, WA 98119
Phone: 206 282-1776
Alt Phone: 888 282-1776
Fax: 206 282-3535
Email: conrad@victorystudios.com
URL: http://www.apsnw.com

An-Amaze-Tion

Area(s) of Specialization: Computer Animation, Digital Audio/Video Editing, Forensic Courtroom Animation, Architectural

Number of Employees: 4+

An-Amaze-Tion is a computer animation and digital audio/video production house specializing in broadcast quality animation. The company works in all facets of the field including, but not limited to: Architectural/Environmental, Broadcast/

Special Effects, CBT-Computer Based Training, Engineering, Forensic, Multimedia, and Marketing/Advertising.

An-Amaze-Tion
5405 Sunlight St.
Simi Valley, CA 93063
Phone: 805 578-9560
Fax: 805-578-9553
Email: prudling@an-amaze-tion.com
URL: http://www.an-amaze-tion.com

Angel Studios

Area(s) of Specialization: CGI, Multimedia

Number of Employees: 90+

Angel Studios creates 3D animation real-time interactive entertainment that mixes high-end technology, creativity, and gameplay. The company's software technology includes physics, adaptive AI, and organic animations. Angel Studios develops a wide variety of immersive interactive entertainment for consoles, PCs, arcades, OEM demos, and location-based entertainment.

Angel Studios
5966 La Place Court, Suite 170
Carlsbad, CA 92008
Phone: 760 929-0700
Fax: 760 929-0719
URL: http://www.angelstudios.com

Animalu Productions

Area(s) of Specialization: 3D Animation, Imaging and Animation for Film/Video/CD-ROM/Gaming Industry

Number of Employees: 2

Animalu Productions creates animation and 3D animation imaging for the CD-ROM, video, film and game industries.

Animalu Productions
633 San Leon
Irvine, CA 92606
Phone: 949 261-1179
Email: animalu@animalu.com
URL: http://www.animalu.com

Animanto

Area(s) of Specialization: Traditional Animation, 3D Animation, 2D Animation

Number of Employees: 6+

A full-service animation studio.

Animanto
624 Cross Ave.
Los Angeles, CA 90065
Phone: 323 5501977
Email: animanto@yahoo.com
URL: http://www.animanto.com

Animation and Effects

Area(s) of Specialization: Design, Production of Effects, Cel and Claymation Animation for Film, Television, Interactive Media

Number of Employees: 2

Animation And Effects creates visuals using cel and claymation techniques among others. Animation and Effects works on a fixed bid basis covering all design services from storyboards to final production.

Animation and Effects
235 Rockaway Beach
Pacificia, CA 94044
Phone: 909 302-8171
Email: Webresponse@animationand
effects.com
URL: http://www.animationandeffects.com

Animax

Area(s) of Specialization: Animation

Number of Employees: 50+

Full-service animation studio.

ANIMAX
3455 S. La Cienega Blvd., Bldg. C
Los Angeles, CA 90016
Phone: 310 559-9651
Fax: 310 559-9428

Email: info@animaxentertainment.com
URL: http://
www.animaxentertainment.com

Animus Films

Area(s) of Specialization: Animation, stop motion

Number of Employees: 5

Animus Films is an independent film production company dedicated to developing and producing commercially appealing. character-driven films for smaller budgets. They productions includes feature as well as documentary films.

Animus Films
914 Hauser Boulevard
Los Angeles, CA 90036
Phone: 323 571-3302
Fax: 323 571-3361
Email: contact@animusfilms.com
URL: http://www.animusfilms.com/

Antigravity Matter

Area(s) of Specialization: Traditional Animation

Number of Employees: 1+

A small animation studio specializing in character design.

Antigravity matter
226 Paris St.
San Francisco, CA 94112
Email: molly@antigravitymatter.com
URL: http://www.antigravitymatter.com

ARG Cartoon Animation Studio

Area(s) of Specialization: Animated Gifs

Number of Employees: 1

ARG Cartoon Animation has animated GIFs, all original, including a dancing cartoon alphabet, online greeting cards, dancing words, an art gallery called Click Media, and the Abnormal Toons. The company produces a CD titled "The RAG! Kartoon Klips" which contains cartoons and animated alphabets.

ARG Cartoon Animation Studio
2790 N. Academy Blvd., Suite 364
Colorado Springs, CO 80917
Phone: 719 559-1945
URL: http://www.artie.com

Artbeats Software Inc.

Area(s) of Specialization: Royalty Free Digital Film Archive

Number of Employees: 18+

The Artbeats Digital Film Library (ADFL) is an approach to stock footage. Their company provides high quality royalty-free, hassle-free digitized stock footage on CD-ROM.

Artbeats Software Inc.
P.O. Box 709
Myrtle Creek, OR 97457
Phone: 800 444-9392
Alt Phone: 541 863-4429
Fax: 541 863-4547
Email: wdoss@artbeats.com
URL: http://www.artbeats.com

Artfoundry

Area(s) of Specialization: Traditional Animation

Number of Employees: 6+

Artfoundry is a multimedia company specializing in 3D Animation graphics, animation, and audio/music for Web, CD-ROM, games, and video.

Artfoundry
950 High School Way, Apt. 3227
Mountain View, CA 94041
Phone: 650 625-1602
Email: info@artfoundry.com
URL: http://www.artfoundry.com

Artichoke Productions

Area(s) of Specialization: Film and Video Production, Audio Production

Number of Employees: 10+

Artichoke Productions was founded in 1981 by Paul Kalbach. Artichoke Productions creates film and video production packages, computer graphics and animation, and has a multimedia studio for film/video/studio.

Artichoke Productions
4114 Linden St.
Oakland, CA 94608
Phone: 510 655-1283
Fax: 510 655-0117
Email: kalbach@artichokepro.com
URL: http://www.artichokepro.com

Atom Films

Area(s) of Specialization: Short Film Distribution

Number of Employees: 140+

Atom acquires licenses to short films, animations, and digital media, and secures distribution via television networks, airlines, theaters, home video and DVD, the Internet, broadband services, and more. The company works with filmmakers, producers, media companies. Since its inception in late 1998, Atom has signed a number of shorts, including the 1999 Academy Award nominee Holiday Romance.

Atom Films
815 Western Ave., Suite 300
Seattle, WA 98104
Phone: 206 264-2735
Fax: 206 264-2742
Email: submissions@atomshockwavecom
URL: http://www.atomfilms.com

ATV-All Things Video

Area(s) of Specialization: Broadcast graphics

Number of Employees: 12+

After 14 years of service to the video production industry in Sacramento, All Things Video offers Closed Circuit System design and sales in addition to Professional and Broadcast services.

All Things Video
2424 Glendale Lane
Sacramento, CA 95825
Phone: 916 973-9100
Alt Phone: 888 973-9149
Fax: 916 480-2722
Email: dAve.@atv.net
URL: http://www.allthingsvideo.net

Available Light, Ltd.

Area(s) of Specialization: Visual Effects, Animation

Number of Employees: 7+

Available Light LTD. creates animation, digital visual effects, rotoscoping, including camera and optical service. The company uses software programs such as Lightwave, some 3D Animation Studio Max, AfterEffects, Digital Fusion, Photoshop and Elastic Reality.

Available Light Ltd.
1125 South Flower Street
Burbank, CA 91502
Phone: 818 842-2109
Email: jv2@migrantfilmworker.com
URL: http://www.availablelightltd.com

Ayres Group

Area(s) of Specialization: Animation

Number of Employees: 14

The company creates animation.

Ayres Group
750 B Street, Suite 42
San Diego, CA 92101
Phone: 619 696-6800
Fax: 619 696-6868
Email: employment@ayres42.com
URL: http://www.ayres42.com

Bandai Entertainment

Area(s) of Specialization: Traditional Animation

Number of Employees: 100+

Bandai Entertainment Inc. is the premier distributor of Japanese animation home video in North America. They have distributed such notable titles like the "Mobile Suit Gundam" series, "Escaflowne," "Cowboy Bebop," and "The Big O." Bandai Entertainment Inc. is a subsidiary of Bandai America Incorporated, who makes the toys for the hit television series, Power Rangers and Digimon. Bandai Entertainment Inc. focuses on home video distribution and licensing. All U.S. operations are headquartered in a large, ultra-modern facility in Cypress, Calif. Bandai Co., Ltd is the third largest toy company in the world comprising 53 subsidiaries in 18 countries. In addition to toys and children's entertainment, Bandai Co.'s global interests include video game software, multimedia, music and full-length feature films, vending machines, trading cards, candies, and licensed apparel.

Bandai Entertainment, Inc.
5551 Katella Ave.
P. O. Box 6054
Cypress, CA 90630
Phone: 714 816-9500

Fax: 714 816-6708
Email: pr@bandai-ent.com
URL: http://www.bandai-ent.com

Bandelier, EFX

Area(s) of Specialization: Commercial Film and Video, Cel Animation, Rotoscoping, 2D Animation and 3D Animation Computer Animation

Number of Employees: 6

The company's animators have produced spots for AT&T, Vlasic Pickles, Kellogg's Cereals, Budweiser, and Kodak. Bandelier uses traditional cels and computer programs to produce 2D Animation, 3D Animation, Rotoscope, stop motion, and CGI animation.

Bandelier, EFX
6808 Academy PKWY East NE
Suite B-1
Albuquerque, New Mexico 87109
Phone: 505 345-8021
Fax: 505 345-8023
Email: allans@bandelier.com
URL: http://www.bandelier.com

Banga U.E. Animation Studio

Area(s) of Specialization: Traditional Animation

Number of Employees: 6+

Independent animation studio that creates its own animated productions and produces animation for third parties.

Banga U.E. Animation Studio
P.O. Box 1310
Hermosa Beach, CA 90254
Phone: 310 937-5123
Email: info@bangaueanimation.com
URL: http://www.bangaueanimation.com

Banned from the Ranch

Area(s) of Specialization: Film and Video Production

Number of Employees: 10+

Banned from the Ranch Entertainment ("BFTR") is a production company connecting digital technology and the entertainment industry for over 18 years.

Banned From the Ranch
1158 26th Street #504
Santa Monica, CA 90403
Phone: 310 490-0045
Fax: 310 470-3250
Email: cc@ranchworksunlimited.com
URL: http://www.bftr.com

Base2 Studios

Area(s) of Specialization: CGI, Film/Video, Multimedia

Number of Employees: 15

Base2 Studios' creates using CGI, film/video and multimedia.

Base2 Studios
2800 North Spear Blvd.
Denver, CO, 80211
Phone: 303 455-0101
Fax: 303 455-1110
Email: info03@base2studios.com
URL: http://www.base2studios.com

BearByte Animation

Area(s) of Specialization: Modeling, Animation, Effects

Number of Employees:

BearByte Animation provides custom 3D animation, modeling, animation, and digital effects to the advertising, entertainment and computer gaming industries. BearByte Animation can provide custom 3D animation models, simple flying logos and photo realistic animated epics.

BearByte Animation
15637 Calle El Capitan
Green Valley, CA 91350
Phone: 805 270-0138
Email: bear@bearbyte.com
URL: http://www.bearbyte.com

BLADE Simulation

Area(s) of Specialization: 3D Animation and 2D Animation

Number of Employees: 1

BLADE Simulation creates access to computer generated modeling and animation. Computer photo-realistic images and animation are used to clarify ideas.

BLADE Simulation
P.O. Box 55656
Seattle, WA 98155
Phone: 206 368-5459
Email: billn@bladesim.com
URL: http://www.bladesim.com

Blizzard Entertainment

Area(s) of Specialization: Research and Development & Design of Computer Entertainment Products

Number of Employees: 130+

Headquartered in Irvine, Calif., Blizzard Entertainment was founded in 1990 under the name Silicon & Synapse. Blizzard Entertainment is a publisher of entertainment software games, including the *Warcraft* series, *Diablo*, and *Starcraft*.

Blizzard Entertainment
P.O. Box 18979

Irvine, CA 92623
Phone: 949 955-0283
Fax: 949 955-0157
Email: sales@blizzard.com
URL: http://www.blizzard.com

Bluelight Animation

Area(s) of Specialization: 2D Animation
and 3D Animation

Number of Employees: 2

Bluelight Animations offers: 3D
Animation motion graphics, Titles,
Logos, Special Effects – Fog, Explosions,
Fire, Rays and More, Character
Animation, 2D Animation and 3D
Animation Morphing, Virtual
Environments, 2D Animation Graphics,
Concept Design, Design and Trouble-
shooting for toy and game construction,
Illustration and Storyboards, Internet -
Web Page Design (including HTML
Programming), Full Raytrace and
Raycast, Final Output To any Format
including Video, Film, and QuickTime.

Bluelight Animation
P.O. Box 5643
Berkeley, CA 94705
Phone: 510 338-1212
Email: info@BlueLightAnim.com
URL: http://www.bluelightanim.com

Blur Studio, Inc.

Area(s) of Specialization: Visual Effects,
Animation, Film and Video

Number of Employees: 11+

Blur specializes in character
development and animation,
photorealistic effects, digital
compositing, and intergalactic battle
sequences.

Blur Studio, Inc.
1589 Venice Blvd.
Venice, CA 90291
Phone: 310 581-8848
Fax: 310 581-8850
Email: Webmaster@blur.com
URL: http://www.blur.com

Bob Lizarraga Animation

Area(s) of Specialization: Traditional
Animation

Number of Employees: 3+

Small studio that specializes in character
design.

Bob Lizarraga Animation
Design/Caricature
4720 Santa Lucia Dr.
Woodland Hills, CA 91364
Phone: 818 884-6999
Fax: 818 884-9137

Email: bobdraw@earthlink.net
URL: http://www.lizarraga.net

Bookartoons

Area(s) of Specialization: Animation

Number of Employees: 6+

Bookartoons is an animation and development creative team in Burbank, CA that develops and produces animated commercials, music videos, TV pilots, development and Web projects.

Bookartoons
859 N. Hollywood Way #258
Burbank, CA 91505
Email: info@bookartoons.com
URL: http://www.bookartoons.com

Brad Marks

Area(s) of Specialization: Traditional Animation

Number of Employees: 6+

Brad Marks International is an executive search firm exclusively dedicated to the entertainment and new media industries.

Brand Marks International
1888 Century Park East, Suite 2010
Los Angeles, CA 90067

Phone: 310 286-0600
Fax: 310 286-0479
Email: bodysnatcher@bradmarks.com
URL: http://www.bradmarks.com

Brain Zoo

Area(s) of Specialization: Animation, Film, Video

Number of Employees: 6+

Brain Zoo Studios is a cutting edge animation and visual effects company with over seven years of experience in the feature film, commercial, music video and gaming industries.

Brain Zoo Studios
16134 Hart St., Suite 200
Van Nuys, CA 91406
Phone: 818 785-1124
Fax: 818 904-1753
Email: info@brainzoostudios.com
URL: http://www.brainzoostudios.com

Brilliant Digital Entertainment

Area(s) of Specialization: 3D Animations for the Internet

Number of Employees:

Brilliant Digital Entertainment is an entertainment content provider and technology developer for the Internet and television markets. The Company is focused on two principal market segments: (1) The development and distribution of 3D Animation, digitally animated interactive content for the Internet, in small file sizes/shorter download times and full-screen images, developed using Brilliant's proprietary software. (2) Technology and tools for the development of Internet ready content. Tools are designed to enable the production of content for distribution via the Internet. These include technologies for lay-up of animation files, automated lip synchronization, data compression and interactive scriptwriting.

Brilliant Digital Entertainment
6355 Topanga Canyon Blvd., Suite 120
Woodland Hills, CA 91367
Phone: 818 615-1500
Fax: 818 615-0995
Email: info@b3Danimation.com
URL: http://www.bde3Danimation.com

Bruce Edwards Productions

Area(s) of Specialization: Animation

Number of Employees: 6+

Small animation studio working on several aspects of animation production.

Bruce Edwards Productions
431 W. Lambert Rd., Suite 308

Brea, CA 92821
Phone: 714 990-2378
Email: bedwards@jps.net
URL: http://www.BruceEdwardsProd.com

Calico Creations, Ltd.

Area(s) of Specialization: CGI, Visual Effects

Number of Employees: 6

For over 23 years, Calico World Entertainment has created traditional and digital animation, visual effects, and design for television, feature films and electronic entertainment. Aligned with World Events Productions, the company is a source for broadcast entertainment, from concept through international distribution.

Calico Creations LTD
10200 Riverside Dr.
N. Hollywood, CA 91602-2539
Phone: 818 755-3800
Fax: 818 755-4643
URL: http://www.calicoworld.com

California Image Associates

Area(s) of Specialization: Production and Post Production

Number of Employees: 22+

Cal Image works in Production and Post Production.

California Image Associates
11333 Sunrise Park Drive
Rancho Cordova, CA 95742
Phone: 916 638-8383
Fax: 916 638-4442
URL: http://www.calimage.com

Camera Control, Inc.

Area(s) of Specialization: Motion Camera Control

Number of Employees: 7

Camera Control Inc., makes live action motion control available to the commercials and visual effects industry in Los Angeles. The facility 'Camera Control' operates two MRMC Milo rigs and has serviced commercials, music videos and feature film projects for over two years. The Milo/Flair system received one of "Academy of Motion Picture Arts & Sciences" technical awards.

Camera Control, Inc.
3317 Ocean Park Boulevard
Santa Monica, CA 90405
Phone: 310 581-8343
Fax: 310 581-8340
Email: info@cameracontrol.com
URL: http://www.cameracontrol.com

Catalyst Productions

Area(s) of Specialization: Production and Post Production, 3D Animation

Number of Employees: 40+

Catalyst Productions is a full-service graphics, 3D animation, video production and post production facility, specializes in creating hi-tech, scientific, and industrial tutorials for a wide range of clients.

Catalyst Productions
1431 Center St.
Oakland, CA 94607
Phone: 510 836-1111
URL: http://catalystproductions.org

Cei, Inc.

Area(s) of Specialization: Traditional Animation

Number of Employees: 6+

Cei, Inc. is a video/DVD/Web animation Production Company specializing in productions for educational/training/children/corporate/product illustrations/advertisement that serve vertical markets. They specialize in multi language/multi ethnic productions for different cultures including African American, Muslim, Arab, Hindu, Spanish.

International, Inc.
92 Corporate Park, C-302
Irvine, CA 92607
Phone: 714 953-5778
Fax: 714 560-0744
Email: Cei3Inc.@aol.com

Cartoon Research

Area(s) of Specialization: Traditional
Animation

Animation history and general reference
source to motion picture industry.

Cartoon Research
7336 Santa Monica Blvd., #650
W. Hollywood, CA 90046
Phone: 323 658-8892
Email: jbeck6540@aol.com
URL: http://www.cartoonresearch.com

Casino of Doom, International

Area(s) of Specialization: Animation,
Graphic Design

Number of Employees: 2+

Jim Fisher has worked professionally as a
graphic artist since 1992 on projects
ranging from magazine covers to
editorial cartoons to corporate branding.
Drawing on his traditional animation
training from college, Jim has recently

focused more on the animated canvas
with a series of well-received Web toons
(available at campchaos.com and
iFilm.com).

Casino of Doom, International
3632 Ocean View Ave.
Los Angeles, CA 90066
Phone: 310 398-1833
Email: casinoofdoom@earthlink.net
URL: http://www.campchaos.comother
shows/casino-of-doom

Centropolis Effects

Area(s) of Specialization: Production and
Post Production, Visual Effects

Number of Employees: 12+

Based on SGI and Intel hardware, CFX
has departments for character
animation, 3D animation camera
tracking, 3D animation computer
graphics effects, 2D animation digital
compositing, 35mm scanning and
recording, and roto/paint. The company
is equipped with Discreet Logic Infernos
along with Cineon Tornadoes and
Cineon Storms. The CG are created with
Softimage, Houdini, and Alias software
as well as a set of proprietary tools. CFX
has produced computer-generated
graphics and digital compositing for
television shows and feature films-
including "Flubber," "Contact," "The

Faculty," "Providence," and "Storm" of the Century. CFX was the lead digital effects house on "Godzilla," contributing over 240 character animation shots to the film and over 160 digital composites.

Centropolis Interactive
10202 West Washington Blvd.
Astaire Building, Suite 2610
Culver City, CA 90232
Phone: 310 204-7300
Fax: 310 204-7301
Email: info@centropolis.com
URL: http://www.centropolis.com

The Chandler Group

Area(s) of Specialization: Production and Post Production, Film and Video Visual Effects

Number of Employees: 10

The Chandler Group is a film-based company to handle visual effects projects from advanced planning to post production. The company is involved in visual effects projects from classics like Star Wars, Blade Runner, and Close Encounters of the Third Kind to the stylistic ventures of Tim Burton's Batman franchise. Blockbusters include: "Godzilla" and "Armageddon." The company creates music videos with artists like Madonna, Elton John, Puff Daddy, Will Smith, TLC, Garth Brooks and Michael Jackson. The company has been involved with commercials for products like Coca-Cola, Kodak, Fed Ex, Skittles, Budweiser and McDonald's.

The Chandler Group
4121 Redwood Ave.
Los Angeles CA 90066.
Phone: 310 305-7431
Fax: 310 306-2532
URL: http://www.cgvfx.com

Channelzero

Area(s) of Specialization: Animation, Sales/Marketing, Film

Number of Employees: 6+

Channelzero was founded in 1999 by Emmy winning Character Designer Dave Warren as a co-op for artists, writers and musicians, dedicated to developing and successfully marketing exciting new and original content for television, film and new media.

Channelzero Entertainment
P.O. Box 13017
Long Beach, CA 90803
Phone: 800 709-9376
Email: info@channelzero.org
URL: http://www.channelzero.org

Characters Ink

Area(s) of Specialization: Animation, Digital Media

Number of Employees: 1+

Characters ink provides 2D animation Key frame animation, inbetweening, clean up, storyboards, backgrounds, traditional or digital. Flash MX, ToonBoom Studio.

Characters Ink
351 Peregrine Ln.
Prescott, AZ 86301
Phone: 928 443-1558
Fax: 928 443-1570
Email: genotoon@juno.com

Chiodo Brothers Productions, Inc.

Area(s) of Specialization: Visual Effects for Film and Video

Number of Employees: 5

Chiodo Brothers Prod., Inc. an foremost independent production companies working in special effects such as stop-motion animation, live action puppetry, make-up effects, miniatures, mechanical props and computer animation. The wizards behind The Teenage Mutant Ninja Turtles "Ninja Turtles: The Next Mutation" television show. The staff fabricated the new turtles and all the villains for The Teenage Mutant Ninga Turtles television show using computer controlled animatronics. The company has worked on a variety of projects, including the Power Rangers feature film and the ground-breaking nine screen, 360 degree film "Dinosaur Adventure," a centerpiece of Iwerks Entertainment's Cinetropolis theme park.

Chiodo Brothers Productions, Inc.
110 W. Providencia Ave.
Burbank, CA 91502
Phone: 818 842-5656
Fax: 818 848-0891
Email: klowns@chiodobros.com
URL: http://www.chiodobros.com

CHOPS & Associates Live Animation

Area(s) of Specialization: Live Animation, Digital Puppeteering

Number of Employees: 8+

CHOPS & Associates Live Animation is the home of Pentium-based Performance Animation, a virtual reality experience that brings 3D Animation characters to life, using real-time animation and video displays. The company's characters are used to attract people to trade show booths, to entertain attendees at sales meetings and to get attention at special events. CHOPS & Associates books performances for 1-5 day events and creates custom 3D Animation characters for animation on the system.

CHOPS & Associates Live Animation
P.O Box 6290
Incline Village, NV 89450
Phone: 888 766-6677
Alt Phone: 775 831-7451
Fax: 775 832-4468
Email: gary@chops.com
URL: http://www.chops.com

Cinema Now

Area(s) of Specialization: Online Distributor of Independent Films

Number of Employees: 10+

Cinema Now was established to be an online community for independent film watchers and filmmakers.

Cinema Now
4553 Glencoe Ave., Suite 200
Marina Del Rey, CA 90292
Phone: 310 314-9506
Fax: 310 773-0071
Email: feedback@cinemanow.com
URL: http://www.cinemanow.com

Cinema Production Service

Area(s) of Specialization: Visual Effects for Film and Video

Number of Employees: 15

Cinema Production Services, Inc. (CPS) was created to miniatures and models. CPS is designed as a free standing resource to commercial filmmakers and all other visual designers working throughout the entertainment industry. The company offers a range of services, from basic stage rental to complete commercial art development and photography. CPS' staff includes model makers, welders, painters and designers.

Cinema Production Service
7631 Haskell Ave.
Van Nuys, CA 91406-2006
Phone: 818 989-2164
Fax: 818 989-2174
Email: cps@cpsfx.com
URL: http://www.cpsfx.com

Cinema Research

Area(s) of Specialization: Title Design, Special Visual Effects and Digital Composition

Number of Employees: 35

Cinema Research creates Title Design and Digital & Special Effects.

Cinema Research
6860 Lexington Ave.
Los Angeles, CA 90038
Phone: 323 460-4111
Fax: 323 962-9429

Cinepartners Entertainment

Area(s) of Specialization: Production and Post Production

Number of Employees: 4

In 1996, Cinepartners Entertainment, Inc. was founded to manage feature films and television programs from Inception to final product. Cinepartners operates in three main areas: creative/production, sales/marketing, and finance.

Cinepartners Entertainment
10801 National Blvd. #103
Los Angeles, CA 90064
Phone: 310 475-8870
Fax: 310 475-0890
Email: cinepartners@jps.net
URL: http://www.cinepartners.net

Cinesite Film Scanning and Recording

Area(s) of Specialization: Visual Effects for Film and Video

Number of Employees: 175

Cinesite, opened in 1992, as a wholly owned subsidiary of Eastman Kodak Company. Cinesite is a full-service digital effects company providing a range of services, including digital compositing, 2D animation & 3D animation effects, wire and object removal, film stock repair and restoration, and digital film scanning and recording. Cinesite serves the motion picture, commercial, and special venue markets. Using both traditional film techniques and computer-generated imagery to build characters, environments and backgrounds, the team employs a range of digital processes to assemble the imagery into a shot. Cinesite has completed visual effects work on such films as "Armageddon," "Dr. Dolittle," "Primary Colors," "The Truman Show," "Lost In Space," "Sphere," "Air Force One," "Event Horizon," "Tomorrow Never Dies," "Jerry Maguire," "Space Jam," "And Smilla's Sense Of Snow."

Cinesite, Inc.
1017 N. Las Palmas Ave., Suite 300
Los Angeles, CA 90038
Phone: 323 468-4238
Fax: 323 468-4485
Email: daphne@cinesite.com
URL: http://www.cinesite.com

COBI Digital

Area(s) of Specialization: All Digital Production Facility

Number of Employees: 4

COBI Digital is owned by California Oregon Broadcasting, Inc., a company that was founded in 1933. COBI, an Oregon corporation, owns five television stations: KOBI-TV in Medford, KOTI-TV in Klamath Falls, KOBI-TV in Coos Bay, KLSR-TV in Eugene, and KEVU-TV in Eugene, as well as Crestview Cable Television in Prineville. COBI Digital became an all-component digital production facility in the Northwest in 1993, and uses Digital Betacam from Sony.

COBI Digital
125 S. Fir Street
Medford, OR 97501
Phone: 888 262-4937
Alt Phone: 541-776-5802
Fax: 541 779-5564
Email: info@cobidigital.com
URL: http://www.cobidigital.com

Colorado Studios

Area(s) of Specialization: Post Production – Film and Television

Number of Employees: 36

Colorado Studios is a production and Post Production facility, with studios at the former site of Stapleton Airport and in downtown Denver. In 1995-96, the TV mini-series "The Shining" was filmed at the Stapleton studio, followed by several independent features. Since 1983, Colorado Studios has held the contract for shooting and editing worldwide for PBS' Newshour. Mountain Mobile Television, a part of Colorado Studios, provides the mobile units for all Rockies, Nuggets, and Avalanche games, plus other events for all the major networks.

Colorado Studios
2400 N. Syracuse St.
Denver, CO 802
Phone: 800 882-6561
Fax: 303 388-9600
Email: info@coloradostudios.com
URL: http://www.coloradostudios.com

Communication Bridges

Area(s) of Specialization: Custom Web Design

Number of Employees: 2+

Communication Bridges produces videos and designs Web sites.

Communication Bridges
1330 Lincoln Ave. # 306
San Rafael, CA 94901

Phone: 415 454-5505
Alt Phone: 888 530-5505
Email: info@combridges.com
URL: http://www.combridges.com
Email: info@combridges.com

Component Post

Area(s) of Specialization: Post
Production for Film and Video

Number of Employees: 3

Component Post is a post production
house in Silicon Valley with a client base
ranging from Apple Computer to Ziff-
Davis.

Component Post
3350 Scott Blvd., Bldg. 63
Santa Clara, CA 95054
Phone: 408 980-5166
Fax: 408 980-9697
URL: http://www.cpost.com

Composite Image Systems/CIS

Area(s) of Specialization: Digital Visual
Effects for Film and Video

Number of Employees: 30

CIS is a digital effects industry with
credits that include "Titanic," "Contact,"
and "Terminator" Along with the many
movies the company has worked on, CIS
also contributed in effects for "Star Trek
Voyager" and the "X-Files."

Composite Image Systems/CIS
1144 N. Las Palmas Ave.
Los Angeles, CA 90038
Phone: 323 463-8811
Fax: 323 962-1859
Email: info@cishollywood.com
URL: http://www.cishollywood.com

Computer Café

Area(s) of Specialization: 3D Animation
and Digital Visual Effects for Film and
Video

Number of Employees: 17

Computer Café is a 3D Animation/
Digital Effects company specializing in
photo realism and character animation.
Clientele range from national ad
agencies and production companies to
major Hollywood studios and television
networks. Some clients include: Walt
Disney Pictures, Touchstone Pictures,
Paramount Pictures, Trimark Pictures,
NBC, DDB Needham Chicago, Chiat
Day Los Angeles, Pittard Sullivan and
Will Vinton Studios. Along with
animation and effects services, their staff
includes storyboard artists, designers,
writers, editors, effects producers and
on-set supervisors.

Computer Café
1207 4th Street, Suite 200
Santa Maria, CA 93455
Phone: 310 260-2320
Fax: 310 260-2420
Email: kenny@syndicate.tv
URL: http://www.computercafe.com

Computer Graphics Systems Development

Area(s) of Specialization: Digital Simulation and Virtual Reality

Number of Employees: 15

Computer Graphics Systems Development Corporation was founded by Roy Latham in 1990. The company provides products and services related to visual simulation and virtual reality. Services include consulting on product design, product evaluation, custom system development, sponsored research, and intellectual property work (including patent preparation, expert witness, and infringement analysis).

Computer Graphics Systems Development
2483 Old Middlefield Way, Suite 140
Mountain View, CA 94043
Phone: 650 903-4920
Fax: 650 967-5252
Email: rlatham@cgsd.com
URL: http://www.cgsd.com/

Continuity Studios

Area(s) of Specialization: 3D Animation, Digital Media

Number of Employees: 20+

Continuity has developed various properties, of its own and others including Buckly o' Hare, Skeleton Warrios, CyberRad, Ms. Mystic, Nighthawk, etc. for TV and Comics. Neal Adams: the Sketch Book was compiled by Arlen Schumer. It spans Adams' comics career, revealing unpublished works, his thought process, and storytelling techniques.

Continuity Studios
4710 W. Magnolia Blvd.
Burbank, CA 91505
Phone: 818 980-8852
Fax: 818 980-8974

Continuity Studios
62 W. 45th Street, 10th Floor
New York, NY 10036
Phone: 212 869-4170
Fax: 212 764-6814
Email: nadams@earthlink.net
URL: http://www.nealadams entertainment.com

Crazy Horse Editorial, Inc.

Area(s) of Specialization: CGI, Film/Video, Multimedia, Animation

Number of Employees: 15

Crazy Horse Editorial is a Post Production company offering creative and technical services for the advertising and promotional communities.

Crazy Horse Editorial, Inc.
912 Colorado Ave.
Santa Monica, Ca 90401
Phone: 310 451-7311
Fax: 310 458-0118
URL: http://www.crazyhorse.com

Creative Industries and Technology

Area(s) of Specialization: Computer Animation, Graphic Design, Interactive Design

Number of Employees: 4

Creative Industries and Technology is multi-faceted computer animation company that offers services including: computer animation, graphic design, and Web design.

Creative Industries and Technology
P.O. Box 7400
Tempe, AZ 85281-7400

Phone: 480 317-0480
Fax: 480 730-0139
Email: cti@ctianimation.com
URL: http://www.citanimation.com

Creative Logik Universe

Area(s) of Specialization: Animation, Digital Media

Number of Employees: 6+

Creative Logik Universe is an innovative studio which offers a broad range of visual effects and 3D animation for the entertainment industry.

Creative Logik Universe
216 S. Jackson St., Suite 201
Glendale, CA 91205
Phone: 818 545-9280
Fax: 818 545-9344
Email: info@creativelogik.com
URL: http://www.creativelogik.com

Creative Studio

Area(s) of Specialization: Animation

Number of Employees: 6+

Studio that does Animation Production, Graphic Design, New Media, Web Animation Production, and Web Site Development.

Creative Studio
17 Brooks Ave.
Venice, CA 90291
Phone: 310 664-6025
Email: pjwalsh68@hotmail.com
URL: http://www.Webhm.comjwalsh

Cyber F/X, Inc.

Area(s) of Specialization: Digital Imaging
Hardware and Software

Number of Employees: 20

Cyber F/X, Inc. located in Southern
California, provides imaging technology.
The company uses Cyberware®
digitizing process to service a wide
variety of clients in the entertainment
and design industries, such as:
Animators, Prop Makers, Designers,
Sculptors, Film Producers, Special
Effects Houses, Interactive CD-ROM
Creators, Theme Park Designers, Music
Video Producers, and Video Game
Developers. The company also uses
CNC-Sculpting™ machines.

Cyber F/X, Inc.
615 Ruberta Ave.
Glendale, CA 91201
Phone: 818 246-2911
Fax: 818 246-3610
Email: info@cyberfx.com
URL: http://www.cyberfx3D
Animation.com

Debut Entertainment, Inc.

Area(s) of Specialization: Production and
Post Production for Film and Video

Number of Employees: 10+

Debut Entertainment produces a wide
range of educational and entertainment
programs, corporate and organizational
promotions and television commercial
for telecommunications, advertising and
entertainment industries. It is also the
post production center for high-profile
Asian-American commercials like AT&T,
California State Lottery, Bank of
America, Sears, Southern California
Edison and many others. In addition, its
computer graphics department produce
DVD titles for feature films in Asian
languages. Debut Entertainment's in-
house recording studio is another
convenience to post production. Voice-
over recording, adding sound effects and
music, making revisions, and final mix
all becomes easier with the finest in
digital audio equipment.

Debut Entertainment, Inc.
923 E. 3rd St., Suite 112
Los Angeles, CA 90013
Phone: 281 324-2700
Fax: 213 626-0395
Email: debutInc@earthlink.net
URL: http://www.debutInc.com

The Design Loft

Area(s) of Specialization: Traditional Animation

Number of Employees: 6+

The Design Loft provides illustration, concept/intellectual property development and animation production services to media entities, including book publishers, television, feature film, video, interactive and online producers.

The Design Loft Studio
4521 N. Vistapark Dr.
Moorpark, CA 93021
Phone: 805 529-3101
Email: pen.and.pencil@juno.com
URL: http://www.Websdirect.
comdesignloft

Design Visualization Partners

Area(s) of Specialization: Computer Graphics

Number of Employees: 15+

Design Visualization Partners creates immersive environments for computer graphics. Their marriage of design skills with technical expertise generates an unparalleled synergy that they apply towards unique design solutions within the computer graphics world. Studio

DVP's work is based in the technology of real-time simulation.

Design Visualization Partners (DVP)
1040 N. Las Palmas Ave., Building 30
Hollywood, CA 90038
Phone: 213 860-3506
Fax: 213 860-3507
URL: http://www.desviz.com

Digital Artist Management, Inc.

Area(s) of Specialization: Traditional Animation

Number of Employees: 6+

Digital Artist Management, Inc. is a full-service agency specializing in creative, technical and executive recruiting, as well as team representation and business development for the interactive entertainment and content development industry.

Digital Artist Management
898 N. Sepulveda Blvd., Suite 175
El Segundo, CA 90025
Phone: 310 414-6800
Fax: 310 414-6804
Email: infodigitalartistmanagement.com
URL: http://www.digitalartist
management.com

Digital Element

Area(s) of Specialization: Animation, CGI

Number of Employees: 6+

Digital Element, Inc. creates cutting edge 3D animation effects for outdoor environments. Their two key product lines are WorldBuilder, a 3D animation modeling and rendering tool for outdoor environments, and Aurora, a Photoshop and After Effects plug-in that does true 3D animation clouds, skies, water, light effects and more. Digital Element also creates nature effects/products on spec as well as animation work.

Digital Element, Inc.
554 56th St.
Oakland, CA 94609
Phone: 510 601-7878
Fax: 510 601-7878
Email: sales@digi-element.com
URL: http://www.digi-element.com

Digiscope

Area(s) of Specialization:

Number of Employees:

Digiscope
2308 Broadway
Santa Monica, CA 90404
Phone: 310 315-6060

Fax: 310 828-5856
Email: mary@digiscope.com
URL: http://www.digiscope.com

DigiCel

Area(s) of Specialization: Traditional Animation

Number of Employees: 6+

DigiCel is the oldest digital ink & paint software company under a new name with new ownership and new software since 1999. They make a full line of 2D animation software for stop motion, pencil test, ink & paint and compositing.

DigiCel
1 Lanterna
Aliso Viejo, CA 92656
Phone: 949 916-8767
Fax: 949 916-8767
Email: info@digicelInc.com
URL: http://www.digicelInc.com

Digital Capture

Area(s) of Specialization: Animation for Web

Number of Employees: 2

Digital Capture is a provider of 3D gnimation GIF animations for Web page design. Based in San Francisco, the company's products were created from original work using various professional CAD applications, broadcast-quality design/animation products, and image editing packages.

Digital Capture
1140 Hampshire
San Francisco, CA 94110
Phone: 415 824-8680
URL: http://www.dcapture.com

Digital Character Group

Area(s) of Specialization: Traditional Animation

Number of Employees: 6+

Digital Character Group produces computer animation for television, feature film and new media applications.

Digital Character Group
P.O. Box 411
Pacific Palisades, CA 90272
Phone: 310 459-4390
Fax: 310 459-5166
Email: info@digitalcharactergroup.com
URL: http://www.digitalcharacter
group.com

Digital Dimension

Area(s) of Specialization: Animation

Number of Employees: 100+

Three Time Emmy Award Winning Animation Studio Specializing in CGI and Related Fields. Digital Dimension has Built a Reputation as an Innovative Provider of Motion Graphics, Visual Effects and Special Effects Animation for the Film, Television, Commercial and Gaming Industries.

Digital Dimension
210 N. Pass Ave.
Burbank, CA 91505
Phone: 818 845-2866
Email: jmorin@digitaldimension.com
URL: http://www.digitaldimension.com

Digital Domain

Area(s) of Specialization: Production and Post Production, Visual Effects

Number of Employees: 450+

Digital Domain is a creative and technological studio to create content and visual imagery.

Digital Domain
300 Rose Ave.
Venice, CA 90291
Phone: 310 314-2800
Fax: 310 314-2888
URL: http://www.d2.com

Digital Factory

Area(s) of Specialization: Motion Picture Sets Building

Number of Employees: 148

Digital Factory is a company that caters to the mechanical needs of the entertainment industry. The company designs and manufactures movie sets in a large scale manufacturing facility.

Digital Factory
28355-410 Industry Drive
Valencia, CA 91355
Phone: 661 775-8616
Fax: 661 775-8617
Alt. Phone: 888 361-3100
URL: http://www.digitalfactory.com

Digital Farm

Area(s) of Specialization: Post Production, Interactive DVD and CD-ROM Authoring, Web Site Design

Number of Employees: 3

Digital Farm is a video, DVD, and multimedia production and post production company. Employees work on projects ranging from corporate promotional videos to broadcast commercials, as well as interactive kiosks, DVD's, CD-ROMs, and Web page support.

Digital Farm
3800 Aurora Ave. N., Suite 280
Seattle, WA 98103
Phone: 206 634-2677
Fax: 206 634-2676
Email: info@digitalfarm.com
URL: http://www.digitalfarm.com

Digital Firepower

Area(s) of Specialization: Digital Environment Creation

Number of Employees: 2-10

Digital Firepower is a team of artists specializing in the creation of virtual environments through the medium of digital matter paintings. The company remains to concentrate on the area of visual effects. With studios in Hollywood and a second in London, the company offers matte work to major studio productions and smaller independent films on both sides of the Atlantic.

Digital Firepower
P.O Box 2937
Los Angeles, CA 90078
Phone: 323 467-9438
Fax: 323 467-9099
URL: http://www.digitalfirepower.com

Digital Imagination

Area(s) of Specialization: Audio and Video Production, Animation, and Interactive Design

Number of Employees: 15

A multimedia based company involved in various aspects of producing multimedia environments, including presentation, hosting sites, audio-video production, animation, e-commerce, and Web design.

Digital Imagination
2801 Townsgate Rd., Suite 101
Westlake Village, CA 91361
Phone: 805 497-7303
Fax: 805 230-9208
URL: http://www.digitalimagination.com/

Digital Wave Productions

Area(s) of Specialization: Visual Effects for Film and Video, CD-ROM and DVD Authoring

Number of Employees: 1

Digital Wave is a video post production boutique, specializing in non-linear AVID editing and 2D animation/3D animation motion graphics. Employees work on a variety of projects, including films, commercials, documentaries, CD-ROMs, and DVDs. Other services include video compression, voice over narration and writing.

Digital Wave Productions
2580 NW Upshur St.
Portland, OR 97210
Phone: 503 227-9283
Alt Phone: 800 858-9283
Fax: 503 227-2636
Email: info@dwavep.com
URL: http://www.dwavep.com

Dimensions 3

Area(s) of Specialization: Stereoscopic Television/Film/Print Media

Number of Employees: 2

Dimensions 3 works in 3D animation glasses, 3D animation TV (3D animation video), 3D animation film (3D animation motion picture), and 3D animation art and 3D animation print media. The company has experience in 3D animation art conversion and 3D animation print media, which have been used for Web sites, in books, magazines, and posters.

Dimensions 3
5240 Medina Rd
Woodland Hills, CA 91364
Phone: 818 592-0999
Fax: 818 592-0987
Email: info@go3Danimation.cc
URL: http://www.3Danimation
company.com

Distant Places

Area(s) of Specialization: Animation

Number of Employees: 6+

An animation studio that does Animation Production, Consulting Services, Game Development, Graphic Design, Software Vendors, Visual Effects Production. 3D Animation Graphics, Animation, Games/Entertainment.

Distant Places
1433 Franklin St., Suite 6
Santa Monica, CA 90404
Phone: 310 453-4748
Email: viklund@renderbox.net
URL: http://www.dplaces.com

DMK Productions, Inc.

Area(s) of Specialization: 3D Animation, Modeling

Number of Employees: 10

DMK Productions provides 3D Animation visualization and presentation graphics, models and scenes suited to the Architecture, Building, Engineering, Land Planning, Product Design, Film and Game Development industries.

DMK Productions
2395 N. Elmdale Ave.
Simi Valley, CA 93065

Phone: 805 583-3901
Fax: 805 583-3911
Email: info@dmkproductions.com
URL: http://www.dmkproductions.com

Downstream

Area(s) of Specialization: Post Production for Film and Video

Number of Employees: 50

DownStream does post production for video and film, merging traditional post production with new media.

Downstream
1650 NW Naito Pkwy., Suite 301
Portland, OR 97209
Phone: 503 226-1944
Fax: 503 226-1283
Email: info@downstream.com
URL: http://www.downstream.com

Dreadnought Pictures

Area(s) of Specialization: Animation

Number of Employees: 10

Dreadnought Pictures is an animation studios. The company focuses on one or two projects at a time. Dreadnought is developing a series of short, computer generated films, for an animated television series or feature film.

Dreadnought Pictures
7010 20th Ave. NE
Seattle, WA 98115
Phone: 206 985-0259
Fax: 206 985-0266
Email: ericf@dreadnought.com
URL: http://www.dreadnought.com

Dream Theater

Area(s) of Specialization: Visual Effects
for Film and Video, Interactive DVD and
CD-ROM Authoring

Number of Employees: 45

Dream Theater is a fully integrated,
digital media production studio
operating two major divisions, Dream
Theater Studios and Dream Theater
Interactive. Dream Theater Studios is the
visual effects unit, developing and
producing high end computer graphic
visual effects and animation for location
based entertainment, feature film,
television, video and game products.
Dream Theater Interactive develops and
produces interactive media for various
delivery pathways including Web, CD-
ROM, DVD, corporate presentations
and kiosk.

Dream Theater
30699 Russell Ranch Road, Suite 190
Westlake Village, CA 91362
Phone: 818 661-1109
Fax: 818 661-1194

Email: info@dreamtheater.com
URL: http://www.dreamtheater.com

DreamWorks SKG

Area(s) of Specialization: Special Effects,
3D Animation, Computer Animation

Number of Employees: 1200

Steven Spielberg, Jeffrey Katzenberg and
David Geffen founded DreamWorks
SKG in October 1994. The company
creates, develops, produces, and
distributes film and music
entertainment. DreamWorks SKG now
produces live-action motion pictures,
animated feature films, network,
syndicated and cable television
programming, home video and DVD
entertainment and consumer products.

DreamWorks SKG
100 Universal City Plz.
Universal City, CA 91608
Phone: 818 733-7000
Fax: 818 733-6155
URL: http://www.dreamworks.com

Driscal Designs

Area(s) of Specialization: Animation

Number of Employees: 6+

Full-service animation studio, from
conception to completion.

Driscal Designs
P.O. Box 1878
Fairfield, CA 94585
Phone: 707 864-1944
Fax: 707 864-1944
Email: info@driscal.com
URL: http://www.driscal.com

Duck

Area(s) of Specialization: Traditional and Experimental Animation for Film and Video

Number of Employees: 30

Duck Soup Studios is a Los Angeles based animation studio doing traditional and experimental animation. with computer special effects and compositing. With many SGI and Mac workstations, the company composites live-action with animation of all forms. As a traditional animation studio the company character animates, in 2D Animation and 3D Animation using all of the available tools.

Duck
2205 Stoner Ave.
Los Angeles, CA 90064
Phone: 310 478-0771
Fax: 310 478-0773
Email: inbox@duckstudios.com
URL: http://www.ducksoupla.com

Duck, You Sucker! Productions

Area(s) of Specialization: Traditional Animation

Number of Employees: 6+

Duck, You Sucker! Productions is a company that creates, designs and develops cartoons for traditional animation and the Internet.

Duck You Sucker! Productions
268 Cabrillo St., Suite A
Costa Mesa, CA 92627
Phone: 949 645-5426
Fax: 949 645-5498
Email: duckyousucker@hotmail.com
URL: http://www.duckyousucker.com

Edmark Corporation

Area(s) of Specialization: New Media development for Educational Purposes

Number of Employees: 200

Using the computer as a learning tool, Edmark combines new multimedia technologies with educational strategies to create educational software products. Their software's combination of guided learning and open-ended exploration allows students to conduct "hands-on" experiments and develop higher-level thinking and problem-solving skills.

Edmark Corporation
Riverdeep, Inc.
500 Redwood Blvd
Novato, CA 94947
Phone: 415 763-4700
Email: info@riverdeep.net

Riverdeep, Inc.
399 Boylston Street
Boston, MA 02116
Phone: 617 778-7600
Fax: 617 778-7601
URL: http://www.riverdeep.net/edmark/

EffectsOne, Inc.

Area(s) of Specialization: Animation

Number of Employees: 6+

Studio offering an array of services: Renderfarm Services (122 CPUs), 3D Animation (Broadcast / Title Graphics), Editing with Final Cut Pro v 4.0 in HD/SD, DVD/CD Authoring, Aerial and Ground Photography.

EffectsOne, Inc.
4091 E. La Palma Ave., #F
Anaheim, CA 92807
Phone: 714 630-4425
Email: sales@efxone.com
URL: http://www.efxone.com

Eggington Productions

Area(s) of Specialization: Animation, Television

Number of Employees: 3+

A small dedicated animation company working on television series for a variety of clients.

Eggington Productions
1009 N. 1140 West
Pleasant Grove, UT 84062
Phone: 801 796-0813
Email: weggingt@eggington.net
URL: http://www.eggington.net

Elektrashock, Inc.

Area(s) of Specialization: Animation, Interactive Design, Visual Effects

Number of Employees: 17

Founded in '97 by Darnell Williams and Rosa Farre and located in Venice CA, ElektraShock is a full-service digital boutique. The staff works in character animation as well as corporate presentation.

Elektrashock, Inc.
1320 Main St.
Venice, CA 90291
Phone: 310 477-9337
Fax: 310 399-4972
URL: http://www.elektrashock.com

Encore Visual Effects

Area(s) of Specialization: Visual Effects

Number of Employees: 100+

Encore creates visual effects.

Encore Visual Effects
6344 Fountain Ave.
Hollywood, CA 90028
Phone: 323 466-7663
Fax: 323 467-5539
Email: ttippets@encorehollywood.com
URL: http://www.encorevideo.com

Energon FX

Area(s) of Specialization: Animation

Number of Employees: 3+

Energon FX is a new startup company in Moorpark, CA specializing in visual effects, game cinematics, and commercials.

Energon FX
7355 Griffith Lane
Moorpark, CA 93021
Phone: 805 657-5586
Email: info@energonfx.com
URL: http://www.energonfx.com

EPX Generator

Area(s) of Specialization: Animation, CGI

Number of Employees: 10+

EPX Generator was founded in 2001 by a team of entertainment executives with extensive expertise in Interactive Entertainment, Feature Films, Television and Documentaries, in concert with the world's foremost historians, archaeologists, architects, gaming programmers, sword masters, technologists and 3D Animation artists with one purpose in mind: To bring the world's greatest ancient civilizations back to life for all platforms.

EPX Generator
835 Grant St., Suite 3
Santa Monica, CA 90405
Phone: 310 384-1680
Email: dv@epxgen.com
URL: http://www.epxgen.com

Eyetronics

Area(s) of Specialization: Traditional Animation

Number of Employees: 30+

Eyetronics provides 3D animation scanning solutions (scanning services, products and custom solutions) for various markets ranging from the movie industry (feature films, VFX) and TV industry (episodics), to the computer games, medical and industrial markets.

Eyetronics 3D animation scanning technology combines 3D animation geometry with high-resolution textures. It can be applied to scan a human face, head or whole body or an object (statues, sculptures, dolls, etc.) ranging from 4 inches to 10 feet.

Eyetronics
811 N. Catalina Ave., Suite 2120
Redondo Beach, CA 90277
Phone: 800 205-9808
Fax: 310 937-9061
URL: http://www.eyetronics.com

Europa Films

Area(s) of Specialization: Visual Effects, Interactive Design, Graphic Design

Number of Employees: 5

Europa is a collective of filmmakers, designers, animators and producers, integrating motion graphics and live action direction with high concept design for feature film main titles, advertising and commercials. The company's clients include: Tristar Pictures, NBC Television, Virgin Interactive, MGM, Aspect Ratio, Dreamworks SKG, Paramount Pictures, and RCA Records.

Europa Films
2057 N. Las Palmas Ave.
Los Angeles, CA 90068

Phone: 323 969-8831
Fax: 323 969-8830
Email: info@europafilms.com
URL: http://www.europafilms.com

Famous3D Animation

Area(s) of Specialization: Animation

Number of Employees: 6+

Famous3D Animation provides cost efficient solutions to capture and create lifelike facial expressions.

Famous3D Animation
1750 Montgomery St.
San Francisco, CA 94111
Phone: 415 835-9445
Fax: 415 954-7199
Email: support@famous3Danimation.com
URL: http://www.famous3Danimation.com

Fat Box, Inc.

Area(s) of Specialization: Post Production, Animation

Number of Employees: 20

Located in San Francisco the company provides 3D animation, CG animation, graphics, and multiple post edit and special effects suites.

Fat Box, Inc.
499 Seaport Court, 2nd floor
Redwood City, CA 94063
Phone: 650 363-8700
Fax: 650 363-8860
Email: info@fatbox.com
URL: http://www.fatbox.com

Flinch Studio

Area(s) of Specialization: Animation,
Web site Design, Digital Media

Number of Employees: 6+

Studio that provides Web Animation
Production, Flash/Internet Animation,
Webisodes, Web sites.

Flinch Studio
8339 Fordham Rd.
Westchester, CA 90045
Phone: 310 315-7200
Email: info@fllnc.h.com
URL: http://www.fllnc.h.com

Flipside Editorial

Area(s) of Specialization: Animation

Number of Employees: 20+

Full-service creative studio.

Flipside Editorial
2403 Main St.
Santa Monica, CA 90405

Phone: 310 399-5959
Fax: 310 399-0012
Email: sleance@flipsidedit.com
URL: http://www.flipsidedit.com

Freak Show Films

Area(s) of Specialization: Animation

Number of Employees: 6+

Freak Show Films is a full-service
animation production company
specializing in stop-motion.

Freak Show Films
651A Scott St.
San Francisco, CA 94117
Phone: 415 776-1076
Email: freakshowsf@hotmail.com
URL: http://www.freakshowfilms.net

Fred Wolf Films

Area(s) of Specialization: Animation

Number of Employees: 10+

Studio that offers Animation
Production, 2D Animation/Traditional,
2D Animation Computer Animation,
Flash/Internet Animation, Short Films,
Television Series, Television Specials.

Fred Wolf Films
4222 W. Burbank Blvd.
Burbank, CA 91505

Phone: 818 846-0611
Fax: 818 846-0979
Email: administration@fredwolffilms.com
URL: http://www.fredwolffilms.com

Freelance Animation

Area(s) of Specialization: Traditional Animation

Number of Employees: 6+

Freelance Animation Production.
Freelance Animation
714 Oak St.
San Francisco, CA 94117
Phone: 415 552-4742

Film Roman

Area(s) of Specialization: Animation

Number of Employees: 400

Film Roman is an animation studio that produces animated television series, specials and feature films. The studio also maintains licensing and merchandising and international distribution arms. Film Roman is working on "The Simpsons," "King of the Hill" and "Bobby's World."

Film Roman, Inc.
12020 Chandler Blvd., Suite 300
N. Hollywood, CA 91607

Phone: 818 761-2544
Email: info@filmroman.com
URL: http://www.filmroman.com

Flamdoodle Animation, Inc.

Area(s) of Specialization: Animation

Number of Employees: 24

Flamdoodle Animation, Inc. is a full-service traditional animation studio providing services from conception to completion for productions in all media, and outputting to all video and film formats at feature film quality. Utilizing the aimo digital system and CD quality, digidesign based audio editing on high-end workstations, the company offers automated lip-synching, inbetweening and digital ink-and-paint.

Flamdoodle Animation Inc.
6 Cuesta LN
Santa Fe, NM 87505-8782
Phone: 505 982-3132
Fax: 505 466-3525
URL: http://www.flamdoodle.com

Flash Film Works

Area(s) of Specialization: Modeling, 3D Animation, Digital Matte Paintings

Number of Employees: 10

Flash Film Works is a beta site for four of the CGI software manufacturers; the company participates in the on-going development of products. Flash Film Works staff includes programmers, animators, 3D animation matte artists and compositors. The company also conducts a training program, teaching all aspects of the visual effects craft.

Flash Film Works
743 Seward Ave.
Hollywood, CA 90038
Phone: 323 468-8855
Fax: 323 468-8040
Email: flash@flashfilmworks.com
URL: http://www.flashfilmworks.com

Flint & Steel Productions, Inc.

Area(s) of Specialization: Web Design

Number of Employees: 1+

Flint & Steel creates interactive Web presentations.

Flint & Steel Productions, Inc.
PMB#12 353-E East 10th St.
Gilroy, CA 95020
Phone: 408 848-8839
Email: all-support@Webhosting.cx
URL: http://www.flintandsteel.net

Flip Your Lid Animation Studios

Area(s) of Specialization: Animation for Film and Web

Number of Employees: 10

Co-founders, Jay Jacoby and Steve Soffer established Flip Your Lid Animation in 1998 to create and produce original animation for television and commercials. In June of 1999, the company launched a new division focusing exclusively on character animation and Web design for the Internet. Flip Your Lid creates advertising and promo campaigns for the entertainment industry including Disney, Fox, Universal, 20th Century Fox, NBC, CBS, Turner Broadcasting, Encore, Paramount, Sony and A&E.

Flip Your Lid Animation Studios
23501 Park Sorrento, Suite 207
Calabasas, CA 91302
Phone: 818 222-0700
Fax: 818 222-9166
Email: jay@flipyourlid.com
URL: http://www.flipyourlid.com

Flying Rhino Productions

Area(s) of Specialization: Film and Video Production, CGI

Number of Employees: 20+

Flying Rhino Productions generates content in the form of Video and Film Production, 2D Animation and 3D Animation, Digital Video and Computer Media for over 8 years. The staff includes Producers, Directors, Writers, Designers, Art Directors, Animators, Artists and Editors. Flying Rhino is equipped with high-end multi-processor NT and Mac workstations, both NT 4.0 and Novell servers, a full digital video and Internet development department, 3 Post Production edit suites and a full audio department.

Flying Rhino Productions
400 Tamal Plaza, Suite 406
Corte Madera, CA 94925
Phone: 415 927-4466
Fax: 415 927-1197
Email: info@delaplaine.com
URL: http://www.flying-rhino.com

Flying Spot, Inc.

Area(s) of Specialization: Post Production

Number of Employees: 25

Flying Spot was founded as a Post Production design boutique in Seattle, Washington in 1992. The Flying Spot creates graphic design and editorials, and series editing, title sequence, and design. Flying Spot now offers seven digital editing suites, nine design and animation suites, super high-resolution 8:8:8 telecine, and Post Production.

Flying Spot, Inc.
1008 Western Ave.
Seattle, WA 98104
Phone: 206 464-0744
Alt Phone: 800 963-7678
Fax: 206 464-0416
Email: info@flyingspot.com
URL: http://www.flyingspot.com

Forum Visual Effects

Area(s) of Specialization: Animation, Film, Television

Number of Employees: 25+

Forum Visual Effects specializes in the creation of photo-realistic effects for feature films and television. In 2002, they branched out to include work for commercials and feature film titles.

Forum Visual Effects
12020 Chandler Blvd., Suite 300
North Hollywood, CA 91607
Phone: 818 761-2544
Fax: 818 508-6420
Email: kvanhook@filmroman.com
URL: http://www.filmroman.com

Four Bars Intertainment

Area(s) of Specialization: Animation

Number of Employees: 6+

Studio that works on Feature Films, Games, Television Series.

Four Bars Intertainment
510 Railway Ave., #335
Campbell, CA 95008
Phone: 408 3649851
Email: mp3bob@aol.com

Foundation Imaging

Area(s) of Specialization: Visual Effects for Film and Video

Number of Employees: 155+

Foundation Imaging, a computer animation/special effects company based in Valencia, California, was founded in 1992 by Ron Thornton and Paul Bryant to create computer visual effects, miniatures and motion control for the entertainment industry. The company has created effects for theme park attractions such as, "Star Trek: The Experience" for the Las Vegas Hilton Hotel and Journey to Atlantis for Sea World/Florida. FI has also created visual effects for Star Trek: Voyager and Star Trek: Deep Space Nine. Foundation Imaging contributed to the making of Tristar Pictures' "Contact." The company creates, designs and produces digital special effects for network and syndicated television projects, feature films, multimedia projects and theme parks around the world.

Foundation Imaging
24933 West Ave. Stanford
Valencia, CA 91355
Phone: 805 257-0292
Fax: 805 257-7966
URL: http://www.foundation-i.com

Four Media Company

Area(s) of Specialization: D-1, 2D Animation and 3D Animation, computer graphics and compositing

Number of Employees: 100+

Four Media Company is a provider of technical and creative services to the entertainment industry. 4MC outsourcing solutions are used in the United States and worldwide by producers, distributors and other owners of television programming, feature films and similar entertainment content. The name Four media Company is derived from the Company's core services in film, video, sound and data.

Four Media Company
2813 West Alameda Ave.
Burbank, CA 91505-4455

Phone: 818 840-7000
Alt. Phone: 800 423-2277
URL: http://www.4mc.com

Fox Animation Studios

Area(s) of Specialization: Animation for Film

Number of Employees: 400+

Fox Animation Studios employs artists, technicians and craftsmen. The company produces classically-animated feature films. As a feature animation facility, the studio houses 83 Silicon Graphics Indy and Indigo computers, plus two Challenge servers and one Onyx server.

Fox Animation Studios
2747 E. Camelback Rd.
Phoenix, AZ 85016
Phone: 602 808-4600
Fax: 602 808-4699
Email: fbcresumes@fox.com
URL: http://www.foxanimation.com

FrankSilas.com

Area(s) of Specialization: Traditional Animation

Number of Employees: 6+

FrankSilas.com is a small animation company in Oceanside California that specializes in animation, whether that be 3D animation or 2D animation, for the Web, for Film, or for Video Games.

FrankSilas.com
4129 Waring Rd. # 11
Oceanside, CA 92056
Phone: 760 806-1810
Email: frank_silas@netzero.net
URL: http://www.franksilas.com

Fred Wolf Films

Area(s) of Specialization: Animation for Films

Number of Employees: 5

The core of Fred Wolf Films' business is in the conceptual development and production of animated films. Red Wolf Films is comprised of two studio locations, one in Burbank, California and the other in Dublin, Ireland. All creative work, concepts, design, script writing, dialogue recording, color, locating and design, storyboards and direction of animation action are executed at the Fred Wolf Films studios. Following these steps, the body of production using all of the above-mentioned pre-production elements is completed in their contracted studio facilities in the Far East and Europe.

Fred Wolf Films
4222 W. Burbank Blvd.
Burbank, CA 91505

Phone: 818 846-0611
Fax: 818 846-0979
Email: administration@fredwolffilms.com
URL: http://www.fredwolffilms.com

Fugitive

Area(s) of Specialization: Animation

Number of Employees: 25+

A full-service animation studio.

Fugitive
4052 Del Rey Ave. Bldg. 108
Marina Del Rey, CA 90292
Phone: 310 577-8900
Fax: 310 577-8902
Email: escape@thefugitives.com
URL: http://www.thefugitives.com

Gentle Giant Studios

Area(s) of Specialization: Digital
Modeling and Scanning, Toy Design,
Maquette Sculpture, Product Animation,
Quicktime VR Studio, Stereolithography,
Complete Mobile Digital Services.

Number of Employees: 20+

Gentle Giant combines computer-based 3D animation, digital scanning, modeling and prototyping technologies with traditional sculpting, molding, casting and painting skills to create models and data for films, games and toys. The company's clients include: Digital Domain, DreamWorks, SKG, Lightstorm Entertainment, LucasFilm Ltd., Marvel Comics, Mattel, Inc., Nickelodeon, Universal Studios, Walt Disney Company, Warner Bros. and Twentieth Century Fox.

Gentle Giant Studios
1115 Chestnut St.
Burbank, CA 91506
Phone: 818 504-3555
Fax: 818 557-8684
Email: cr.gentlegiant@usa.net
URL: http://www.gentlegiantstudios.com/

Giant Killer Robots

Area(s) of Specialization: Animation,
CGI, Multimedia

Number of Employees: 5

Giant Killer Robots is a digital effects company formed by animators Mike Schmitt, Peter Oberdorfer and John Vegher to create high-quality computer animation for film and television. The company deals with all aspects of the entertainment industry, creating effects for movies, commercials and video games.

Giant Killer Robots
576 Natoma Street
San Francisco, CA 94103
Phone: 415-863-9119

Fax: 415 863-9108
Email: info@giantkillerrobots.com
URL: http://www.giantkillerrobots.com/

Gigawatt Studios

Area(s) of Specialization: Interactive Design for Games, Web, and CD-ROM

Number of Employees: 27

Gigawatt Studios is a digital production studio located in Hollywood, CA. Gigawatt has the technical, creative, and production facilities to create interactive game entertainment, multimedia and Web site development. Gigawatt is represented by International Creative Management, and has established relationships with publisher's and distributors in the interactive multimedia and game industry. Gigawatt has been contracted to develop high-end 3D animation graphic adventures for the PC platform as well as location based interactive entertainment.

Gigawatt Studios
6255 Sunset Boulevard
Hollywood, CA 90028
Phone: 323 856-5245
Fax: 323 856-5240
Email: designjobs@gwatt.com
URL: http://www.gwatt.com

Gosch Productions

Area(s) of Specialization: Film and Video Production, Audio Production

Number of Employees: 20

Gosch Productions provides a full-service film/video production house and sound stage to initiate and complete production seamlessly under one roof.

Gosch Productions
5144 Vineland Ave.
North Hollywood, CA 91601
Phone: 818 509-3530
Fax: 818 509-3534
Email: gosh@speakeasy.net
URL: http://www.gosch.net

Grafx

Area(s) of Specialization: Web Design, Video, Training

Number of Employees: 10

Grafx was founded in 1982 and Incorporated in 1984. Its first products were early interactive presentation production and delivery tools such as PC Paint and GRASP. Grafx has served technology companies by providing marketing, sales and training materials.

Grafx
P.O. Box 2097

Capistrano Beach, CA 92624-0097
Phone: 949 361-3475
Fax: 949 248-0439
Email: info@gfx.com
URL: http://www.gfx.com

Graphic Arts

Area(s) of Specialization: Animation

Number of Employees: 60+

The labor union for creative artists, writers and technicians in animation and computer graphics in southern California.

Graphic Arts, Local 839 IATSE
4729 Lankershim Blvd.
North Hollywood, CA 91602-1864
Phone: 818 766-7151
Fax: 818 506-4805
Email: mpsc839@mindspring.com
URL: http://www.mpsc839.org

H-gun Labs-Unplugged

Area(s) of Specialization: Animation

Number of Employees: 10+

The company creates 2D animation and 3D animation computer animation Chicago and San Francisco. H-Gun West (the San Francisco location) produces much of the work in-house. H-Gun West is a MAC/SGI-based facility, utilizing 2D animation and 3D animation programming.

H-Gun Labs
587 Shotwell
San Francisco, CA 94110
Phone: 415 648-4386
Fax: 415 920-3911
URL: http://www.hgun.com
Email: info@hgun.com

Hairless Dog Production

Area(s) of Specialization: Animation, CGI, Video

Number of Employees: 6+

Hairless Dog Production specializes in digital animation for Web and CD application. Services include scripting, character design, and animation as well as traditional graphic design and copywriting.

Hairless Dog Productions
P.O. Box 86824
San Diego, CA 92138
Phone: 619 269-9368
Email: bwarr1@cox.net
URL: http://members.cox.net/bwarr3

Hammerhead Productions

Area(s) of Specialization: Film and Video Production

Number of Employees: 11

Hammerhead Productions, founded in February, 1995, is a digital film production company. The company is involved in creating digital visual effects used in making the company's own films, producing films for other studios. The company writes scripts and software.

Hammerhead Productions
Studio City, CA
Phone: 818 762-8641
Fax: 818 762-7311
Email: jobs@hammerhead.com
URL: http://www.hammerhead.com

Happy Trails Animation llc

Area(s) of Specialization: Animation All Types

Number of Employees: 5

Situated in Portland, Oregon, animators Andy and Amy Collen create, produce and direct traditional, digital, and mixed media. The company offers cel animation, DV photo manipulation, character and background design, pastels, inks and watercolors, sand and other materials, paper cutout animation, flat clay animation, and various forms of computer technology. Full production from storyboard to finished master. Soundtracks are often composed by musician and soundman Greg Ives, who has played with Miles Davis, Dizzy Gillespie, and Quincy Jones.

Happy Trails Animation LLC
11900 SW 116th Ave.
Portland, OR 97223
Phone: 503 590-7377
Fax: 503 590-7111
Email: hta@happytrailsanimation.com
URL: http://www.happytrailsanimation.com/Web site/home.html

Hellcat Productions

Area(s) of Specialization: Traditional Animation

Number of Employees: 6+

A small animation studio that has produced the movie and series Blood of the Samurai.

Hellcat Productions
4961 Ea Rd.
Kapaa, HI 96746
Phone: 808 823-9160
Fax: 808 823-9160
Email: AYamasato@aol.com
URL: http://www.bloodofthesamurai.com

Helium Productions, Inc.

Area(s) of Specialization: 3D Animation Computer Animation, CGI

Number of Employees: 11

Full service animation studio offering a wide range of services. Helium's infrastructure is built around Silicon Graphics hardware and several software platforms. With a capacity of seven animation seats, each staff member works on SGI Octane workstation including the loaded SGI Challenge render farm; the company's facility contains a total of 30 CPUs available.

Helium Productions, Inc.
2690 N. Beachwood Drive
Hollywood, CA 90068
Phone: 323 467-9323
Fax: 323 467-9396
URL: http://www.heliumproductions.com

Hippoworks.com

Area(s) of Specialization: Animation, Graphic Design

Number of Employees: 6+

Provider of cartoonlets, Webisodes, e-cards, and interactive entertainment and educational animations that are distributed across the Web.

Hippoworks.com
520 Altair Place
Venice, CA 10011
Phone: 310 581-1665
Email: denis@hippoworks.com
URL: http://www.hippoworks.com

HIT Entertainment

Area(s) of Specialization: Animation

Number of Employees: 100+

Large animation company offering a wide range of animation products.

HIT Entertainment
9300 Wilshire Blvd., 2nd Fl.
Beverly Hills, CA 90212
Phone: 310 724-8979
Fax: 310 724-8978
URL: http://www.hitentertainment.com

Hi-Test Productions, Inc.

Area(s) of Specialization: Traditional Animation

Number of Employees: 6+

Hi-Test Productions, Inc. is a full-service station. Since starting in 1984 by award winning producer/director Russell Calabrese, Hi-Test has been producing animation, illustration, audio and music for many satisfied clients.

Hi-Test Productions, Inc.
11542 Otsego St.
North Hollywood, CA 91601
Phone: 818 623-0584
Fax: 818 623-0563
Email: info@Hi-TestProductions.com
URL: http://www.Hi-TestProductions.com

Hornet Animation

Area(s) of Specialization: 3D Animation, Digital Effects, Motion Graphics

Number of Employees: 1+

Hornet Animation develops, produces and creates computer animation, visual effects and motion graphics, for use in feature films, title sequences, logo treatments, music videos, editing and broadcast sports events. The design team composed creates intricate 3D Animation models and designs realistic textures, life-like animations, and complex compositing.

Hornet Animation
5777 West Century Blvd., Suite 1640
Los Angeles, CA 90045
Phone: 310-641-9464
Fax: 310 641-2117
Email: michaelf@hornetInc.com
URL: http://www.hornetInc.com

Houlamation

Area(s) of Specialization: Animation, Digital Media

Number of Employees: 6+

Animation studio that produces 3D animation, animation on the Web and multimedia.

Houlamation
415 1/2 5th Ave. West
Kirkland, WA 98033
Phone: 425 739-0293
Email: houlamation@hotmail.com
URL: http://www.houlamation.com

House of Moves Motion Capture Studios

Area(s) of Specialization: CGI

Number of Employees: 20-25

House of Moves, in its fifth year of operation, provides motion capture services, stock 3D animation data, and custom 3D animation tools for the entertainment industry. The company has completed hundreds of animation projects including: electronic games, TV commercials, feature films, broadcast television series and online character animation/content for the Web. Motion capture technology, originally designed as a way for orthopedic surgeons to pinpoint irregularities in the human gait, has evolved into a technology whereby a human performance can be digitized and utilized to drive the motion of 3D animation characters. While motion capture is usually limited to humanoid characters, House of Moves has successfully captured other types of characters as well.

House of Moves Motion Capture Studios
5318 McConnell Ave.
Los Angeles, CA 90066
Phone: 310 306-6131
Fax: 310 306-1351
Email: jobs@moves.com
URL: http://www.moves.com

Howard A. Anderson Company

Area(s) of Specialization: Tiles, Optical, Digital Film Effects, Second Unit Photography

Number of Employees: 22+

Howard Anderson Company provides the following capabilities for clients' projects: motion picture Post Production, special photographic effects, title and logo design/animation, computerized motion control animation camera, composites from blue screen photography, complete insert stage, and 2nd Unit/location photography crews, storyboards, matte paintings/composites, miniatures, effects supervision, and supervision for blue screen photography, silicon graphics-MAC/IBM, 3D Animation graphic design, computer animation, wire and rig removal, digital compositing, image warping and morphing, digital effects capabilities, multi-layer composites, blue/green/non-screen, roto-scoping, motion tracking (single and multiple point), image retouching, matte painting and image manipulation, and scratch/dirt removal/restoration, warping and morphing of images, and 3D Animation title or logo design and animation.

Howard A. Anderson Company
5161 Lankershim Blvd., Suite 120
North Hollywood, CA 91601
Phone: 818 623-1111
Fax: 818 623-7761
Email: reception@haopticals.com
URL: http://www.haopticals.com

Hulabee Entertainment

Area(s) of Specialization: Traditional Animation

Number of Employees: 6+

Hulabee Entertainment is a digital media company created to provide unrivaled quality interactive entertainment to children and families worldwide. The company develops and publishes software and services designed for Windows, Macintosh, the Internet and other devices.

Hulabee Entertainment
218 Main St.
Box 370
Kirkland, WA 98033
Phone: 425 739-2700
Fax: 425 739-2701
Email: info@Hulabee.com
URL: http://www.hulabee.com

Illusive Reality

Area(s) of Specialization: Animation, Graphic Design

Number of Employees: 10+

Illusive Reality provides visually stunning and accurate 3D animation sequences that bring to life the complexities of science and technology in a way that everyone can understand. Illusive Reality also provides high-end visualizations of medical and other instrumentation designs as well as corporate Image animations.

Illusive Reality Animation
1364 Sunbeam Circle
San Jose, CA 95122
Phone: 408 293-7620

Fax: 408 904-5506
Email: jftupper@earthlink.net

Image G/Ikongraphics

Area(s) of Specialization: Motion Control Cinematography

Number of Employees: 30

Image G is a provider of motion control cinematography and related special effects services to the entertainment, advertising, and multimedia industries. Founded by Tom Barron in 1984, the company has worked in computer-controlled camera technology and developed new techniques to create ever more sensational visual effects.

Image G/Ikongraphics
10900 Ventura Blvd.
Studio City, CA 91604
Phone: 818 761-6644
Fax: 818 761-8397
Email: info@imageg.com
URL: http://www.imageg.com

Imaginary Forces

Area(s) of Specialization: Film and Video Production, Interactive Design

Number of Employees: 80+

Imaginary Forces (IF) is the fusion of thought, images, movement and sound.

As storytellers, the company's purpose is to challenge convention and find solutions for the media in which it works: film, broadcast, print, site and interactive design.

Imaginary Forces
6526 Sunset Boulevard
Hollywood, CA 90028
Phone: 323 957-6868
Fax: 323 957-9577
Email: jobs@imaginaryforces.com
URL: http://www.imaginaryforces.com

Imagination Workshop

Area(s) of Specialization: Computer Generated Animations

Number of Employees: 1

Jack Walsh's Computer Generated Animations is a Web gallery that offers projects ranging from commercial broadcast animations/visual effects to fully immersive computer generated three-dimensional worlds.

Imagination Workshop
19822 Collins Rd.
Santa Clarita, CA. 91351
Phone: 661 298-9615
Email: t4c@thevine.net
URL: http://www.smartlink.net/~jwalsh

IM DEAD Co.

Area(s) of Specialization: Animation

Number of Employees: 2+

Small animation studio offering a variety of animation products from a Web game to an entire animation show.

Im Dead Co.
31021 Elk Morton Dr.
Kent, WA 98042
Phone: 253 631-0507
Email: imdeadco@aol.com
URL: http://imdeadco.0catch.com4

Industrial Light And Magic

Area(s) of Specialization: Visual Effects, Film and Video Production, CGI

Number of Employees: 1,000+

When George Lucas founded industrial Light and Magic in 1975, he pointed the way to a new kind of filmmaking in which extraordinary worlds, unforgettable creatures and epic battles could be achieved, all with, meticulous realism. Just north of San Francisco, Industrial Light and Magic is currently working on a number of projects.

Industrial Light and Magic
Lucas Digital, Ltd. LL
P.O. Box 2459

San Rafael, CA 94912
Phone: 415 448-2000
Fax: 415 456-0833
URL: http://www.ilm.com

Inertia Pictures, Inc.

Area(s) of Specialization: Interactive
Design, Visual Effects

Number of Employees: 6

Inertia Pictures is a full-service digital
entertainment, design, and production
company located in Santa Monica,
California. Inertia offers all sorts of
different design solutions using
technology for online animation, 3D
animation computer graphics, concept
design for television, games, feature
films, and theme park films and toys.

Inertia Pictures, Inc.
13428 Maxella Ave., Suite 671
Santa Monica, CA 90404
Phone: 310 745-1650
Fax: 310 829-7291
Email: Webmaster@intertia.com
URL: http://www.inertia.com

Infinite Dimensions Studios

Area(s) of Specialization: Web
Development, Animation, Video, Game
Characters

Number of Employees: 25

Infinite Dimensions Studios help
customers create Web sites, films,
television programs or live Internet
shows. The company has experience in
traditional television and film, and
expertise in computer generated content.

Infinite Dimensions Studios
33 Sorrento Way
San Rafael CA, 94901
Phone: 415 454-6806
Fax: 415 456-2623
Email: bellis@idscorp.net
URL: http://www.idscorp.net/

Inkwell Images

Area(s) of Specialization: Traditional
Animation

Number of Employees: 6+

Inkwell Images is an award-winning
intellectual properties company
specializing in motion picture/video
production, including project
development, animation and live action
for educational, industrial, documentary,
and entertainment outlets; and
inventions and product development.

Inkwell Images
4015 Edenhurst Ave.
Los Angeles, CA 90039

Phone: 323 666-4077
Fax: 323 666-4079
Email: inkwellim@aol.com
URL: http://www.inkwellimagesink.com

International Cartoons and Animation Center, Inc.

Area(s) of Specialization: Cartoon Development

Number of Employees: 100

International Cartoons & Animation Center, Inc. (ICAC, Inc.) is an animation studio specializing in producing direct-to-video, lip-synched, multilingual children's animated cartoons. The company's productions are generated in six different languages (English, Arabic, French, Malay, Urdu and Turkish). The staff redraws the characters to lip-synch to each language. The company's original stories promote positive and universal family values. The videos feature classical 2D animation style. ICAC, Inc. continues to expand in production capabilities and international marketing and sales.

International Cartoons and Animation Center, Inc.
1823 E 17th St., Suite 203
Santa Ana, CA 92705
Phone: 714 953-5778
Fax: 714 560-0744

Email: ICACINC.@aol.com
URL: http://www.familytoons.com

Intrepidus Worldwide

Area(s) of Specialization: Interactive Design

Number of Employees: 2

Intrepidus is a privately owned company with offices in Santa Monica, California operating through two separate groups: broad based media production and entertainment management.

Intrepidus Worldwide
3000 West Olympic Blvd.
Santa Monica, CA 90404
Phone: 310 453-4800
Fax: 310 453-4801
Email: info@intrepidus.com
URL: http://www.intrepidus.com

Isle of Night Productions

Area(s) of Specialization: Traditional Animation

Number of Employees: 6+

Isle of Night Productions is a "concept to delivery" digital media company, specializing in animation and visual effects. Founded by world-renown magician Nicholas Night, ION Productions creates original animation concepts for TV and Web and uses today's digital tools combined with theatrical illusions to create stunning, cost-efficient special effects in their original and industrial productions.

Isle of Night Productions, LLC
25705 Windjammer Dr.
San Juan Capistrano, CA 92675
Phone: 949 240-1924
Email: nn@nicholasnight.com
URL: http://www.nicholasnight.comion

Island Fever Productions, Inc.

Area(s) of Specialization: Computer Animation, Illustration, Film, Web

Number of Employees: 2

Island Fever Productions, Inc. creates 3D animation and 2D animation computer animations, models, illustrations and graphics for a variety of venues including: feature films, TV, commercials, architects, display firms, industrial design firms, company informational films and brochures, court forensics, and individuals.

Island Fever Productions, Inc.
824 11th. Street, Suite #8
Santa Monica, CA 90403
Phone: 310 656-3011
Fax: 310 656-3021
Email: info@island-fever.com
URL: http://www.kjdesign.net

iWerks Entertainment

Area(s) of Specialization: Animation

Number of Employees: 50+

Large multimedia studio offering a wide range of services.

iWerks Entertainment
4520 W. Valerio St.
Burbank, CA 91505-1046
Phone: 818 841-7766
Fax: 818 841-7847
Email: sales@iwerks.com
URL: http://www.iwerks.com

JibJab Media, Inc.

Area(s) of Specialization: Animation, CGI, Digital Media

Number of Employees: 6+

Animation studio offering a variety of services.

JibJab Media, Inc.
Raleigh Studios
1600 Rosecrans Ave.
Bldg 6A, Suite 4
Manhattan Beach, CA 90254
Phone: 310 727-2677
Fax: 310 727-2678
Email: getinfo@jibjab.com
URL: http://www.JibJab.com

Jim Keeshen Productions, Inc.

Area(s) of Specialization: Animation

Number of Employees: 2+

Story consultant and pre-visualization specialist and designer of 2D animation and 3D animation characters.

Jim Keeshen Productions, Inc.
P.O. Box 251435
Los Angeles, CA 90025
Phone: 310 478-7230
Fax: 310 478-5142
Email: animatics@aol.com

Joseph Abbati

Area(s) of Specialization: Film/Video, Multimedia, CGI

Number of Employees: 1

Joseph Abbati is an art director and designer. The company creates advertisements, packaging, logos, sales brochures, and Web page designs. Clients have included: Colossal Films: Time-Warner, Organic Online, WorldCom, Intel, Hewlett Packard, Mac Home Journal, Parenting Magazine, Visages, Generra, Code Bleu Jeans, Delta Burke Design, The North Face, and Marjorie Baer.

Joseph Abbati
1931 Mason Street
San Francisco, CA 94133-2725
Phone: 415 673-2341
Email: jlabbati@creative.net
URL: http://www.creative.net/~jlabbati/

Kenimatlon Animation Services

Areas(s) of Specialization: Film Animation Service

Number of Employees: 1+

Kenimation Animation Services creates titles, aerial images, montages, and animation.

Kenimation Animation Services
1424 N. Wilcox Ave.
Hollywood, CA 90028
Phone: 323 462-2679
Email: kenru@thegrid.net

Klasky Csupo, Inc.

Area(s) of Specialization: Animation

Number of Employees: 400+

Klasky Csupo, Inc. created television shows as Rugrats, Duckman, Aaahh!!! Real Monsters and The Simpsons. With an Eastern European flare, the animators of Klasky Csupo produce television shows, commercials, music videos and title designs. The company is owned and operated by founders Arlene Klasky and Gabor Csupo.

Klasky Csupo, Inc.
1258 N. Highland Ave.
Hollywood, CA 90038
Phone: 323 468-5978
Fax: 323 468-3021
Email: Webmaster@klaskycsupo.com
URL: http://www.klaskycsupo.com

Kleiser-Walczak Construction Co.

Area(s) of Specialization: CGI, Visual Effects for Film and Video

Number of Employees: 40

Kleiser-Walczak Construction Co. produces computer generated animation and visual effects for feature films, special venue attractions, commercials and interactive media. This team works out of production studios in Hollywood, Manhattan, and Massachusetts.

Kleiser-Walczak Construction Co.
6105 Mulholland Hwy.
Hollywood, CA 90068
Phone: 323 467-3563
Fax: 323 467-3583
Email: marie@kwcc.com
URL: http://www.kwcc.com

KMC Films, Inc.

Area(s) of Specialization: Animation

Number of Employees: 6+

Studio offering Animation Production; 2D Animation/Traditional, 2D Animation Computer Animation, 3D Animation Computer Animation, Flash/Internet Animation; Animated Web Graphics, Feature Films, Television Series.

KMC Films, Inc.
20300 Ventura Blvd., #305
Woodland Hills, CA 91364
Phone: 818 346-3589
Fax: 818 346-4534
Email: kmcfilms@hotmail.com

Kurtz & Friends Films

Ares(s) of Specialization: Cel Animation, Special Effects, Film

Number of Employees: 15+

Kurtz & Friends Films works in special effects, cel animation and film titles.

Kurtz & Friends Films
2312 W. Olive Ave.
Burbank, CA 91506
Phone: 818 841-8188
Fax: 818 841-6263

Email: kurtz99@ix.netcom.com
URL: http://www.kurtzandfriends.com

L@it2D Animation

Area(s) of Specialization: Film and
Television Production, Interactive
Design

Number of Employees: 4

L@it2'd is a digital entertainment design
company, running the gamut from
concept to delivery of content for
Broadcast Television, Film, and
Interactive media. The company
combines organic design with
technology.

L@it2D Animation
6815 W. Willoughby Ave., Suite 102
Los Angeles, CA 90038
Phone: 323 856-0700
Fax: 323 856-0704
Email: info@Lati2D Animation.com
URL: http://www.lati2D Animation.com

Landor Associates

Area(s) of Specialization: Web Design,
Graphic Design

Number of Employees: 1500+

Landor Associates is an international
image management consultancy with 49
years in the design business and offices
in 14 countries with over 500 employees
worldwide, specializing in corporate
identity, environmental and packaging
design. Project teams are
interdisciplinary, made up of designers,
architects, production specialists,
marketing professionals, naming experts
and market research professionals. The
company creates visual identity systems.

Landor Associates
1001 Front Street
San Francisco, CA 94111
Phone: 888 252-6367
Fax: 415 365-3190
Email: more_info@landor.com
URL: http://www.landor.com

Landmark Entertainment Group

Ares(s) of Specialization: TV and
Themepark Design

Number of Employees: 30+

Since its inception in 1980, Landmark
Entertainment Group has been creating
forms of entertainment for the
expanding global audience. Landmark
Entertainment Group is a diversified
entertainment company that has worked
internationally since 1980. Founded by
Gary Goddard and Tony Christopher,
Landmark creates, develops, and
produces live entertainment, film and

television productions, licensing and merchandising properties, interactive development, as well as theme parks and attractions for the theme park and leisure industry.

Landmark Entertainment Group
5200 Lamkershin Blvd.
North Hollywood, CA 91601
Phone: 818 753-6700
Fax: 818 753-6767
Email: hr@landmarkusa.com
URL: http://www.landmarkusa.com

Laser Media, Inc.

Area(s) of Specialization: Digital graphics, Laser Productions

Number of Employees: 15

LaserMedia is a laser effects firm established in 1974, now producing laser effects for entertainment, promotion and theme park installations. Laser Media works in laser display technology, animation and special effect lighting.

Laser Media, Inc.
6383 Arizona Circle
Los Angeles, CA 90045
Phone: 310 338-9200
Fax: 310 338-9221
Email: lmilasers@aol.com
URL: http://www.lasermedia.com

Laserpacific Media Corporation

Area(s) of Specialization: Post Production for Film and Video, Interactive Design

Number of Employees: 100+

Laserpacific implements technology and services to the television, motion picture and digital media industries. Laserpacific's facilities offer every service necessary to assist the creators of motion picture film and digitally captured content prepare creative assets for distribution via analog or digital broadcast, file servers, DVD, Laser Disc, DVD-Rom, CD-ROM, by satellite or the Internet. Laserpacific was a force in the television industry's transition from analog, film-based methods to electronic and digital postproduction techniques, (Electronic Laboratory).

Laserpacific Media Corporation
Phone: 323 462-6266
Fax: 323 464-6005
Email: info@laserpacific.com
URL: http://www.laserpacific.com

LifeMode Interactive, Inc.

Area(s) of Specialization: Traditional Animation

Number of Employees: 6+

LifeMode Interactive, Inc. is a pioneering software company producing high-end tools and solutions designed primarily for fellow computer and video game developers, yet ready to aid many other applications wherever virtual 3D animation actors showing lifelike behavior are required or desirable. The line-up of current and future products is conceived as a revolutionary software suite, the Life Studio, allowing for painless production of what they call 'five-dimensional' games, the fifth dimension being the sought after human factor: visual credibility, advanced artificial intelligence, user's emotional involvement. Their strongest skills are in ultra-realistic human characters and complex nature and urban environments.

LifeMode Interactive, Inc.
283 Dalewood Way
San Francisco, CA 94127
Phone: 650 592-9229
Fax: 801 469-6576
Email: info@lifemi.com
URL: http://www.lifemi.com

Lightfoot Ltd, Inc.

Area(s) of Specialization: Animation, Digital Media

Number of Employees: 20+

Lightfoot Ltd, Inc. offers animation and digital media equipment, supplies & training for schools and teachers. Founded on the belief that money spend on teacher training would bring higher returns for the students, Lightfoot Ltd, Inc. focus is on the teacher and how to supply them with the tools, training and lesson plans to make life easier.

Lightfoot Ltd, Inc.
36125 Travis Ct.
Temecula, CA 92592
Phone: 909 693-5165
Fax: 909 693-5166
Email: ltfoot@lightfootltd.com
URL: http://www.lightfootltd.com

Lippy, Inc.

Area(s) of Specialization: Animation, Television, Film, Digital Media

Number of Employees: 6+

Founded in 1992 by Creative Director/ Executive Producer, Michael Lipman, Lippy, Inc. has pioneered traditional character animation for New Media CD-ROMs, Flash-based Web-isodic cartoons, video games, and broadcast television.

Lippy
310 Rydal Ave.
Mill Valley, CA 94941
Phone: 415 383-1927

Fax: 415 383-1443
Email: Info@lippy.com
http://lippy.com

Phone: 415 621-1300
Email: betsy@littlefluffyclouds.com
URL: http://www.littlefluffyclouds.com

Little Fluffy Clouds, Inc.

Area(s) of Specialization: Animation and Design

Number of Employees: 2+

Little Fluffy Clouds was founded in May 1996 by English designer/producer, Betsy De Fries and Dutch director Jerry van de Beek. The company specializes in all forms of digital animation and design, offering story boarding, character development and creative design, special effects, editing, compositing and New Media. LFC presents a complete design and production facility for broadcast and Web-based graphics. In 1997 Coca-Cola "Pictogram" was awarded a Creativity 27 Gold, Mainstay "Up…Down…Up…" received a bronze Clia and a London International Advertising Award for Best Animation. Both spots were featured in the 1997 SIGGRAPH Computer Animation Festival, where Betsy and Jerry also presented a Sketches forum on non-realistic rendering techniques.

Little Fluffy Clouds, Inc.
Pier 29 Annex
San Francisco, CA 94111

Liquid Light Studios

Area(s) of Specialization: Animation for Film and Video, Animated Shorts

Number of Employees: 6

Liquid Light Studios is a 3D animation design and animation studio located in West Los Angeles. Established in January, 1996, Liquid Light Studios worked within the broadcast arena which has led to such credits as Ally McBeal's Dancing Baby, promos for E! Entertainment Television, and character animation for "The Rosie O'Donnell Show." Liquid Light also applied its discipline of 3D animation to film and architecture. Its recent animated short, "Pronto Saldremos del Problema," won the award for "Best Animated Short Film" in Mexico City.

Liquid Light Studios
1093 Broxton Ave., Suite 220
Los Angeles, CA 90024
Phone: 310 443-5551
Fax: 310 443-5542
Email: info@liquidlightstudios.com
URL: http://www.liquidlightstudios.com

Loko Pictures

Area(s) of Specialization: Paper Manipulation, painting on Glass, Cel Animation, Sand Animation

Number of Employees: 4

Loko Pictures is an animation studio based in Los Angeles formed by a collaboration of animators/artists with a variety of animation styles. Loko Pictures has produced intro. ID jobs, title sequences, and animation for CD-ROMs & interactive Web based documents. Loko offers traditional cell, cut out, sand, and 3D animation computer animation.

Loko Pictures
548 South spring St., Suite 921
Los Angeles, 90013
Phone: 213 622-4398
Fax: 213 622-2177
URL: http://www.lokopic.com

LOOK! Effects, Inc.

Area(s) of Specialization: Visual Effects for Film and Video

Number of Employees: 25

LOOK! has 2D animation and 3D animation artists with experience as visual effects supervisors and artists of both feature film and commercial projects, including the opening sequence of *Armageddon* and *Volcano*.

LOOK! Effects, Inc.
1611A El Centro Ave.
Los Angeles, CA 90028
Phone: 323 469-4230
Fax: 323 469-4931
Email: driscoll@lookfx.com
URL: http://www.lookfx.com

LucasArts Entertainment Co.

Area(s) of Specialization: Interactive Entertainment Software

Number of Employees: 500 +

LucasArts was founded in 1982 by filmmaker George Lucas to provide an interactive element in his vision of a multi-faceted game company. The work produced combines storytelling, character development and settings. LucasArts Entertainment Company LLC is one of five Lucas companies. Lucas Digital Ltd. LLC, comprised of Industrial Light & Magic and Skywalker Sound, provides visual effects and audio Post Production services to the entertainment industry. Lucasfilm Ltd. includes George Lucas' feature film and television activities, as well as THX, Lucas Licensing Ltd. is responsible for the merchandising of all Lucasfilm's film and television properties. Lucas Learning

Ltd. offers interactive software products that provide learning opportunities through exploration and discovery.

LucasArts Entertainment Co.
P.O Box 10307
San Rafael, CA 94912
Phone: 415 472-3400
Alt. Phone: 888 532-4263
Fax: 415 444-8240
Email:Webjedi@lucasarts.com
URL: http://www.lucasarts.com

Lucasfilm Ltd. and Lucas Licensing Ltd.

Area(s) of Specialization: Digital Effects

Number of Employees: 1,100

Based in Marin County, California, Lucasfilm Ltd. is an independent production company, having produced five box office hits and won 17 Academy Awards. The company includes all of the George Lucas' feature film and television activities, and houses the business affairs, finance, information technology and services, research library/archives, Internet, Skywalker Ranch operations, marketing, and human resources divisions.

Lucasfilm Ltd
P.O. Box 10307
San Rafael, CA 94912
Phone: 415 444-8438

Fax: 415 662-2460
URL: http://www.lucasfilm.com

Lucas-THX

Area(s) of Specialization: Sound Effects

Number of Employees: 500+

THX quality film presentation in the exhibition and consumer electronics industry. The Professional THX Sound System is currently in over 1,400 theaters worldwide. There are more than 80 THX disc titles on the market.

THX Division
P. O. Box 10327
San Rafael, CA 94912
Phone: 415 492-3900
Fax: 415 492-3988
Email: cinema@thx.com
URL: http://www.thx.com

Lumens

Area(s) of Specialization: DVD Production, Computer Animation, Software Development

Number of Employees: 4

Lumens Studios' DVD production staff works on DVD titles, and has clients that include: Buena Vista Home Video, Warner Bros., TriMark, Anchor Bay, Fox, and Image Entertainment. The company's software, Afterburn, delivers 3D animation photorealistic volumetric effects to the 3D Animation Studio MAX community. Afterburn can turn MAX 2 Particle system to realistic clouds, fire, smoke, explosions, and nebula.

Lumens
820 Grant Ave.
Novato, CA 94945
Phone: 415 897-1801
Fax: 707 546-8912
Email: jon@lumens.com
URL: http://www.lumens.com

Lunarfish

Area(s) of Specialization: Interactive Design and Animation

Number of Employees: 2

Lunarfish creates animation and interactive design.

Lunarfish
San Francisco & Los Angeles
Phone: 888 445-0246
Fax: 888 445-0247
Email: info@lunarfish.com
URL: http://www.lunarfish.com

Lyric Media

Area(s) of Specialization: Production, Animation, Multimedia Development, Software

Number of Employees: 2

Lyric Media provides video production, computer animation & multimedia development services. Lyric also provides custom 3D animation software development services, particularly in support of 3D Animation Studio MAX. The company is located in Silicon Valley.

Lyric Media
215 Alexander Ave.
Los Gatos, CA 95030
Phone/Fax: 408 395-8444
Email: info@lyric.com
URL: http://www.lyric.com

M80 Interactive Marketing

Area(s) of Specialization: Interactive Design and New Media

Number of Employees: 20+

M80 is an Internet marketing company specializing in music, films, and other new media. M80 Interactive Marketing was launched in the summer of 1998 by former Maverick Recording Company Head of New Media Dave Neupert. M80 uses the street team model that is currently used by most major labels and translates it to the Internet.

M80 Interactive Marketing
2400 Hyperion Ave.
Los Angeles, CA 90027
Phone: 323 644-7097
Fax: 323 644-7010
Email: jeff@m80im.com
URL: http://www.m80im.com

Macromedia, Inc.

Area(s) of Specialization: Interactive Design

Number of Employees: 1000+

Macromedia is focused on Web designers, consumers, and the enterprise, delivering Internet products and technologies designed for the Web. Macromedia's Web Publishing products are showcased on the company's Web sites. To address the training and education needs of the enterprise, Macromedia is building upon its Web Publishing to create new Web Learning solutions.

Macromedia, Incorporated
600 Townsend Street
San Francisco, CA 94103
Phone: 415 252-2000
Fax: 415 626-0554
URL: http://www.macromedia.com

Magic Box Productions, Inc.

Area(s) of Specialization: Virtual Reality & Interactive Media

Number of Employees: 50

Magic Box Productions, Inc. provides consulting services, focusing on computer graphics, animation, multimedia, virtual reality and the Internet. Magic Box and Magic Bow productions include design services in the fields of digital media and multimedia entertainment and display systems.

Magic Box Productions, Inc.
345 N. Maple Dr., #222
Beverly Hills, CA 90210
Phone: 310 550-0243
Email: Webmaster@mbp.com
URL: http://www.mbp.com

Magico

Area(s) of Specialization: 3D Animations and Images

Number of Employees: 1

Magico's clients include: Disney, LucasArt, Time Warner, CAPCOM, Sega, 3D Animation O, San Francisco Production Group (General Motors television ads), and Midland Production. Work is done in Alias Power Animator

Stopmotion animator at Curious Pictures works on animating a head for a scene in HBO's "A Little Curious". Courtesy of Garth Gardner Photo Archive.

with Studio Paint for texturing. The animator also uses Amazon Paint, Composer and Mac.

Magico
Phone: 510 339-2554
Email: info@magico.net
URL: http://www.magico.net

Mainframe USA, Inc.

Area(s) of Specialization: Animation

Number of Employees: 6+

Studio offering Animation Production, 3D Animation Computer Animation, Television Series.

Mainframe USA, Inc.
2049 Century Park East, Suite 2130
Los Angeles, CA 90067
Phone: 310 556-2221
Fax: 310 556-0975
Email: info@reboot.com
URL: http://www.mainframe.ca

Manex Entertainment

Area(s) of Specialization: 3D Animation, Visual Effects

Number of Employees: 80

Manex Interactive is the special effects of Manex Entertainment combined with digital multimedia design and production. Manex Interactive draws from its visual effects heritage to work on the Internet and other interactive projects. Manex has created effects for feature films and commercials such as: "Mission Impossible 2," "Bless the Child," "Romeo Must Die," "Jordan to the Max," "Crouching Tiger," "Deep Blue Sea," "American Beauty," "The Matrix," "What Dreams May Come," and "Muppets From Space."

Manex Entertainment
4751 Wilshire Blvd., Suite 202
Los Angeles, CA 90010
Phone: 323 936-6822
Fax: 323 936-7968
Email: studios@manex-group.com
URL: http://www.mvfx.com

Mantis Motion Productions

Area(s) of Specialization: Animation, Film

Number of Employees: 6+

Optical motion capture studio providing capture of body, face and hands for game development, commercials, live events and feature film production.

Mantis Motion Productions
9324 S Hawley Park Rd., Suite C
West Jordan, UT 84088
Phone: 801 282-6694
Email: info@mantismotion.com
URL: http://www.mantismotion.com

Master Designs Computer Graphics

Area(s) of Specialization: Model Building and Visual Effects

Number of Employees: 2

Master Designs Computer Graphics was first formed to provide computer work (CAD) and computer-aided machining (CAM) for in-house model shops and small companies. Master Designs has added digital graphics to its line of services, such as photo manipulation, 3D Animation modeling, rendering, animation, and special effects. The company builds many types of models which include: architectural, study, detailed (museum), topographical, or even accident reconstruction models, models that may be used for presentation, movie special effects, display, or even legal purposes.

Master Designs Computer Graphics
P.O. Box 26172
Tempe, AZ 85285-6172
Phone: 480 966-7983
Fax: 480 966-7984
Email: robertk@Masterdesigns.com
URL: http://www.masterdesigns.com/

Matte World Digital

Area(s) of Specialization: Visual Effects

Number of Employees: 100

Specializing in the creation of realistic digital and traditional special visual effects, Matte World Digital offers digital 2D animation and 3D animation computer graphics and compositing, a full model shop for miniature creation, complete motion control facilities and blue and green screen stages combined with artistic vision.

Matte World Digital
24 Digital Drive #6
Novato, CA 94949
Phone: 415 382-1929
Fax: 415 382-1999
Email: info@matteworld.com
URL: http://www.matteworld.com

The Media Staff

Area(s) of Specialization: Recording for Audio

Number of Employees: 4+

The Media Staff helps clients with communications such as: audiobook and voice-over recording, scoring and sweetening, foreign language conversions, video production and non-linear editing. The company records, edits, scores, mixes and sweetens commercials, corporate videos, and radio drama.

The Media Staff
8425 West 3rd Street, Suite 401
Los Angeles, CA 90048
Phone: 323 658-8996
Fax: 323 658-8990
Email: info@themediastaff.com
URL: http://www.themediastaff.com

Media X

Area(s) of Specialization: Interactive Design

Number of Employees: 30

MediaX Corporation is a multimedia development and publishing company with expertise in real-time, 3D animation multimedia/interactive and online technology. MediaX has grown from a two-person studio to a turnkey multimedia house with more than 15 employees. In 1996, MediaX became a publicly held company when it merged with ZeitgeistWerks in Los Angeles. The client list, past and present, includes: EMI/Capital Records, MCA, Dow Jones/ Wall Street Journal, New Line Cinema, Toshiba, Apple Computer, Inc. and Iwerks.

Media X/ Los Angeles
8522 National Boulevard, Suite 110
Culver City, CA 90232
Phone: 310 815-8002
Fax: 310 815-8096
Email: info@media-x.com
URL: http://www.media-x.com/
Media X/ Santa Cruz
303 Potrero Street, 42-302
Santa Cruz, CA 95060
URL: http://www.mediax.com

Media Architects

Area(s) of Specialization: Animation, Sales/Marketing

Number of Employees: 6+

Media Architects is a full-service advertising agency and multimedia design firm that specializes in developing creative marketing and advertising tools for new and existing businesses. They offer audio & video production, media buying services, script writing, Web site design, Web site marketing, search engine optimization, corporate identity development,

animations, jingles and wide-range of creative services.

Media Architects
3207 E. Poinsettia Dr., Suite 53
Phoenix, AZ 85028
Phone: 602 569-3435
Email: info@media-architects.net
URL: http://www.media-architects.net

Merwin Creative

Area(s) of Specialization: Creative Design for Film, Interactive Design

Number of Employees: 27

For the past 18 years, Merwin Created has worked on major corporate product launches and full image campaigns to neighborhood public affairs.

Merwin Creative
419 Occidental Ave. South, Suite 208
Seattle, WA 98104
Phone: 206 621-7552
Fax: 206 343-0271
URL: http://www.merwlnc.reative.com

Mesmer Animations Labs

Area(s) of Specialization: Animation

Number of Employees: 50+

Mesmer Animations Labs is a resource center for the Information Age. They are an Authorized Training Center for game art, computer graphics, animation and special effects software from the big three: Discreet, Alias and Softimage. With classroom instruction, on-site custom training, Web based distance learning and printed books and courseware.

Mesmer Animation Labs
1116 N.W. 54th St., Suite A
Seattle, WA 98107
Phone: 800 237-7311
Fax: 206 782-8101
Email: info@mesmer.com
URL: http://www.mesmer.com

Method

Area(s) of Specialization: Visual Effects for Film and Video

Number of Employees: 4

Method specializes in visual effects for commercials and music videos. The company's services range from pre-production planning, pre-visualization and set supervision to compositing, matte painting and 2D animation and 3D animation and modeling.

Method
1546 Seventh St., Second Fl.
Santa Monica, CA 90401
Phone: 310 899-6500
Fax: 310 899-6501

Email: contact@methodstudios.com
URL: http://www.methodstudios.com

Metrolight Studios

Area(s) of Specialization: Visual Effects for Film and Video, 3D Animation

Number of Employees: 30+

Metrolight Studios Inc. uses computer animation tools to tell a story a filmmaker can imagine, or visualize a message a broadcaster requires, using the capabilities of CGI studios.

Metrolight Studios, Inc.
5724 W. 3rd St., #400
Los Angeles, CA 90036
Phone: 323 932-0400
Fax: 323 932-8440
URL: http://www.metrolight.com

Metropolis Digital, Inc.

Area(s) of Specialization: Video Games

Number of Employees: 20+

Working in console and PC games, Metropolis Digital has expertise in game development, digital effects, content creation, and entertainment software publishing. The company has in-house proprietary development tools coupled with the management experience of its key executives who have brought to market arcade and console games - among them, the legendary Street Fighter IITM series.

Metropolis Digital, Inc.
12 S. First St., Suite 1000
San Jose, CA 95113
Phone: 408 286-2900
Fax: 408 286-2970
Email: resume@metro3D Animation.com
URL: http://www.metro3D
Animation.com

Mike Young Productions, Inc.

Area(s) of Specialization: Animation

Number of Employees: 3+

An independent animation production studio specializing in 2D Animation, 3D Animation, and CGI animation.

Mike Young Productions, Inc.
20335 Ventura Blvd., Suite 225
Woodland Hills, CA 91364
Phone: 818 999-0062
Fax: 818 999-0172
Email: info@mikeyoungproductions.com
URL: http://
www.mikeyoungproductions.com

Mirage Media

Area(s) of Specialization: Film and Video Production and Post Production

Number of Employees: 6+

Established in 1983, Mirage Media is a full-service video production company offering services from the initial concept through the completed video production. The company assists in production from field shooting to professional pre & post production.

Mirage Media
1301 Post St.
San Francisco, CA 94109
Phone: 415 495-3477
Fax: 415 447-1996
URL: http://www.videomirage.com

Mixin Pixls

Area(s) of Specialization: Animation

Number of Employees: 5

Digital design and animation studio Mixin Pixls opened its doors in January 1998. The company was launched by Co-Founder/Henry Artist Mark Dennison and Co-Founder/Animation Director Harri Paakkonen. The Mixin Pixls team creates animation and effects for numerous clients including Intel, Budweiser, Dirt Devil, Frito Lay, Pontiac, Spirit, Honda, United Airlines, Kraft and Pacific Life.

Mixin Pixls
1335 4th Street, Suite 200
Santa Monica, CA 90401
Phone: 310 917-9141
Fax: 310 917-9142
Email: mpixls@mixinpixls.com
URL: http://www.mixinpixls.com

Mobility, Inc.

Area(s) of Specialization: Digital
Animation for Film and Video

Number of Employees: 10+

Mobility is a digital animation studio
providing full-service 3D animation and
2D animation for the feature film,
HDTV and commercials. Mobility
contributed to the Academy Award
winner for Visual Effects, What Dreams
May Come. The company staff can
structure. The ability to re-configure
software and hardware needs
appropriate to particular productions.
Mobility combines digital effects with
small teams and flexible software and
hardware infrastructure.

Mobility Inc.
555 Rose Ave., #8
Venice, CA 90291
Phone: 310 664-9664
Fax: 310 664-9554
Email: nfo@mobus.com
URL: http://www.mobus.com

Modern VideoFilm

Areas of Specialization: Computer
Animation, Visual Effects and Motion
Control

Number of Employees: 700

Modern Videofilm work in visual effects,
computer animation and motion
control.

Modern VideoFilm
4411 W. Olive Ave.
Burbank, CA 91505
Phone: 818 840-1700
Fax: 323 850-6151
URL: http://www.mvflnc.com/

MoonStone Studio

Area(s) of Specialization: Animation,
Web site Design, Digital Media

Number of Employees: 6+

MoonStoneStudio is a Web Site Design
and Development Company delivering
high quality professional Web sites.

MoonStone Studio
1524 Silverlake Blvd.
Los Angeles, CA 90026
Phone: 323 229-5505
Email: luna@moonstonestudio.com
URL: http://www.moonstonestudio.com

Mondo Media

Area(s) of Specialization: Animation for Video/Film/Web

Number of Employees: 120

Founded in 1988 and based in San Francisco Mondo Media is a new media company that creates, develops, and syndicates animated entertainment for the Web, television and the interactive television markets. The production facility is staffed by more than 100 artists, animators, writers, producers and business staff.

Mondo Media
135 Mississippi Street
San Francisco, CA 94107
Phone: 415 865-2700
Fax: 415 865-2645
Email: jobs@mondomedia.com
URL: http://www.mondominishows.com

Montana Edit, Inc.

Area(s) of Specialization: Post Production for Film and Video, Interactive Design

Number of Employees: 2

Montana Edit is a film and video edit studio in 1992. The company serves the entertainment and advertising communities with Avid edit systems and training and with personal service and support.

Montana Edit, Inc.
1131 Montana Ave.
Santa Monica, CA 90403
Phone: 310 451-9933
Fax: 310 453-3332
Email: info@montanaedit.com
URL: http://www.montanaedit.com

Motion City Films

Area(s) of Specialization: Film and Video Production and Post, Interactive Design

Number of Employees: 10+

Motion City Films offers a full range of production services utilizing new media tools. For 3D animation the company uses the Electric Image Animation System, Form-Z, and Extreme 3D Animation. For 2D animation the staff uses the Production Bundle of Adobe After Effects with all of the additional plug-ins.

Motion City Films
1620 Broadway, Suite A
Santa Monica, CA. 90404
Phone: 310 434-1272
Fax: 310 434-1273
Email: witt@motioncity.com
URL: http://www.motioncity.com

Moving Media

Area(s) of Specialization: 2D Animation and 3D Animation for TV, Web Design

Number of Employees: 2

Moving Media designs and create computer animation.

Moving Media
1045 17th Street, Studio C
San Francisco, CA 94107
Phone: 415 861-1759
Fax: 415 861-8712
Email: info@movingmedia.com
URL: http://www.MovingMedia.com

Neptune Media World

Area(s) of Specialization: Animation, 2D Animation, 3D Animation, CGI

Number of Employees: 20

Neptune Media World does multimedia including 2D Animation/3D Animation graphics and animation, interactive software (especially for educational/training purposes), video editing and compositing, design, and software training.

Neptune Media World
Modesto, CA 95350
Email: sg42@yahoo.com
URL: http://www.neptunemediaworld.com

New Hollywood, Inc.

Area(s) of Specialization: Animation Camera Services, Special Effects, Titles, Cinemascope Animation

Number of Employees: 1+

Since 1979, New Hollywood, Inc. has served the animation, Motion Picture, Television, Music Video, and Commercial fields. The areas of participation include: Editorial; Title Design and Execution; Post Production Supervision; Special Effects Supervision and Execution; Animation Production and Camera Service.

New Hollywood, Inc.
1302 N. Cahuenga Blvd.
Hollywood CA 90028.
Phone: 323 466-3686
URL: http://home.sprintmail.com/~ozziez/

Nexus Multimedia

Area(s) of Specialization: Animation, Digital Media

Number of Employees: 6+

A versatile multimedia company specializing to date in extraordinarily realistic architectural renderings, backgrounds and animations as well as Web site design, voice-over, copywriting and multimedia production work.

Nexus Multimedia
520 E. Portland St.
Phoenix, AZ 85004
Phone: 602 256-0448
Fax: 602 256-0461
Email: mail@nexusmultimedia.com
URL: http://www.nexusmultimedia.com

Nickelodeon Digital

Area(s) of Specialization: Animation, Film/Video

Number of Employees: 100+

A Viacom International, Inc. company. Nickelodeon Animation Studios produces and creates several cartoon shows. The company's feature film such as "The Rugrats Movie."

Nickelodeon Digital
231 W. Olive St.
Burbank, CA 91502
Fax: 818 736-3539
Nickelodeon Digital
1515 Broadway, 20th floor
New York, NY 10036-8901
Phone: 212 258-7727
URL: http://www.nick.com

North by Northwest Productions

Area(s) of Specialization: Film and Video Production and Post, Interactive Design

Number of Employees: 35+

North By Northwest Productions is a team of more than 40 people who create, write, shoot, edit, mix, compose, illustrate, animate, multimediate, produce, direct and consult on film, video and interactive multimedia projects.

North by Northwest Productions/
Spokane
903 W. Broadway
Spokane, WA 99201
Phone: 509 324-2949
Fax: 509 324-2959

North by Northwest Productions/Boise
601 W. Broad Street
Boise, ID 83702
Phone: 208 345-7870
Fax: 208 345-7999
Email: sjibben@nxnw.net
URL: http://www.nxnw.net

Novocom, Inc.

Area(s) of Specialization: Post Production and Visual Effects

Number of Employees: 15

Novocom provides broadcast branding / identities and design and Post Production compositing and visual effects. The company is headquartered in

Los Angeles with satellite offices in Hollywood (Paramount Pictures Studios), London, and Singapore. Clients include worldwide television networks, DTH Systems, and cable companies, movie studios, production companies, distributors, advertising agencies, and multimedia content producers, as well as freelance producers, directors, and editors.

Novocom, Inc.
5401 Beethoven St.
Los Angeles, CA 90066
Phone: 310 448-2500
Fax: 310 448-2525
Email: info@novo.com
URL: http://www.novo.com

nPower Software

Area(s) of Specialization: Traditional Animation

Number of Employees: 6+

nPower Software empowers 3D Animation artists, designers and engineers by connecting end users with advanced technology tools. nPower Software builds unique solutions based on proprietary technology. They focus on providing tools to facilitate creativity, simplify design processes, improve ease of use, and reduce design time and cycles.

nPower Software
13064 Trail Dust Ave.
San Diego, CA 92129
Phone: 858 538-3800
Fax: 858 538-3800
Email: Support@nPowerSoftware.com
URL: http://www.nPowerSoftware.com

Oddities Wild

Area(s) of Specialization: Traditional Animation, Film, Television

Number of Employees: 6+

Oddities Wild is dedicated to coming up with original concepts to be used for both prime time and children's television series.

Oddities Wild
70 Strawberry Hill Ave., #D1C
Stamford, CT 06902
Phone: 203 961-9229
Email: imaginethis@comic.com

Omni Video

Area(s) of Specialization: Post Production, Graphic Design, Animation Services

Number of Employees: 7

Omni Video offers full-service broadcast equipment rental, as well as comprehensive post production, graphic design and animation services. The company serves a wide client base that includes advertising agencies, local production companies, independent producers and corporate communication groups. Located near downtown Portland, Oregon, Omni is a broadcast rental facility specializing in a vast range of equipment from industrial to electronic cinematography.

Omni Video
911 NE Davis St.
Portland, OR 97232
Phone: 800 258-OMNI
Alt Phone: 503 233-1989
Fax: 503 230-1172
Email: info@omni-video.net
URL: http://www.omni-video.com

Oregon3D Animation

Area(s) of Specialization: Traditional Animation

Number of Employees: 6+

Oregon3D Animation focuses on continuing education for professionals working in the animation, post production and visualization industries.

Oregon3D Animation, Inc.
9875 S.W. Beaverton-Hillside Hwy.
Beaverton, OR 97005-3393
Phone: 503 626-9000
Fax: 503 641-5671

Email: info@oregon3Danimation.com
URL: http://www.oregon3Danimation.com

168 Design Group

Area(s) of Specialization: Computer graphics and design

Number of Employees: 20

The company creates design packages for television.

168 Design Group
60 Broadway
San Francisco, CA 94111
Phone: 415 837-0168
Fax: 415-693-4203
URL: http://www.168designgroup.com

Pacific Data Images

Area(s) of Specialization: Visual Effects and Animation for Film and Video

Number of Employees: 350

Founded in 1980 by Carl Rosendahl, PDI started out creating broadcast graphics, and in 1985 expanded into commercials and then to feature film effects. The company provides Hollywood with 3D Animation visual effects and animation.

Pacific Data Images
3101 Park Boulevard

Palo Alto, CA 94306
Phone: 650 846-8100
Fax: 650 846-8101
URL: http://www.pdi.com

Pacific Ocean Post Studios

Area(s) of Specialization: Video Editing
and Encoding, Sound, DVD Mastering.

Number of Employees: 150+

Pacific Ocean Post Studios authors DVD
disks. The Cinram/Pop DVD Center is
fully equipped to address all the
functions necessary to assemble, script,
and multiplex elements created by POP
Sound and POP Video and transmit data
streams directly to Cinram for
manufacture. To optimize the DVD
creation process, Pacific Ocean Post
Video edits the video and format (if
necessary) and performs MPEG-2 VBR
encoding of video elements.

Pacific Ocean Post Studios
730 Arizona Ave.
Santa Monica, CA 90401
Phone: 310 458-9192
Fax: 310 587-1222
Email: dclark@popsound.com
URL: http://www.popstudios.com

Paradesa Media

Area(s) of Specialization: Interactive
Design

Number of Employees: 20

The company develops Web sites,
intranets, extranets and creates
multimedia programming for broadcast
and cable television, laser disc, CD-ROM
and online services. Paradesa Media
offers development services for both
public and private sites, including:
interface and graphic design,
information design, Web site
development and maintenance,
development of intranet applications
and databases. Clients include Bank of
America, Genstar Instant Space, Piper
Jaffray, Thelen, Marin, Johnson &
Bridges, The California Trust, West
Coast Industries, Bay Area Multimedia
Partnership, and Studio Z.

Paradesa Media
375 Alabama Street
San Francisco, CA 94110
Phone: 415 487-2020
Fax: 415 487-2030
Email: joshua@finertechnologies.com
URL: http://www.paradesa.com

Paradise F.X.

Area(s) of Specialization: Visual Effects

Number of Employees: 10

Paradise FX develops new technology
and applies it to the most technically
challenging projects. Paradise F.X. is

committed to developing and photographing the Motion Picture, Theme park, and Special Venue industries ideas. Paradise FX designed a 3D Animation Dual camera system and has several other Large Format 3D Animation systems in development.

Paradise F.X.
7011 Hayvenhurst Ave.
Richmond, CA 94804
Phone: 818-785-3100
Fax: 818-785-3313
Email: info@paradisefx.com
URL: http://www.paradisefx.com

Pixel Liberation Front, Inc.

Area(s) of Specialization: Digital Production, Animation, CGI, Visual Effects

Number of Employees: 20+

PLF is a visual effects company, offering the specialties of pre-visualization and 3D animation integration in addition to experience in 3D animation and virtual environments creation. With offices in Los Angeles and New York, and a team of digital artists, PLF offers solutions to visual effects production coast to coast.

Pixel Liberation Front/New York
150 W. 28 St. #1003
New York, NY 10001

Phone: 212 239-1455
Fax: 212 239-3201

Pixel Liberation Front/Los Angeles
1316 1/2 Abbot Kinney Blvd.
Venice, CA 90291
Phone: 310 396-9854
Fax: 310 396-9874
Email: plf@thefront.com
URL: http://www.thefront.com

Planet Blue

Area(s) of Specialization: 3D Animation and Visual Effects

Number of Employees: 12

Since 1988, Planet Blue has been working in the creation and seamless integration of visual effects and animation with live action for commercials, features, television, music videos and the Internet.

Planet Blue
1250 6th Street
Santa Monica, CA 90401-1633
Phone: 310 899-3877
Fax: 310 899-3787
Email: info@planetblue.com
URL: http://www.planetblue.com

Pixologic, Inc.

Area(s) of Specialization: Animation, CGI, Film

Number of Employees: 6+

Pixologic presents ZBrush: an award-winning, innovative painting product that simplifies the science behind generating computer graphics. Services include: Animated Web Graphics, Commercials, Feature Films, Games, Short Films.

Pixologic, Inc.
336 West 31st St.
Los Angeles, CA 90007
Phone: 213 748-0990
Fax: 213 748-9888
Email: info@pixologic.com
URL: http://www.ZBrush.com

PowerProduction Software

Area(s) of Specialization: Animation, Film, Television

Number of Employees: 10+

PowerProduction Software is a leading developer of state-of-the-art desktop computer software tools for interactive multimedia authoring and the media industry. The company works extensively with the film, entertainment and advertising industries and is primarily known for its storyboarding software tools.

PowerProduction Software
15732 Los Gatos Blvd., Suite 300
Los Gatos, CA 95032
Phone: 408 281-7724
Fax: 253 595-8480
Email: info@powerproduction.com
URL: http://www.powerproduction.com

Prime Post

Area(s) of Specialization: Film/Video, Sound, Multimedia

Number of Employees: 25-30

Prime Post was established in 1991 to provide post production services to the film and television industries. Prime Post provides online & off-line editing, AVID, film to tape transfer, duplication and standards conversion, digital media, motion control, aspect ratio conversion, closed captioning, domestic & international fiber optic and satellite transmission services. Studio clients include Miramax Films, Buena Vista, USA Networks, Universal Studios, CBS, and Showtime Networks. Other clients include DavisGlick Productions, Carsey-Werner Productions, Quentin Tarantino, Tribune Entertainment, Artist View Entertainment, Strom/Magallon Entertainment, Cinequanon Pictures,

Tylie Jones and Associates, Gross Productions, Two Headed Monster Productions, Moxie Pictures, Klasky-Csupo Productions, A Band Apart Commercials, Dreamworks SKG, and many others.

Prime Post
3500 Cahuenga Blvd West
Los Angeles, CA 90068
Phone: 323 878-0782
Fax: 323 878-2781
Email: info@primepost.com
URL: http://www.primepost.com

The Production Group

Area(s) of Specialization: Film/Video, Multimedia

Number of Employees: 12

Located in Hollywood, The Production Group Studios is a full-service, turn-key video production facility. The company provides everything from facilities, equipment and crews to production office space, field production packages, coordination service and more.

The Production Group Studios
1330 Vine Street
Hollywood, CA 90028
Phone: 323 469-8111
Fax: 323 962-22182
Email: rnasch@production-group.com
URL: http://www.production-group.com

Protozoa, Inc.

Area(s) of Specialization: 3D Animation

Number of Employees: 30

Protozoa is a production studio using proprietary performance-animation software, "ALIVE," which is used by broadcasters worldwide, and is suited to 3D Animation on the Web. Protozoa-designed "ALIVE"-driven characters have been seen on television, at live events, and on the Web. The company has over ten years experience in 3D Animation motion-capture animation. The company builds real-time digital puppets for Cartoon Network, Disney, the BBC, MTV.

Protozoa, Inc.
2727 Mariposa St., Studio 100
San Francisco, CA 94110
Phone: 415 522-6500
Fax: 415 522-6522
URL: http://www.protozoa.com

Puget Sound Center

Area(s) of Specialization: Animation, Sales/Marketing

Number of Employees: 25+

PSC was founded in 2000 by an innovative partnership of leading high tech corporations, education, and government, and has recently become Discreet's finest 3D Animation and Multimedia Training Center.

Puget Sound Center
Canyon Park Business Center
22002 26th Ave. Southeast
Bothell, WA 98021
Phone: 425 640-1950
Fax: 425 640-1953
Email: info@pugetsoundcenter.org
URL: http://pugetsoundcenter.org

Puppet Studio

Area(s) of Specialization: Animation, Post Production

Number of Employees: 6+

Puppet Studio designs, builds and performs three dimensional characters for films, TV and commercials.

Puppet Studio
10903 Chandler Blvd.
North Hollywood, CA 91601
Phone: 818 506-7374
Email: pup8stdo@aol.com
URL: http://www.thepuppetstudio.com

Pyros Pictures, Inc.

Area(s) of Specialization: Animation, Digital Media, CGI

Number of Employees: 15+

Pyros Pictures, Inc. has been creating special effects, animation, and graphics for over 20 years in the feature film, broadcast TV, and computer gaming industries.

Pyros Pictures, Inc.
3197 Airport Loop Dr., Bldg. A
Costa Mesa, CA 92626
Phone: 714 708-3400
Fax: 714 708-3500
Email: gpyros@pyros.com
URL: http://www.pyros.com

Random Task

Area(s) of Specialization: Multimedia Design and Production

Number of Employees: 2+

Random Task is a full-service design and production company, working with clients in a variety of media.

Random Task
4216 Santa Monica blvd.
San Francisco, CA 94103
Phone: 415 865-1465
Fax: 415 865-1475
Email: careers@sbigroup.com
URL: http://www.razorfish.com

Razorfish – San Francisco
340 Main Street
Venice, CA 90291-2524
Phone: 310 581-5599

Fax: 310 581-5598
URL: http://www.razorfish.com

Reality Check

Area(s) of Specialization: CGI,
Multimedia, Animation

Number of Employees: 10-20

Reality Check creates in 3D Animation.
Reality Check works with clients from
concept and design, to full
implementation and integration.

Reality Check
723 Cahuenga Blvd.
Los Angeles, CA 90038
Phone: 323 465-3900
Fax: 323 465-3600
Email: info@realityx.com
URL: http://www.realityx.com

Rejobi

Area(s) of Specialization: Special Effects
for Web, Audio

Number of Employees: 5

Rejobi Interactive Communications,
established in February of 1996, work in
the area of business development,
product marketing, computer-graphics
design, applications development, mass-
communication technologies, interactive
multimedia, CD-ROM and laptop

presentation publishing, Internet access
technologies and World Wide Web site
design and marketing.

Rejobi
2520A Warren Drive,
Rocklin, CA 95677
Phone: 916 439-6146
Email: vscheunemann@rejobi.com
URL: http://www.rejobi.com

Renegade Animation, Inc.

Area(s) of Specialization: Traditional
Animation, Web-based Animation

Number of Employees: 12+

In 1992, Renegade Animation was
created with a simple goal in mind: to
cure the sick, feed the hungry, provide
shelter to those without shelter, and
promote world peace through the
miracle of cel animation. Advertising
projects include soft drinks, breakfast
cereals, fast food and toys. Inks and
paints are used in the preparation of
their animation.

Renegade Animation, Inc.
204 N. San Fernando Blvd.
Burbank, CA 91502
Phone: 818 556-3395
Fax: 818 556-3398
Email: lisa@renegadeanimation.com
URL: http://www.renegadeanimation.com

ReZ.n8 Productions, Inc.

Area(s) of Specialization: CGI, Animation

Number of Employees: 30

From network branding campaigns to photo-realistic effects, to a treatment of a simple logo, ReZ.n8 creates design and animation.

ReZ.n8 Productions, Inc.
6430 Sunset Blvd., Suite 100
Los Angeles, CA 90028
Phone: 323 957-2161
Fax: 323 464-8912
URL: http://www.rezn8.com

RichCrest Animation Studios

Area(s) of Specialization: Animation, Film

Number of Employees: 50+

RichCrest Animation Studios is an independent producer of high quality, animated motion pictures and direct-to-video programs. Richard Rich, director of Disney's "The Fox and the Hound" and "The Black Cauldron" started Rich Animation in 1986. Since that time, they have produced over 70 half hour videos and seven feature length films. Rich Animation produced the three "Swan Princess" films, distributed by Turner and Columbia TriStar, and "The King and I," released theatrically in 1999 by Warner Bros. "The Scarecrow" is a current release of Warner Family Entertainment, and their production of "The Trumpet of the Swan" was a theatrical release of TriStar Pictures this past May. In addition, their "Animated Hero Classics" series enjoyed a successful two-year run on HBO. They are currently involved in a co-production with TLC Entertainment for a series of 5 half hour videos entitled "The Kids 10 Commandments."

RichCrest Animation Studios
333 N. Glenoaks Blvd., Suite 300
Burbank, CA 91502
Phone: 818 846-0166
Fax: 818 846-6074
Email: ttobin@studiorich.com

Right Hemisphere

Area(s) of Specialization: Animation, 2D Animation, 3D Animation, Digital Media

Number of Employees: 6+

Right Hemisphere is a leader in graphical information management, offering solutions that help companies unlock and leverage their complex 2D animation, 3D animation and CAD data across the entire enterprise.

Right Hemisphere
2740 W. Magnolia Blvd., Suite 305
Burbank, CA 91505

Phone: 818 557-0003
Fax: 818 557-0120
Email: sales@righthemisphere.com
URL: http://www.righthemisphere.com

Rhonda Graphics, Inc.

Area(s) of Specialization: Video/Film
Computer Animation and Visual Effects

Number of Employees: 6

Rhonda Graphics is a company of artists
and technicians creating computer
animation and visual effects for video
and film projects. Based in Phoenix,
Arizona, the company collaborates with
commercial, broadcast and corporate
clients to create television commercials,
film effects, show opens, broadcast
graphics, opens for sporting events and
programs, as well as compositing,
retouching, and a variety of other visual
effects. The company works with
advertising agencies, directors,
production companies and clients
around the world, from Los Angeles to
Kansas City, and New York to Tokyo.

Rhonda Graphics Inc.
1730 E. Northern Ave., Suite 204
Phoenix, AZ 85020
Phone: 602 371-8880
Fax: 602 371-8832
Email: Webmaster@rhonda.com
URL: http://www.rhonda.com

Rhythm and Hues

Area(s) of Specialization: CGI,
Computer Animation

Number of Employees: 500+

The designers at Rhythm and Hues
actively seek input and advice from
others, but ultimately a single individual
is responsible for the final design
decisions. Their space is physical
counterpoint to the aesthetic problems
their designers are solving. Sunlight and
shadow play off intersecting planes and
surfaces. Recruiting

Rhythm and Hues Studios, Inc.
5404 Jandy Place
Los Angeles, CA 90066
Phone: 310 448-7500
Fax: 310 448-7600
Email: recruitment@rhythm.com
URL: http://www.rhythm.com

Rijn & Reisman

Area(s) of Specialization: 3D Animation
Art, Imaging

Number of Employees: 5

Rijn & Reisman work in the specialized
area of crafting and producing
miniatures, models, sculptures, and
maquettes (small, preliminary models of
sculptures) for clients such as Universal

Studios, Warner Bros., 20th Century Fox, Walt Disney, Paramount Pictures, Tim Burton Productions, Landmark Entertainment Group, and Rhythm & Hues. The staff of artisans create three-dimensional models, sculptures and maquettes. The company resume includes such feature films as Amistad, Junior, Mars Attacks, An American Werewolf in Paris, and Wild Wild West and major theme parks as: Universal Studios Hollywood, Florida, and Japan, Disneyland, the Disney Stores, Disney's Animal Kingdom, Sega GameWorks, Warner Bros. Stores, among many others.

Rijn & Reisman
10737 Chandler Blvd.
N. Hollywood, CA 91601
Phone: 818 509-0531
Alt Phone: 818 509-0580
Fax: 818 509-1369
Email: arenare@pacbell.net
URL: http://www.rijnreisman.com

Ring of Fire

Area(s) of Specialization: Animation, Visual Effects

Number of Employees: 16+

A creative digital effects and design studio, Ring of Fire was launched in 1996 to specialize in visual effects supervision, 2D animation compositing, CGI, and design for commercial, television and feature film projects. Catering to ad agencies, production companies and editorial houses, the Ring of Fire team is made up of visual effects supervisors, as well as Inferno, Henry and 3D animation artists.

Ring of Fire
8300 Melrose Ave., Suite 204
West Hollywood, CA 90069
Phone: 323 966-5410
Email: amy@ringoffire.com
URL: http://www.ringoffire.com

Rocket Pictures, Inc.

Area(s) of Specialization: CGI, Multimedia, Film/Video, Animation

Number of Employees: 10

Rocket Pictures is a media production and design firm specializing in film, broadcast, sports, entertainment and corporate communications. The company was founded in 1988 by Les Fitzpatrick and Dan Pepper and has clients such as Airborne Express, Alaska Airlines, DDB Needham, Microsoft, Millenium Arts, MTV, Fox Searchlight Pictures, Fox Sports, Weyerhaeuser and WongDoody.

Rocket Pictures, Inc.
1114 Post Ave.
Seattle, WA 98101
Phone: 206 623-7678
Fax: 206-623-6349
Email: info@rocket-pictures.com
URL: http://rocket-pictures.com

Rough Draft Studios, Inc.

Area(s) of Specialization: Animation,
Film, Video

Number of Employees: 20+

Rough Draft Studios, Inc.(RDS) was
founded in 1991. RDS houses a state-of-
the-art production facility, specializing
in both traditional and 3D animation, in
their 30,000 sq. foot Glendale crib.
Rough Draft has produced over one
hundred half-hours of prime time
animation including Futurama, Baby
Blues, and The Maxx. Previous work
includes Beavis & Butthead Do America,
The Naked Truth/Title Sequence, Spy Vs.
Spy, The Critic, music videos, and
commercials.

Rough Draft Studios, Inc. (RDS)
209 N. Brand Blvd.
Glendale, CA 91203
Phone: 818 507-0491
Fax: 818 507-0486
URL: http://www.roughdraftstudios.com

Route 66 Productions, Inc.

Area(s) of Specialization: Animation,
CGI, Multimedia, Film/Video

Number of Employees: 15

Route 66 Productions is a business
communications company that produces
live events and media for corporate use.
The headquarters is located near Los
Angeles International Airport and has
8,000 square feet of production
workspace. The company has ten years
experience producing new product
introductions, business meetings, video
conferences, interactive training
presentations, inspirational videos, and
trade show displays and kiosks for
companies like Sony, McDonald's, GTE,
Microsoft, Lexus, Guess, Apple
Computer, Honda, ITT and many more.

Route 66 Productions, Inc.
3215 La Cienega Ave.
Culver City, CA 90232
Phone: 310 815-2424
Fax: 310 815-2420
Email: admin@route66la.com
URL: http://www.digital66.com

Sad World Animation

Area(s) of Specialization: Traditional
Animation, 3D Animation

Number of Employees: 6+

Sad World Animation delivers top quality 3D animation modeling and animation.

Sad World Animation
1425 SW Clay #1
Portland, OR 97201
Phone: 503 241-1270
Email: delang@teleport.com
URL: http://www.sad-world.com

San Francisco Production Group

Area(s) of Specialization: Animation, CGI, Multimedia, Film/Video

Number of Employees: 6

SFPG is an animation and special effects service for Web and multimedia developers, video producers and video directors. The company started with HTTP://WWW sites, interactive kiosks, CD-ROM's and interactive television applications. Working entirely on the desktop, the company provides special effects and animations to video producers and directors, and creates content modules for Web and multimedia developers.

San Francisco Production Group
550 Bryant Street
San Francisco, CA 94107

Phone: 415 495-5595
Fax: 415 543-8370
Email: Webmaster@sfpg.com
URL: http://www.sfpg.com

Scansite

Area(s) of Specialization: 3D Animation Scanning. Digital Scanning

Number of Employees: 10

In addition to using 3D Animation digitizing technologies, Scansite offers a range of services including scanner sales & training, NURBS model construction, engineering, analysis and verification, rapid prototyping and consulting.

Scansite
1 Madrone Ave.
Woodacre, CA 94973-0695
Phone: 415 472-9500
Fax: 415 472-9545
Email: support@scansite.com
URL: http://www.scansite.com

Scarlet Letters

Area(s) of Specialization: Titles Design for Motion Pictures

Number of Employees: 5

Working in the motion picture and television title graphics field for over 12 years, Scarlet Letters helps clients with titles from the small screen of the computer to the big screen of the theater.

Scarlet Letters
6430 Sunset Boulevard, Suite 1001
Hollywood, CA 90028
Phone: 323 461-5959
Fax: 323 461-1758
Email: scarlet@ciagroup.com
URL: http://www.ciagroup.com/

Screaming Pixels

Area(s) of Specialization: Animation, Visual Effects, Industrial Design

Number of Employees: 5

Screaming Pixels develops its own production work and is working on a children's CGI series for British Television. The company's product design experience runs wide from ceramics to tightly engineered products, products are shown at photographic levels from the very first stages of development. By developing designs in the CGI environment the company has the ability to reflect changes in color and form, and give a virtual 360 degree view of the product.

Screaming Pixels
648 Buena Vista Drive
Santa Barbara, CA 93108

Phone: 805 565-0822
Fax: 805 565-4633
Email: enquiry@screamingpixels.com
URL: http://www.screamingpixels.com

Screaming Wink Productions

Area(s) of Specialization: Animation, Video

Number of Employees: 6+

A studio that has made award winning educational videos for the past 10 years.

Screaming Wink Productions
P.O. Box 373
Hakalau, HI 96710
Phone: 808 963-5482
Email: info@screamingwink.com
URL: http://www.screamingwink.com

Secret Weapon Inc.

Area(s) of Specialization: Animation, Video, Film

Number of Employees: 10+

Secret Weapon Inc. is a leading art and animation studio located in the heart of the Bay Area's electronic entertainment community. The top-shelf client roster includes Sony Computer Entertainment America, 3D Animation O, Electronic Arts, Nexon, Blue Shift, Little Beast and PhiloTV.

Secret Weapon
4 W. 4th Ave.
Lower Lobby
San Mateo, CA 94402
Phone: 650 401-8878
Email: info@secretweapon.org
URL: http://www.secretweapon.org

Shadow Caster

Area(s) of Specialization: CGI,
Animation.

Number of Employees: 3+

Shadow Caster is a visual effects and entertainment company based in Santa Barbara, California. The company produces imagery for the film, television, and multimedia industries. Shadow Caster was founded by a core group of artists with experience in the design and creation of computer generated visual effects.

Shadow Caster
136 W. Canon Perdido, Suite B-2
Santa Barbara, CA 93101
Phone: 805 884-1818
Fax: 805 884-9576
Email: plloyd@shadowcaster.com
URL: http://www.shadowcaster.com

Sierra, Inc.

Area(s) of Specialization: CGI,
Multimedia, Animation

Number of Employees: 480+

Sierra, Inc. is one of the developers and publishers of interactive entertainment and productivity software for personal computers. Sierra has been in the computer software field for nearly 20 years.

Sierra, Inc.
3060 139th Ave. SE, Suite 500
Bellevue, WA 98005
Phone: 425 649-9800
Fax: 425 641-7617
Email: careers@vugames.com
URL: http://www.sierra.com

Silicon Graphics, Inc./ Computer Systems Business Unit

Area(s) of Specialization: Multimedia,
CGI

Number of Employees: 3,000

SGI is one of the leaders in high-performance computing technology. The company's systems, ranging from desktop workstations and servers to powerful supercomputers in the world, deliver advanced computing and 3D animation visualization capabilities to scientific, engineering, and creative professionals and large enterprises. In addition, SGI creates software for design, Internet, and entertainment applications. SGI works in several industries, including manufacturing, government, entertainment, communications, energy, the sciences, and education.

Silicon Graphics, Inc./Computer Systems Business Unit
2011 Northshoreline Blvd.
Mountain View, CA 94043
Phone: 650 960-1980
Fax: 650 960-0197
Fax: 650 960-3393
URL: http://www.sgi.com

SimEx Digital Studios

Area(s) of Specialization: Traditional Animation, 2D Animation, 3D Animation, CGI

Number of Employees: 40+

Full-service animation production servicing the television commercial and specialty venue film industries. Specializing in 2D animation cel and 3D animation CGI character work.

SimEx Digital Studios
3250 Ocean Park Blvd., Suite 100
Santa Monica, CA 90405
Phone: 310 664-9500
Fax: 310 664-9977
Email: allen@simexds.com
URL: http://www.simexds.com

Slappy Pictures

Area(s) of Specialization: Animation

Number of Employees: 6+

Slappy Pictures is an independent animation production studio providing traditional 2D animation, stop-motion, and CGI animation for TV, film, commercial, Internet and game projects.

Slappy Pictures
23962 Dovekie Circle
Laguna Niguel, CA 92677
Phone: 949 448-0653
Email: contact@slappypictures.com
URL: http://www.slappypictures.com

Smashing Ideas Animation

Area(s) of Specialization: Animation for Web, Broadcast Television, Multimedia

Number of Employees: 31

Smashing Ideas Animation creates animation for broadcast television and the Web.

Smashing Ideas Animation
1604 Dexter Ave. N.
Seattle, WA 98109
Phone: 206 378-0100
Fax: 206 378-5704
Email: evanc@smashingideas.com
URL: http://www.smashingideas.com

Socketoo Media

Area(s) of Specialization: Traditional Animation, Post Production

Number of Employees: 6+

Socketoo Media is a new company providing North American exposure for foreign language productions.

Socketoo Media
2462 Glencoe Ave.
Venice, CA 90291
Phone: 310 822-1749
Email: socketoomedia@aol.com

Sockeye Creative, Inc.

Area(s) of Specialization: Film/Video, CGI, Multimedia

Number of Employees: 7

Sockeye Creative Inc. is production studio that combines film and video with graphic design. Sockeye is a small studio located in Portland's historic Union Station. The three principles are Tom Sloan, Andy Frser, and Peter Metz.

Sockeye Creative, Inc.
800 NW 6th Street, Suite 211
Portland, OR 97209
Phone: 503 226-3843
Fax: 503 227-1135
Email: tsloan@sockeyecreative.com
URL: http://www.sockeyecreative.com

Sojourn Design

Area(s) of Specialization: Animation, CGI, Post Production

Number of Employees: 6+

Character design, illustration and graphic design from concept to finish.

Sojourn Design
187 W. Mission Ave.
Ventura, CA 93001
URL: http://www.sojourndesign.com

SOL Design FX

Area(s) of Specialization: CGI, Film/Video, Multimedia

Number of Employees: 35+

SOL Design is a small boutique company using a combinations of high-tech and traditional methods to create designs and effects works for advertising companies. The company's clients include Janet Jackson, Puff Daddy, and Smashing Pumpkins.

SOL Design FX
515 N. State Street, 26th Floor
Chicago, IL 60610
Phone: 312 706-5500
Fax: 312 706-5501
Email: neal@soldesignfx.com
URL: http://www.soldesignfx.com

Sony Computer Entertainment America

Area(s) of Specialization: Computer Game Console Game and Console Development

Number of Employees: 750

Sony Computer Entertainment America, a division of Sony Computer Entertainment America Inc., distributes and markets the PlayStation game console in North America, develops and publishes software for the PlayStation game console, and manages the U.S. third party licensing program. Based in Foster City, California, Sony Computer Entertainment America Inc. is a wholly-owned subsidiary of Sony Computer Entertainment Inc.

Sony Computer Entertainment America
919 East Hillsdale Blvd., 2nd Floor

Foster City, CA 94404
Phone: 1-800-345-SONY
URL: http://www.scea.com

Sony Pictures Imageworks

Area(s) of Specialization: Film/Video, CGI, Multimedia, Animation

Number of Employees: 350

Sony Pictures Imageworks is a digital production company dedicated to visual effects and computer animation. The company has lent its groundbreaking talent and technology to such films as "Big Daddy," "Patch Adams," "Snow Falling on Cedars," "Godzilla," "City of Angels," "Contact," "Anaconda," "Michael," "The Ghost and the Darkness," "James and the Giant Peach" and "Starship Troopers," Paul Verhoeven's "The Hollow Man"; two films for Robert Zemeckis, "Cast Away" and "What Lies Beneath"; Mike Nichols' "What Planet Are You From?" and Imageworks President Ken Ralston's directorial debut, "Jumanji II."

Sony Pictures Imageworks
9050 West Washington Blvd.
Culver City, CA 90232
Phone: 310 840-8000
Fax: 310 840-8888
URL: http://www.spiw.com

Southern Exposure

Area(s) of Specialization: Multimedia

Number of Employees: 4

An artist-run organization, Southern Exposure reaches out to diverse audiences, and serves as a forum and resource center that provides support to the Bay Area's arts and educational communities.

Southern Exposure
401 Alabama Street
San Francisco, CA 94110
Phone: 415 863-2141
Fax: 415 863-1841
Email: soex@soex.org
URL: http://www.soex.org

Spaff Animation

Area(s) of Specialization: Animation

Number of Employees: 100

The company produces animation.

Spaff Animation
10119 1/2 Riverside Drive
Toluca Lake, CA 91602
Phone: 818 761-6744
Fax: 818 761-9608
Email: mail@spaffanimation.com
URL: http://www.spaffanimation.com

Spank Interactive

Area(s) of Specialization: Animation, Modeling, Digital Video, Special Effects, Simulations, Web Design

Number of Employees: 2

Spank Interactive specializes in creating work that interactively that draw on the senses and personify information. Communication of ideas and information must be immediate, accessible and coherent. The company's root demographic offers a cohesive approach to helping clients explore and implant new media opportunities.

Spank Interactive
4041 Damant Court
North Highlands, CA 95660
Phone: 916 334-8385
Fax: 916 334-8385
Email: info@spank.com
URL: http://www.spank.com

Spazzco

Area(s) of Specialization: Animation, Web design

Number of Employees: 3

Spazzco specializes in animation using traditional techniques as well as the most popular 2D animation and 3D animation digital character animation tools. Other services include: Flash 4 Animation, Traditional Cel Animation, 3D Animation Max Character Studio animation, Storyboards and background studies.

Spazzco
610 22nd Street, #314
San Francisco, CA 94107
Phone: 415 551-2692
Fax: 415 551-1080
Email: info@spazzco.com
URL: http://www.spazzco.com

Spicy Cricket Animation

Area(s) of Specialization: 3D Animation for Film/Video/Games

Number of Employees: 1

Spicy Cricket Animation is a 3D Animation site for beginners and industry professionals alike. With easy-to-use links and reference pages, Angie Jones, the site's creator, offers case-study instruction on 3D animation character design and an insider's suggestions on career advancement.

Spicy Cricket Animation
3189 Shearer Ave.
Cayucos, CA 93430-1856
Email: angie@spicycricket.com
URL: http://www.spicycricket.com

Spumco, Inc.

Area(s) of Specialization: Animation

Number of Employees: 100+

Spumco is a production company founded by animation maverick John Kricfalusi. Kricfalusi was once the understudy of Ralph Bakshi, working as creative director on the rejuvenated Mighty Mouse series. John Kricfalusi with his Spumco teammates, created such multimedia as the rock video for Bjork's "I Miss You" and the cartoon series made exclusively for the Internet, with characters: George Liquor, Jimmy The Idiot Boy, and Sody Pop. The company markets comic books, dolls, and novelty products from this series, and also other work, exclusively through the Web site.

Spumco, Inc.
415 E. Harvard Street, Suite 204
Glendale, CA 91205
Phone: 818 550-5960
Fax: 818 550-0320
URL: http://www.spumco.com

Stan Winston Studio

Area(s) of Specialization: Special Effect Model Making

Number of Employees: 100

For 25 years, Stan Winston and a team of artists and technicians have been creating characters, creatures and monsters for motion pictures and television. Live action character and make-up effects have been used in films such as: "The Lost World: Jurassic Park," "Terminator," "Predator," "Aliens" and "Interview with the Vampire." The company's illustrators, sculptors, technicians, painters, engineers and fabricators have created everything from dinosaurs and gorillas to alien life forms from the other side of the universe.

Stan Winston Studio
17216 Saticoy Street
P.O. Box 346
Van Nuys, CA 91406
Phone: 818 782-0870 Ext. 132
Fax: 818 782-0807
Email: info@swfx.com
URL: http://www.swfx.com

Stargate Films, Inc.

Area(s) of Specialization: Animation, CGI, Film/Video, Multimedia

Number of Employees: 25-30

Stargate Films studio works in film, video, and computer technologies to totally integrate multimedia production studio. The company integrates technical filmmaking with special effects and live action production.

Stargate Films, Inc.
1103 W. Isabel St.
Burbank, CA 91506
Phone: 818 972-1100
Fax: 818 972-9411
Email: info@swfx.com
URL: http://www.stargatefilms.com

Station X Studios, LLC

Area(s) of Specialization: CGI, Animation, Multimedia, Film/Video

Number of Employees: 66+

Station X Studios, LLC was founded in 1997 by a team of animators, programmers, systems administrators, and production personnel to create a complete entertainment studio. The company creates visual effects for film, TV, and commercials, develop revolutionary new software for the visual effects industry, and develops and produces film and television projects. Besides various commercials and in-house productions, the company created over 200 shots for the feature film "Dungeons and Dragons," which the company is co-producing.

Station X Studios
1717 Stewart Street
Santa Monica, CA 90404
Phone: 310 828-6460
Fax: 310 828-4101
URL: http://www.stationxstudios.com

Super Custom Workshop

Area(s) of Specialization: Animation, CGI, Television, Digital Media

Number of Employees: 6+

3D Animation CGI animation, visual effects and mixed media design and production for video games, theme parks, museums, features, TV commercials, broadcast and new media.

Super Custom Workshop
3520 Hughes Ave., #115
Los Angeles, CA 90034
Phone: 310 980 9838
Email: info@supercustom.org
URL: http://www.supercustom.org

Super 78 Studios

Area(s) of Specialization: Animation

Number of Employees: 10+

A full-service animation studio.

Super 78 Studios, Inc.
1344 N. Highland Ave.
Hollywood, CA 90028
Phone: 323 464-7878
Fax: 323 464-7879
URL: http://www.super78.com

Super-fi, Inc.

Area(s) of Specialization: Animation, Digital Media

Number of Employees: 6+

Launched in October 2001, digital content studio Super-Fi produces animation and design-based cross-platform content for commercials, broadcast design, music videos, film and branded online entertainment.

Super-fi, Inc.
37 W. 20th, No. 1005
New York, NY 10011
Phone: 212 924-6536
Email: ny@super-fi.com
URL: http://www.super-fi.com

Swankytown

Area(s) of Specialization: Animation, Multimedia, CGI

Number of Employees: 10+

Swankytown.com is a digital media company creating customized comedy advertainment. The company licenses original Flash animation, streaming video content, animated interactive games, e-cards as well as provides traditional media support. Swankytown Partners was officially formed in 1998 to create comedic entertainment.

Swankytown.com was formed in 1999 as a virtual studio, creating digitally produced comedy content for Web-sites and other media. Swankytown's first endeavor, the digital short comedy film, "New Testament," was released worldwide in 1998.

Swankytown
4470 Sunset Blvd., Suite 300
Los Angeles, CA 90027
Phone: 323 466-8600
Fax: 323 466-8800
Email: info@swankytown.com
URL: http://www.swankytown.com

SWAY Digital Studio

Area(s) of Specialization: Animation, 3D Animation, Post Production, Digital Media

Number of Employees: 50+

SWAY digital studio was founded by Clio award-winning animation and visual effects supervisor, Mark Glaser. SWAY employs the latest digital technology and the highest caliber artistic talent in the production of 3D animation, visual effects, and all-digital 2D Animation. SWAY provides the advertising and film industries with innovative solutions for the creation of sophisticated imagery and animation for their projects. SWAY offers an array of high-end services including photo-real CGI, character animation, effects, pre-visualization, shoot planning/supervision, and compositing.

SWAY Digital Studio
1100 Glendon Ave., Fl. 17
Los Angeles, CA 90024
Phone: 310 689-7237
Fax: 310 689-7272
Email: info@swaystudio.com
URL: http://www.swaystudio.com

S.W. Conser

Area(s) of Specialization: Traditional Animation

Number of Employees: 2+

Contractor for animation, illustration and storyboarding services, with digital capabilities but an emphasis on traditional styles.

S.W. Conser
Happy Trails Animation
11900 S.W. 116th
Tigard, OR 97223
Phone: 503 407-9740
Fax: 847 724-8261
Email: conser@earthlink.net
URL: http://www.conchnet.net

Sylvan Design & Animation

Area(s) of Specialization: Traditional Animation, 2D Animation, 3D Animation

Number of Employees: 6+

Services offered include 3D animation modeling and animation, precision product modeling, 3D Animation forensic reconstruction, texture-mapping and lighting, cross-sections and schematics, 2D animation & 3D animation illustration, drawing, and storyboarding.

Sylvan Design & Animation
508 Webster St.
Petaluma, CA 94952
Phone: 707 479-0763
Fax: 707 658-1999
Email: tom@sylvandna.com
URL: http://www.sylvandna.com

Talking Screens

Area(s) of Specialization: Animation

Number of Employees: 1+

A small animation studio offering a wide range of media services.

Talking Screens
San Ramon, CA 94583
Phone: 916 722-3798
Email: info@talkingscreens.com
URL: http://www.talkingscreens.com

Taylor Entertainment Group

Area(s) of Specialization: Animation, Film, Digital Media

Number of Employees: 10+

Taylor Entertainment Group LLC is partnered with Topanga, California-based Work Of Art Studio to produce Flash animation trailers for clients such as MGM Studios. The company also creates original characters, concepts and scripted animations that they own for distribution and co-production over the Web as well as television and film.

T-Bone Films, Inc.

Area(s) of Specialization: Film/Video, Multimedia, CGI

Number of Employees: 2+

Formed in 1993 by Executive Producer Craig Caryl and Director Evan Stone, T-Bone Films has evolved from it sports filmmaking roots into a full-service creative shop. The company has collaborated with MTV to produce shows including the 1996 #1 MTV Sports Segment "Junk State." Channel One News hired T-Bone to produce documentaries for an in school programming Network. T-bone provides services to clients from Airwalk to Disney Interactive.

T-Bone Films, Inc.
1234 21st Street
Santa Monica, CA 90404
Phone: 310 453-4822
Fax: 310 453-4849
Email: info@t-bone.com
URL: http://www.t-bone.com

TFX, Inc.

Area(s) of Specialization: CGI, Multimedia

Number of Employees: 20-35

In 1992 Allen Pike and Charley Zurian a fully integrated automotive and product prototyping facility in Southern California using digital technologies as well as traditional design approaches. Employees at TFX experience in the fields of design, engineering, sculpting, and the visual arts.

TRANSFX a.k.a. TFX
8300 Waters Rd.
Moorpark, CA 93021
Phone: 805 532-1526
Fax: 805 532-1645
Email: transfx@transfx.com
URL: http://www.transfx.com

Tigar Hare Studios

Area(s) of Specialization: 2D Animation and 3D Animation Computer Animation/Special Effects for Film/Commercials/Television

Number of Employees: 16

Tigar Hare Studios is a high-end 3D animation computer animation and graphics design studio. The company services clients in commercial, broadcast, feature film, special venue markets, computer gaming, convergence media, and Web animation.

Tigar Hare Studios
4735 N. Sepulveda Blvd., Suite 426
Sherman Oaks, CA 91403
Phone: 818 907-6663
Fax: 818 907-0693
Email: recruitment@tigarhare.com
URL: http://www.tigarhare.com

Tippet Studios

Area(s) of Specialization: CGI, Film/Video, Multimedia, Animation

Number of Employees: 125+

With sixteen years, fifteen feature films, and six Oscar nominations, Tippet studios has a staff of more than 125 artists, designers, engineers, and animators. Tippett Studio is an animation and visual effects studio under the guidance of Phil and his partners, Jules Roman (Vice President and Executive Producer) and Craig Hayes (Creative Director and Visual Effects Supervisor).

Tippet Studios
2741 Tenth St.
Berkeley, CA 94710
Phone: 510 649-9711
Fax: 510 649-9399
Email: info@tippett.com
URL: http://www.tippett.com/

Tom T. Animation

Area(s) of Specialization: Animation

Number of Employees: 6+

An artist run animation production company with the top name and most highly experienced animation artists in Los Angeles. Organized in unique cooperation with the Cartoonists' Guild, MPSC. Local 839, this studio is dedicated to the concept and practice of "the best talent in the World for the best price in town." The President/Producer/Director, Tom Tataranowicz, is a veteran of having run the operations and creative elements of companies such as Filmation, Marvel, Sunwoo.

Tom T. Animation, Inc.
4729 Lankershim Blvd., 2nd Fl.
North Hollywood, CA 91602
Phone: 818 980-6012
Fax: 818 980-6034
Email: BikerMiceT@aol.com

Threshold Digital Research Labs

Area(s) of Specialization: Animation, Film, Television, Digital Media

Number of Employees: 10+

Threshold Digital Research Labs (TDRL) is a groundbreaking global digital animation and visual effects production studio. The company produces original full-length digitally animated feature films. TDRL also has a production services division that creates and produces digital visual effects and digital animation for movies, television, Web sites, games, IMAX movies, theme parks and location based entertainment for major studios, networks and advertisers.

Threshold Digital Research Labs
1649 11th St.
Santa Monica, CA 90404
Phone: 310 452-8899
Fax: 310 452-0736

Tony Toonz

Area(s) of Specialization: Traditional Animation

Number of Employees: 2+

A small animation studio that works on television and video.

Tony Toonz
123 Early Ct.
Prince George County, VA 23801
Phone: 804 733-7469
Email: TON520JAC@AOL.COM

Toonshoppe

Area(s) of Specialization: Animation, 3D Animation, Television

Number of Employees: 6+

Toonshoppe provides 3D animation & flash animation to TV, Internet, and feature film. Recent productions include flash-for-television for Starz/Encore.

Toonshoppe
940 N. Orange, Suite 118
Hollywood, CA 90038
Phone: 323 467-1145
Fax: 707 988-8449
Email: info@toonshoppe.com
URL: http://www.Toonshoppe.com

Tooned In

Area(s) of Specialization: 3D Animation and Cel Animation

Number of Employees: 12+

Tooned In is an animation studio located in Seattle, Washington. The company specializes in melding technology with traditional animation techniques, maintains a small permanent staff of artists and technologists, and employs a large number of freelance artists from the Seattle, Los Angeles, and other parts of the country. In addition to the U.S. based animation team, the company has a software consulting and animation production partnership with Wang Film Productions in Taipei, Taiwan.

Tooned In
218 Broadway East, Suite 202
Seattle, WA 98102
Phone: 206 323-1426
Fax: 206 323-1427
Email: info@toonedin.com
URL: http://www.toonedin.com

Tooniversal

Area(s) of Specialization: Cel Animation, Live Action Film, Special Effects

Number of Employees: 50

The Tooniversal Company is an independent producer and distributor of motion pictures, both live-action and animated. Tooniversal also has a live-action production and distribution division, Premiere Pictures International. The company represents both animation and live-action production facilities, and also distributes films from various countries in a number of territories worldwide including the United States. For many years, Tooniversal has been a producer of limited edition animation art. Clients include the Warner Bros. Studio Stores and more than 150 animation art galleries in the U.S. and Canada.

The Tooniversal Company
21755 Ventura Blvd., #101
Woodland Hills, CA 91364
Phone: 310 230-7684
Fax: 801 365-7267
URL: http://www.tooniversal.com

Total Video Co.

Area(s) of Specialization: Film/Video, Multimedia, CGI

Number of Employees: 25

Total Video Co. has been creating videos for more than 20 years serving its corporate and broadcast clients. The company creates video news releases, new product roll-outs, national sales meetings, commercials, and corporate documentaries.

Total Video
432 North Canal Street, Suite 12
South San Francisco, CA 94080
Phone: 650 583-8236
Fax: 650 583-4708
Email: info@totalvideo.com
URL: http://www.totalvideo.com

Train Simple

Area(s) of Specialization: Animation, CGI, Video

Number of Employees: 6+

Train Simple is a new media training company specializing in computer graphics.

A Train Simple Company, Inc.
1334 3rd St., Suite 309
Santa Monica, CA 90401
Phone: 888 577-8333
Fax: 310 395-2151
Email: sales@trainsimple.com
URL: http://www.trainsimple.com

The Truly Dangerous Company

Area(s) of Specialization: Motion Simulator, Puppets, Creature Effects

Number of Employees: 2

The Truly Dangerous Company is two people—Trey Stokes and Maija Beeton—who provide production and design services to the entertainment industry.

The Truly Dangerous Company
9818 Commerce Ave.
Tujunga, CA 91042
Phone: 818 353-5556
Fax: 818 353-4140
URL: http://www.trudang.com

Turtle Rock

Area(s) of Specialization: Animation

Number of Employees: 6+

Turtle Rock creates hilarious Web animations and videos for entertainment, education and marketing.

Turtle Rock New Media
1388 Haight St., Suite 88
San Francisco, CA 94117
Phone: 415 681-8830
Email: info@turtlerock.com

Twiddle Productions

Area(s) of Specialization: Animation, Post Production

Number of Employees: 6+

Twiddle productions is a full-service production house that deals with all aspects of animation, graphic design, comic book art production and Web design.

Twiddle Productions
9000 Harrat St., Suite 7
West Hollywood, CA 90069
Phone: 310 271-7173
Fax: 909 798-7332
Email: hr@twiddleproductions.com
URL: http://www.twiddleproductions.com

Urban Vision Entertainment

Area(s) of Specialization: Japanese Animation

Number of Employees: 9

Urban Vision Entertainment, Inc., a production/distribution company based in Los Angeles, formed in July, 1996 to help introduce the alternative animation genre known as anime or Japanimation to mainstream media. The company primarily produces/acquires Japanese animation for direct-to-home video release and distributes to the home video market. The company also has a broad-based licensing division which includes such endeavors as theatrical and television releases and interactive games.

Urban Vision Entertainment
5120 Goldleaf Circle
Los Angeles, CA 90056
Phone: 323 292-0147
Email: info@urban-vision.com
URL: http://www.urban-vision.com

Valve Software

Area(s) of Specialization: CGI,
Multimedia, Animation

Number of Employees: 40+

Valve is an entertainment software
company founded by Gabe Newell and
Mike Harrington and based in Kirkland,
Washington. Valve's debut product was a
PC game called "Half-Life," released in
November, 1998. "Half-Life" was named
"Best PC Game Ever" in the November
1999 issue of PC Gamer, the world's
bestselling PC games magazine.

Valve Software
P.O. Box 1688
Bellevue WA 98009
Phone: 425 889-9642
Fax: 425 889-9642
Email: contact@valvesoftware.com
URL: http://www.valvesoftware.com

Vicon

Area(s) of Specialization: Animation, Film

Number of Employees: 20+

Vicon is a leading developer of optical
motion capture systems. For 18 years
Vicon has been providing professionals
with the latest tools to accurately capture
the subtleties of human motion for
medical research, engineering, game
development, broadcast, and film. Vicon
Motion Systems is a wholly owned
subsidiary of OMG Ltd.

Vicon Motion Systems
9 Spectrum Pointe Dr.
Lake Forest, CA 92630
Phone: 949 472-9140
Fax: 949 472-9136
Email: moveme@vicon.com
URL: http://www.vicon.comView Studio

The Video Agency, Inc./TVA

Area(s) of Specialization: Film/Video,
Animation, Multimedia

Number of Employees: 23+

TVA is a full-service film / video
production and duplication company
close to Universal Studios. Housed in a
17,500 sq. ft. facility with blue screen
sound stages, motion control, digital
editing bays, audio recording studio,
TVA produces television programs,
corporate motion pictures, computer
animation and visual effects, special
venue films, WaterScreen attractions, TV
commercials, direct-mail video, etc., in

every major language. The company specializes in traditional film/video uses as well as other emerging technologies.

The Video Agency Inc./TVA Productions
10900 Ventura Blvd.
Studio City, CA 91604
Phone: 818 505-8300
Fax: 818 505-8370
Email: info@tvaproductions.com
URL: http://www.tvaproductions.com

Video Arts, Inc.

Area(s) of Specialization: Film/Video, CGI, Animation, Multimedia

Number of Employees: 15+

Video Arts is a digital studio providing for clients' production needs. The company specializes in design, animation, editing and special effects for advertising, corporate communications and broadcast clients.

Video Arts, Inc.
724 Battery St., Suite 5400
San Francisco, CA 94111
Phone: 415 788-0300
Fax: 415 788-3331
Email: ksalyer@vidarts.com
URL http://www.vidarts.com

View Studio

Area(s) of Specialization: Animation, Television, Film

Number of Employees: 6+

View Studio is a digital effects and graphic design studio with a unique environment that nurtures the creative process. Projects include design and special effects for commercials, television, film, the Internet and interactive media.

View Studio, Inc.
6715 Melrose Ave.
Hollywood, CA 90038
Phone: 323 965-1270
Fax: 323 965-1277
Email: info@viewstudio.com
URL: http://www.viewstudio.com

Viewpoint

Area(s) of Specialization: 3D Animation Modeling

Number of Employees: 300

Viewpoint Digital is recognized for creating and publishing a library of 3D animation digital content, and providing unparalleled custom modeling services-helping create digital effects for films, television programs, advertisements, games and Web sites. Viewpoint's work is featured in major motion pictures including The World Is Not Enough, Mystery Men and Pushing Tin, and has had starring roles in numerous films such as "Antz," "Star Trek: Insurrection," "Independence Day," "Air Force One" and "Godzilla." Viewpoint's work can also be seen in characters and props for game titles including Interstate '82, Pandora's Box, Civilization: Call to Power and Gauntlet: Legends; television programs such as Star Trek Voyager and Jonny Quest; advertisements for Dodge, McDonalds, Taco Bell and Nike; and 3D animation-enabled Web sites for The Sharper Image, Autobytel.com and Ticketmaster.com.

Viewpoint
13348 Beach Ave.
Marina Del Rey, CA 90292
Phone: 310 280-2000
Alt. Phone: 800-328-2738
Fax: 310 845-9412
Email: info@viewpoint.com
URL: http://www.viewpoint.com

Viewport Images

Area(s) of Specialization: Computer Graphics, Animation

Number of Employees: 5+

Viewport Images is a computer graphics and animation production facility specializing in 3D Animation /2D Animation graphics and effects for the entertainment, interactive, multimedia and visualization industries. Viewport Images was established in 1986 by John Howard with experience in the design and production of computer graphics and visual effects for feature films, video, theatrical ID's, cable and network broadcast graphics packages.

Viewport Images
109 N Naomi St.
Burbank, CA 91505
Phone: 818 559-8705
Email: info1@viewportimages.com
URL: http://www.viewportimages.com/

Virtualmagic Animation

Area(s) of Specialization: Animation, CGI, Multimedia

Number of Employees: 20-30

VirtualMagic Animation is a service for 2D animation digital ink, paint and compositing production. Founded in 1992, the company is a resource for television and film production companies, major studios and ad agencies. Working with USAnimation, Softimage Toonz, Media Pegs and other software packages on Hewlett-Packard, Silicon Graphics and Windows NT platform the company provides clients with comprehensive digital ink & paint services.

Virtualmagic Animation
4640 Lankershim Blvd., Suite 201
North Hollywood, CA 91602
Phone: 818 623-1866
Fax: 818 623-1868
URL: http://www.virtualmagicusa.com

Visible Productions

Area(s) of Specialization: CGI, Multimedia, Animation

Number of Employees: 20

Visible Productions develops custom biomedical animations, illustrations, and interactive multimedia for the healthcare and educational markets. Based on the National Library of Medicines' "Visible Human Project," VP's anatomical content can be used to create: anatomical imagery that is used to conduct biomedical research, simulate surgical procedures, and educate students, patients, and healthcare professionals.

Visible Productions
116 N. College Ave., Suite 7
Fort Collins, CO 80524
Phone: 970 407-7240
Fax: 970 407-7248
Email: vip@visiblep.com
URL: http://www.visiblep.com

Visionary Studio

Area(s) of Specialization: Digital Animation, Illustration

Number of Employees: 5

Visionary Studio was founded by Tim Haskins to do illustration of books. The company offers one-on-one classes in drawing, animation, Web design, and digital coloring/special fx.

Visionary Studio
3535 NE 141st
Portland, OR 97230
Fax: 503 256-4578
URL: http://www.visionarystudio.com

Vision Crew Unlimited

Area(s) of Specialization: Animation, CGI, Multimedia, Film/Video

Number of Employees: 10

Vision Crew Unlimited was founded in 1994 to provide visual effects for feature films, commercials, and television. Building miniature fabrication and mechanical effects, VCU has expanded into a full-service visual effects facility.

Vision Crew Unlimited
5939 Rodeo Rd.
Los Angeles, CA 90016
Phone: 310 558-0450
Fax: 310 558-0437

Email: admin@visioncrew.com
URL: http://www.visioncrew.com

Vision Scape Imaging, Inc.

Area(s) of Specialization: 3D Animation, Digital Effects

Number of Employees: 30

Vision Scape Imaging, Inc. is a leading production studio dedicated to creating 3D animation and digital effects for the feature film, commercial and electronic game industries. The company's staff writes code, creates software plug-ins and explores new applications.

Vision Scape Imaging, Inc.
5125 Convoy St., Suite 121
San Diego, CA 92111
Phone: 858 391-1300
Alt Phone: 800 507-5678
Fax: 858 391-1301
URL: http://www.thelab3D Animation.com

Visual Concept Engineering, Inc./VCE

Area(s) of Specialization: Film/Video, CGI, Multimedia

Number of Employees: 10-12

VCE (Visual Concept Entertainment) began in 1982 after founder Peter Kuran finished work as animation supervisor for Industrial Light and Magic (ILM) on George Lucas' "The Empire Strikes Back." VCE has worked on over 200 theatrical motion pictures including both "Addams Family" films and all three "Robocop" features. The latest feature work from VCE was seen in "Idle Hands," "Starship Troopers," "Courage Under Fire," and "Nixon."

Visual Concept Engineering, Inc./VCE
13300 Ralston Ave.
Sylmar, CA 91342
Phone: 818 367-9187
Fax: 818 362-3490
Email: vcelnc.@aol.com
URL: http://www.vce.com

Visual Magic Images, Inc.

Area(s) of Specialization: 3D Animation Computer Animation, Digital Visual Effects

Number of Employees: 8+

VMI is a boutique visual effects production studio specializing in high end digital animation and effects. The company provides a full range of computer generated and digital effects services for the producers of: Feature Films, Ride Films, Commercial, Multimedia, Ride Film Libraries, Theme Parks and Theater Design. Whether a simple logo treatment or complex visual effects for a feature film or interactive game, the VMI creative team works with a client from the creative concept to the final project completion.

Visual Magic Images
929 E. 2nd Street, Suite 201
Los Angeles, CA 90012
Phone: 213 680-3336
Fax: 213 628-2111
Email: Email: info@visual-magic.com
URL: http://www.visual-magic.com

The Voices In Your Head

Area(s) of Specialization: Animation, Sound

Number of Employees: 6+

A company offering voice services for animation.

The Voices In Your Head
1140 N. Formosa
Editorial 323
West Hollywood, CA 90036
Phone: 323 850-2887
Email: granlund@attbi.com
URL: http://
www.thevoicesinyourhead.com

Wallace Creative, Inc.

Area(s) of Specialization: 3D Animation, CGI

Number of Employees: 2

Wallace Creative Inc. provides concept and content development, directorial and full production capabilities, 2D animation and CGI character and graphic animation, design and art direction and cinematic storyboarding. The company creates work for the Internet, commercial broadcast, video, multimedia, music videos, gaming, film and print.

Wallace Creative, Inc.
1705 NW 25th. Ave.
Portland, OR 97210
Phone: 503 224-9660
Fax: 503 224-9667
Email: info@wallyhood.com
URL: http://www.wallyhood.com

Walt Disney Feature Animation

Area(s) of Specialization: Animation, Multimedia, Film/Video, CGI

Number of Employees: 1,000+

More than 75 years ago, Walt Disney led a crew of artists to create 37 full-length animated films. Walt Disney Feature Animation has a library of classics. Through the collaborative efforts of 2,000 artists and crew members at animation studios in Los Angeles, Orlando, and Paris, the Feature

Animation groups are creating ten new stories. Walt Disney Animation combines traditional and digital artists with technology, administration, and production management teams.

Walt Disney Feature Animation
500 South Buena Vista Street
Burbank, CA 91521-7454
Phone: 407-828-3110
Fax: 818 558-2547
URL http://disney.go.com

Warner Bros. Television & Classic Animation

Area(s) of Specialization: Feature Films to Television, Home Video, Animation, Comic Books.

Number of Employees: 9000

WARNER BROS., is a fully integrated, broad-based entertainment company, involved in the creation, production, distribution, licensing and marketing of all forms of entertainment and attendant businesses. Warner Bros., a Time Warner Entertainment Company, works in every aspect of the entertainment industry from feature films to television, home video, animation, comic books, product and brand licensing, retail stores and international theaters. With the acquisition of Turner Entertainment by Time Warner in October 1996, the classic MGM (pre-1986) and RKO titles, as well as animation from Hanna-Barbera, Ruby-Spears and MGM, were added to the Warner Bros.-managed library.

Warner Brothers
4000 Warner Blvd
Burbank, CA 91522
Phone: 818 954- 6000
URL: http://www.warnerbros.com

Western Images

Area(s) of Specialization: CGI, Multimedia, Animation, Film/Video

Number of Employees: 40

Western Images, a digital production and design studio, handles projects ranging from commercial to theatrical, music video, long-form and broadcast design. Western's animators, artists, designers, editors and colorists are accessible as resources from the early stages of project planning through delivery, collaborating with clients (and each other) to produce results.

Western Images
600 Townsend St., Suite 300W
San Francisco, CA 94103
Phone: 415 252-6000
Fax: 415 621-6780
URL: http://www.westernimages.com

Whamo Entertainment

Area(s) of Specialization: Animation

Number of Employees: 50+

MarVista Entertainment is the beneficiary of Whamo Entertainment 's library which contains 3000 hours of television programming. MarVista continues Whamo's business strategy, but adds to its core business the production and acquisition of live-action feature films, television movies and series. MarVista's headquarters are in Los Angeles with production and sales offices in Barcelona, Spain and Boston.

Whamo Entertainment
1850 S. Sepulveda Blvd.
Los Angeles, CA 90025
Phone: 310 477-0338
Fax: 310 477-0338
Email: info@whamoentertainment.com
URL: http://www.whamoentertain-ment.com

Wholesome Products

Area(s) of Specialization: Traditional Animation

Number of Employees: 6+

Stop motion/mixed medium production company focusing on developing projects for director/creators Stephen Holman and Josephine Huang.

Wholesome Products
348 1/2 N. Spaulding Ave.
Los Angeles, CA 90036
Phone: 323 939-2397
Fax: 323 939-2374
Email: wholesomeprod@aol.com

Wild Brain, Inc.

Area(s) of Specialization: Multimedia, Animation, CGI

Number of Employees: 300

Founded in 1994, Wild Brain, Inc. is an animation studio in the heart of the San Francisco Bay Area. Wild Brain's client list includes names in entertainment and advertising: Universal, Microsoft, Twentieth Century Fox, Coca-Cola, Disney, Nike, Warner Bros., Levi Strauss, LucasArts, Nickelodeon and HBO.

Wild Brain, Inc.
660 Alabama Street
San Francisco, CA 94110
Phone: 415 553-8000
Fax: 415 553-8009
Email: info@wildbrain.com
URL: http://www.wildbrainInc.com

William Moffitt Associates

Area(s) of Specialization: Film/Video, Digital Production

Number of Employees: 4

William Moffitt Associates is a full-service communications company specializing in film, video and digital production for clients world wide. The company services a client's company or organization in the boardroom, on TV, or over the Internet.

William Moffitt Associates
747 North Lake Ave.
Pasadena, CA 91104
Phone: 626 791-2559
Fax: 626 791-3092
Email: lynne@wmadigital.com
URL: http://www.wmadigital.com/

Will Vinton Studio

Area(s) of Specialization: Dimensional Animation

Number of Employees: 400

In 1975, Closed Mondays, a clay animated film Will Vinton co-created with Bob Gardiner, won the Academy Award for Best Animated Film. The studio worked on Rip Van Winkle, Creation, The Great Cognito and created special visual effects in the Disney feature Return to Oz. The studio has also done work on such films as Legacy, The Little Prince, Martin the Cobbler and Dinosaur. Will Vinton Studios has two Academy Award winning directors, and has won six prime-time Emmy Awards and numerous CIio awards.

Will Vinton Studio
1400 NW 22ND Ave.
Portland, OR 97210
Phone: 503 225-1130
Fax: 503 226-3746
Email: info@vinton.com
URL: http://www.vinton.com

Wired Digital

Area(s) of Specialization: CGI, Multimedia

Number of Employees: 170+

Wired Digital creates a range of dynamic online products that help people put emerging technologies to use in their personal and professional lives. Their online services provide technology-oriented information and cutting-edge tools that people can use day to day. Wired Digital is headquartered in San Francisco with satellite offices in New York, Chicago, and Los Angeles.

Wired Digital
660 Third Street
Fourth Floor

San Francisco, CA 94107
Phone: 415 276 8400
Fax: 415 276 8499
URL: http://hotwired.lycos.com/home/digital

Wow Studio, Inc.

Area(s) of Specialization: Animation

Number of Employees: 6+

Animated cartoon studio specializing in interactive flash animation.

Wow Studio, Inc.
1217 Yale St.
Santa Monica, CA 90404
Phone: 310 453-7832
Fax: 310 453-0384
Email: wwolsen@adelphia.net

WSI Multimedia

Area(s) of Specialization: Animation, Digital Media

Number of Employees: 10+

A full-service animation studio.

WSI Multimedia
9225 Harrison Park Ct.
Indianapolis, IN 46216
Phone: 317 544-0499
Fax: 317 544-2192
Email: rick.myers@wsystems.com
URL: http://www.wsimultimedia.com

Xaos, Inc.

Area(s) of Specialization: Multimedia, Film/Video, CGI

Number of Employees: 20-25

Xaos was founded with the belief that a company could be successful based on true artistic expression. Just as some painters choose to grind their own pigments or make their own brushes, they wrote a body of software with which to create their imagery, and gathered a handful of talented painters and sculptors who could do what they set out to do. Their facility offers opportunities to work on diverse projects including commercials, broadcast IDs, feature films, special venue and large-format cinema.

Xaos, Inc.
444 De Haro St.
San Francisco, CA 94107
Phone: 415 558-9267
Fax: 415 558-9160
Email: brian@xaostools.com
URL: http://www.xaostools.com/

XtrackrZ, Inc.

Area(s) of Specialization: Animation, CGI

Number of Employees: 3+

A small studio that does 3D Animation Character Animation utilizing the latest in technology.

XtrackrZ, Inc.
4262 Vinton Ave.
Culver City, CA 90232
Phone: 310 704-3036
URL: http://www.xtrackrz.com

Yearn to Learn

Area(s) of Specialization: Animation, CGI, Television

Number of Employees: 25+

Yearn to Learn have developed an extensive multimedia property to act as a conduit for scientific and educational content, focusing initially on a CGI animated television series to interactively educate through intelligent character, situation and slapstick comedy 'The Timely Adventures of Bones and Whatsit.' Yearn to Learn has successfully pitched and received the commitment of a presenting public television station and are currently in the process of arranging a presentation to the full PBS network (100 million viewers weekly).

Yearn to Learn
P.O. Box 1928
Laguna Beach, CA 92652
Phone: 949 715 1718

Fax: 208 655 0222
Email: info@yearn2learn.com
URL: http://www.yearn2learn.com

Zoom Cartoons Entertainment

Area(s) of Specialization: Animation, Television, CGI.

Number of Employees: 6+

A full-service animation company for any job, big or small: Features, Television, Interactive, Games, Commercials.

Zoom Cartoons Entertainment, LLC
1201 W. 5th St., Suite M300
Los Angeles, CA 90017
Phone: 213 202-5959
Fax: 213 202-5960
Email: toonz@zoomcartoons.com
URL: http://www.zoomcartoons.com

Zona Productions, Inc.

Area(s) of Specialization: Multi Camera Productions

Number of Employees: 5

Small studio offering post production services.

Zona Productions, Inc.
215 S. La Cienega Blvd. #204

Beverly Hills, CA 90211
Phone: 310 652-4070
Fax: 310 652-0390
Email: info@zonaproductions.com
URL: http://www.zonaproductions.com/

Zooma Zooma

Area(s) of Specialization: Film/Video

Number of Employees: 7

A bi-coastal production company specializing in commercials, music videos and short films. Established 8 years ago, Zooma Zooma's goal is to create an exciting production company for unique, young filmmakers to showcase talent.

Zooma Zooma
804 Main St., Suite 200
Venice, CA 90291
Phone: 310 829-3269
Fax: 310 453-0636
Email: eknable@aol.com
URL: http://www.zoomazooma.com

Zygote Media Group

Area(s) of Specialization: Modelers

Number of Employees: 15-25

Zygote Media Group, Inc. is a Utah-based company providing 3D animation computer data (models and texture maps) for use in commercial 3D animation modeling, rendering, and animation software packages (3D animation applications). The name "Zygote" signifies the first stage of life, just as computer modeling is the first stage of a 3D animation computer animation. The name also conveys Zygote's main expertise and targeted market niche: building organic types of models.

Zygote Media Group
679 N. 1890 West, Suite 45A
Provo, UT 84601
Phone: 801 765-4141
Alt Phone: 800 267-5170
Fax: 801 765-4343
Email: customsales@zygote.com
URL: http://www.zygote.com

Canada

Alias-Wavefront

Area(s) of Specialization: CGI, Multimedia, Animation

Number of Employees: 500+

As the one of the world's leading innovators of 2D animation and 3D animation graphics technology, Alias|Wavefront develops advanced software for the film and video, games and interactive media, industrial design and visualization markets. Based in Toronto, Alias|Wavefront is a wholly owned, independent software subsidiary of Silicon Graphics, Inc.

Alias-Wavefront
Global Headquarters – Toronto
210 King Street East
Toronto, ON M5A 1J7
Phone: 800 447-2542
416 362-9181
Fax: 416 369-6140
URL: http://www.aw.sgi.com

Animatoon Film Group, Inc.

Area(s) of Specialization: Animation

Number of Employees: 6+

Animated television series development company.

Animatoon Film Group, Inc.
1055 W. Hastings St., Suite 1400
Vancouver, BC V6E 2E9
Phone: 604 697-0360
Fax: 604 697-0361
Email: info@ideationcorp.net

Association of BC Animation Producers

Area(s) of Specialization: Animation

Association for animation producers.

Association of BC Animation Producers
928 Davie St.
Vancouver, BC V6Z 1B8
Phone: 604 734-2866
Fax: 604 734-2869
Email: abcap@hotmail.com
URL: http://www.abcap.org

ATI Technologies, Inc.

Area(s) of Specialization: Animation, Graphic Design

Number of Employees: 100+

From desktops to laptops, workstations to handheld devices, video game consoles to integrated solutions, ATI has established itself as a world leader in the design and manufacture of innovative 3D animation graphics solutions.

ATI Technologies, Inc.
33 Commerce Valley Dr. East
Thornhill, ON L3T 7N6
Phone: 905 882-2600
Fax: 905 882-2620
Email: sales@ati.com
URL: http://www.ati.com

Atomic Cartoons

Area(s) of Specialization: Animation, 2D Animation

Number of Employees: 10+

Atomic Cartoons is a high-end animation production studio. Their specialties are traditional 2D animation production, pre-production, and co-production. Atomic also specializes in content creation and development as well as streaming and broadcast Flash animation.

Atomic Cartoons, Inc.
928 Davie St.
Vancouver, BC V6Z 1B8
Phone: 604 734-2866
Fax: 604 734-2869
Email: info@atomiccartoons.com
URL: http://www.atomiccartoons.com

Audio Visions Productions

Area(s) of Specialization: Film/Video, Multimedia, Sound, Animation

Number of Employees: 1

MPSL is Toronto's full-service video and digital media production center. Since 1981, MPSL has provided quality video production services to the broadcast and corporate television production industries. Production, video editing, computer animation, duplication, standards conversion, teleprompting services and CD-ROM/DVD production are all carried out in their six-thousand square foot facility, which is conveniently located near the center of Toronto, just minutes from downtown. Linear and non-linear off-line edit suites, video duplication and international standards conversion facilities, and digital workstations for animation, CD-ROM/DVD production, video capture and multimedia file conversion to video provide all the services required by video and multimedia producers.

Audio Visions Productions
885 Don Mills Rd., Suite 208
Toronto, ON M3C 1V9
Phone: 416 449-7614
Fax: 416 449-9239
Email: info@mpsl.com
URL: http://www.mpsl.com

AurenyA Entertainment Group

Area(s) of Specialization: Animation, 3D Animation, Television, Film

Number of Employees: 10+

AurenyA Entertainment Group is a team of highly-skilled and talented artists, animators and technical directors that produces world-class 3D animation--animation used in production and co-production of TV and Feature Films.

AurenyA Entertainment
Suite 930, 665-8th St. Southwest
Calgary, AB T2P 3H7
Phone: 403 215-1088
Fax: 403 215-1089
Email: info@aurenya.com
URL: http://www.aurenya.com

AXYZ

Area(s) of Specialization: Animation

Number of Employees: 10+

A full-service animation studio.

AXYZ
425 Adelaide St. West
Toronto, ON M5V 1S4
Phone: 504 504-0425
Fax: 504 504-0045
Email: info@axyzfx.com
URL: http://www.axyzfx.com

Bardel Animation, Ltd.

Area(s) of Specialization: 2D Animation Traditional Animation.

Number of Employees: 12+

Bardel Animation, one of Western Canada's largest 2D animation houses, has gained a reputation for excellence in producing everything from festival shorts to feature films. Phases of production, from design and storyboarding to AVID editing and digital ink and paint, are done in-house.

Bardel Animation, Ltd.
509 Richards St.
Ground Floor
Vancouver, BC V6B 2Z6
Phone: 604 669-5589
Fax: 604 669-9079
Email: info@bardelentertainment.com
URL: http://www.bardelanimation.com

Barking Bullfrog Cartoon Company, Inc.

Area(s) of Specialization: Multimedia

Number of Employees: 2

Barking Bullfrog Cartoon Company Inc. is a multifaceted animation company providing creative and dynamic production services for television and multimedia programming. Established in 1996 by partners Ian Freedman and Mark Freedman, Barking Bullfrog Cartoon Company Inc. continues the tradition of quality animation services achieved by the partners previously their own respective companies.

Barking Bullfrog Cartoon Company, Inc.
#101-480 Smithe St.
Vancouver, BC V6B 5E4
Phone: 604 551-8709
Fax: 604 689-0715
Email:
frogresources@barkingbullfrog.com
URL: http://www.barkingbullfrog.com

Beaubien

Area(s) of Specialization: Animation

Number of Employees: 2+

Small animation studio.

Beaubien
6634 St Denis
Montreal, QC H2S 2R9
Email: info@yummyyolks.com
URL: http://www.yummyyolks.com

Beevision Productions, Inc.

Area(s) of Specialization: Animation, 2D Animation, 3D Animation, Post Production, Film, Television, Web site Design

Number of Employees: 6+

A full-service design studio offering a wide range of media services.

Beevision Productions, Inc.
366 Adelaide St East, #425
Toronto, ON M5A 3X9
Phone: 416 868-1700
Fax: 416 868-9512
Email: info@beevision.com
URL: http://www.beevision.com

Bitcasters

Area(s) of Specialization: Animation, CGI

Number of Employees: 6+

Bitcasters designed, coded and delivered some of the top games on Disney's Zoog Web site as well as the tremendously successful ClickClub at Family Channel.

Bitcasters
364 Richmond St. West, 5th Fl.
Toronto, ON M5V 1X6
Phone: 416 351-0889
Fax: 416 351-9884
Email: info@bitcasters.com
URL: http://www.bitcasters.com

Black Walk Productions

Area(s) of Specialization: Animation, Video, Television

Number of Employees: 40+

Studio offering a wide range of animation services and other media services.

Black Walk Productions
99 Sudbury St., Unit 99
Toronto, ON M6J 3S7
Phone: 416 533-5864
Fax: 416 533-2016
Email: info@blackwalk.com
URL: http://www.blackwalk.com

Blackfly Group, Inc.

Area(s) of Specialization: Animation, Film, Video

Number of Employees: 10+

This company was founded in 1995 to produce odd little films and specials, mostly for folks like The Discovery Channel, mostly about science – and fiction – and the starship-empowering energies that can erupt whenever the two meet. Initially, some thirty films and series were produced, using digital cameras, editing systems, and incredibly low-budget techniques (two filmmakers - Michael Lennick and his spousal unit Shirley Gulliford - one minivan, one dog, and many roadmaps.) Since then, the company has slowly grown to become a major supplier of science-related documentaries.

Blackfly Group, Inc.
411 Richmond St. East, Suite 205
Toronto, ON M5A 3S5
Phone: 416 594-3665
Fax: 416 363-8960
Email: michael@foolishearthling.com
URL: http://www.foolishearthling.com

Boomstone Animation, Inc.

Area(s) of Specialization: Animation

Number of Employees: 6+

A full-service animation studio offering animation services from storyboarding to production.

Boomstone Animation, Inc.
290 Picton Ave., Suite 201
Ottawa, ON K1Z 8P8
Phone: 613 725-3843
Fax: 613 725-9327
Email: info@boomstone.com
URL: http://www.boomstone.com

Boomstone Entertainment, Inc.

Area(s) of Specialization: Pre-Production

Number of Employees: 5

Boomstone has had the privilege of lending their talents on a number of animated productions. They are constantly developing new and exciting animation styles and concepts to offer to the marketplace. Mr. Dodo can be found on the end credits of the Stellar Entertainment Inc.'s live action feature film, "Undercover Angel."

Boomstone Entertainment, Inc.
311 Richmond Rd., Suite #302
Ottawa, ON K1Z 6X3
Phone: 613 725-3843
Fax: 613 725-9327
Email: info@boomstone.com
URL: http://www.boomstone.com

Bone Digital Effects

Area(s) of Specialization: Animation & Digital Compositing

Number of Employees: 4

Since 1997, Bone Digital Effects has provided 3D animation, visual effects, video production, multimedia and Internet related services to producers of film, television, and corporate communications. Their goal is to maintain a position in the market place as an affordable provider of high end post production and communication development. Their studio now operates from a 28,000 sq. ft. production facility located in the heart of Toronto's film district.

Bone Digital Effects
33 Villiers Street suite 107
Toronto, ON M5A 1A9
Phone: 416 469-3406
Fax: 416 469-3506
URL: http://www.bonedigitaleffects.com/

Bowes Production, Inc.

Area(s) of Specialization: Stop-motion animation

Number of Employees: 5-

Created to specialize in Clay Animation, Bowes Production Inc. has expanded to cover a wide variety of stop-motion techniques, using mediums such as clay, rubber foam latex, silicones, foam core, sand, nuts, bolts, and an endless amount of found objects. Bowes Productions is one of the fastest growing and innovated stop-motion animation studios in Western Canada, producing commercials, television productions, children's programming, station IDs, short films, music videos and various other specialized projects. Clients include: McDonalds, Milton Bradley, General Mills, Mattel, CBC Canada, YTV Canada, and Fuji Television Corporation Japan.

Bowes Production, Inc.
4776 Buxton St.
Burnaby, Vancouver BC V5H 1J3

Phone: 604 871-0338
Fax: 604 433-0340
Email: info@bowesproductions.com
URL: http://www.bowesproductions.com/

Bullet Digital Post

Area(s) of Specialization: Animation, Television, Film

Number of Employees: 50+

In 1994 the company's founders, Bob Munroe, John Mariella, Kyle Menzies and actor, director, writer William Shatner created C.O.R.E. with the underlying philosophy that a studio designed by artists for artists produces the best environment for creating exceptional work. Eight years, 50 Features Films, 15 Television Series and 20 MOWs' later the studio has expanded to house a crew of more than 50 Animators, Visual Effects Supervisors, Production Managers and R & D Software Engineers.

Bullet Digital Post
219 Dufferin St., Suite 100B
Toronto, ON M6K 3J1
Phone: 416 536-9100
Fax: 416 536-2898
Email: janine@bulletdigital.com
URL: http://www.bulletdigital.com

Buzz Image Group, Inc.

Area(s) of Specialization: Post Multimedia

Number of Employees: 15

Since its establishment in 1988, Buzz Image Group has been a leader in the creation and processing of visual imagery, offering state-of-the-art services in video post production, animation and 2D animation/3D animation visual effects for the film and television industries. Widely recognized for its outstanding expertise and creativity, the Buzz team employs the most advanced technologies to achieve and maintain the highest standards of quality.

Buzz Image Group, Inc.
Group Image Buzz Inc.
312 Sherbrooke Street East
Montreal, QC H2X 1E6
Phone: 514 848-0579
Alt. Phone: 800 567-0200
Fax: 514 848-6371
Email: info@buzzimage.com
URL: http://www.buzzimage.com

CADgraf Multimedia

Area(s) of Specialization: Animation, Graphic Design

Number of Employees: 6+

CADgraf Multimedia specializes in 3D animation character modeling and animation, with a focus on corporate and product branding.

CADgraf Multimedia
40 MariCt. St.
Cantley, QC J8V 2V2
Phone: 819 827-3057
Email: cadgraf@videotron.ca
URL: http://www.cadgrafmultimedia.com

Calibre Digital Pictures

Area(s) of Specialization: Animation, Film, Television

Number of Employees: 50+

Established in 1988, Calibre Digital Pictures is an industry leader in animation, visual effects, compositing and matte painting. The studios combine technology and technique, assembling the latest hardware and software with the brightest and most talented minds in the business. They provide creative and technical expertise across a broad range of disciplines including 30-second commercials and full-length features.

Calibre Digital Pictures
65 Heward Ave.
Bldg A, S 201
Toronto, ON M4M 2T5
Phone: 416 531-8383

Fax: 416 531-8083
Email: info@calibredigital.com
URL: http://www.calibredigital.com

Canuck Creations

Area(s) of Specialization: Traditional Animation

Number of Employees: 10+

A full-service animation studio offering many services.

Canuck Creations
401 Richmond St. West, Suite 111
Toronto, ON M5V 3A8
Phone: 416 979-5687
Fax: 416 979-5570
Email: info@canuckcreations.com
URL: http://www.canuckcreations.com

Catapult Productions

Area(s) of Specialization: Traditional Animation

Number of Employees: 10+

Catapult Productions creates entertainment using computer character animation.

Catapult Productions
477 Richmond St. West, Suite 1001
Toronto, ON M5V 3E7
Phone: 416 504-9876

Fax: 416 504-6648
Email: mayerson@catapult
productions.com
URL: http://www.catapultproductions.com

Cellar Door Productions

Area(s) of Specialization: Animation,
Film, Video, Sales/Marketing

Number of Employees: 30+

Cellar Door Productions specializes in
developing, financing and producing
quality, value-based animated and live-
action productions with national and
international partners.

Cellar Door Productions
3 Malahu Dr.
Charlottetown, PE C1A 8A5
Phone: 902 628-3880
Fax: 902 628-2088
Email: productions@cellardoor.tv
URL: http://www.cellardoor.tv

Chuck Gammage Animation Inc.

Area(s) of Specialization: Animation, 2D
Animation

Number of Employees: 20+

Chuck Gammage Animation Inc. is a
full-service, 2D animation production
house led by internationally-acclaimed
animator Chuck Gammage. From
storyboarding to digital ink & paint,
direction to character design, the studio
sets the standard and continues to push
the animation envelope with a talented
team of classical animators and
assistants.

Chuck Gammage Animation
317 Adelaide St. West, Suite 910
Toronto, ON M5V 1P9
Phone: 416 593-9627
Fax: 416 593-9629
Email: info@cganim.com
URL: http://www.cganim.com

CineGroupe

Area(s) of Specialization: Traditional
Animation

Number of Employees: 6+

Small animation studio offering a wide
range of services.

CineGroupe
1010, St-Catherine St. East, 6th Fl.
Montreal, QC H2L 2G3
Phone: 514 849-5008
Fax: 514 849-5001
Email: info@cinegroupe.ca
URL: http://www.cinegroupe.com

The Collideascope Animation Studio

Area(s) of Specialization: Animation, Film, Digital Media

Number of Employees: 20+

The Collideascope Animation Studio was built to accommodate the production demand in the industry for high quality classical and digital animation. The studio uses the latest in animation techniques and tools to produce cutting-edge high quality 2D animation.

Collideascope Digital
Productions, Inc.
P.O. Box 34002
Scotia Square RPO
Halifax, NS B3J 3S1
Phone: 902 429-8949
Fax: 902 429-0265
Email: andrea@collideascope.com
URL: http://www.collideascope.com/default2.htm

Comet Entertainment Inc.

Area(s) of Specialization: Animation, CGI, Television, Sales/Marketing

Number of Employees: 6+

Comet Entertainment Inc. creates, designs, builds and delivers long and short form animation content for broadcasters, online media, and game titles for next generation consoles and PCs.

Comet Entertainment, Inc.
1129 Woodbine Ave.
Toronto, ON M4C 4C6
Phone: 416 421-4229
Fax: 416 425-5931
Email: info@cometentertainment.com
URL: http://www.cometentertainment.com

Coolstreak Cartoons, Inc.

Area(s) of Specialization: Animation, Digital Media

Number of Employees: 6+

Coolstreak Cartoons, Inc. specializes in the development of Macromedia Flash productivity tools and provides animation services to business clients.

Coolstreak Cartoons
25 Jean Brillant
Roxboro, QC
Email: info@toondoctor.com
URL: http://www.toondoctor.com

C.O.R.E. Digital Pictures

Area(s) of Specialization: Film/Video, CGI, Multimedia, Animation

Number of Employees: 30+

C.O.R.E. is a digital animation and special effects company with studios in Toronto, Canada. They design and produce digital visual effects for feature films, television series, commercials, and movies of the week. During the past decade their artists have individually won more than 50 national and international awards. They received the 1995 International Monitor Award and the 1996 Gemini Award for their work on the television series TekWar.

C.O.R.E. Digital Pictures
488 Wellington St. W., Suite 600
Toronto, ON M5V 1E3
Phone: 416 599-2673
Fax: 416 599-1212
Email:info@coredp.com
URL: http://www.coredp.com

C4 Digital Entertainment

Area(s) of Specialization: Traditional Animation

Number of Employees: 10+

Established in early 2000, C4 Digital has proven its excellence by completing major projects for Bandai America Inc. and Toymax Inc. Services cover all aspects of CGI including: Computer Animation, Character Design, 3D Animation Modeling, Digital Image Production, Digital Effects and Web Design.

C4 Digital Entertainment
#120 11960 Hammersmith Way
Richmond, BC V7A 5C9
Phone: 604 204-2692
Fax: 604 204-2691
Email: contact@c4digital.ca
URL: http://www.c4digital.ca

Crush, Inc.

Area(s) of Specialization: Animation

Number of Employees: 10+

Full-service animation studio.

Crush, Inc.
439 Wellington St. West
Toronto, ON M5V 1E7
Phone: 416 345-1936
Fax: 416 345-1965
Email: joann@crushinc.com
URL: http://www.crushinc.com

Cuppa Coffee Animation

Area(s) of Specialization: Animation, Multimedia, Film/Video

Number of Employees: (on contract, number varies)

Cuppa Coffee is an experimental animation company based in Toronto. Owner and Executive Producer Adam Shaheen founded the company in 1992 with limited animation experience and enough money for first and last months rent. Since that time, Cuppa has grown in size and stature, winning over clients with their distinctive blend of cutting-edge animation styles.

Cuppa Coffee Animation
400-215 Spadina Ave.
Toronto, ON M5V 1X3
Phone: 416 340-8869
Fax: 416 340-9819
Email: info@cuppacoffee.com
URL: http://www.cuppacoffee.com

Digimata

Area(s) of Specialization: Animation

Number of Employees: 30+

A full-service animation studio.

Digimata
36 Woodycrest Ave.
Toronto, ON M4J 3A7
Phone: 416 462-3388
Fax: 416 462-2718
Email: digimata@digimata.com
URL: http://www.digimata.com

Di-O-Matic, Inc.

Area(s) of Specialization: Animation, 3D Animation

Number of Employees: 20+

Di-O-Matic is a young, but rapidly growing software development company based out of Montreal, Canada. It was co-founded in October 2000 by Laurent M. Abecassis, an award-winning artist and animator as well as veteran Discreet Training Specialist. The company's goal is a straightforward one: To simplify the process of 3D Animation content creation for animators by providing sophisticated, yet artist-friendly tools.

Di-O-Matic, Inc.
5045 MacDonald, Suite 31
Montreal, QC H3X 2V2
Phone: 514 570-2256
Fax: 514 489-4558
Email: info@di-o-matic.com
URL: http://www.di-o-matic.com

Disada

Area(s) of Specialization: Animation, TV

Number of Employees: 10+

Founded in 1971, Disada specializes in quality animation, whether traditional, computer (which they pioneered as early as 1983) and now Flash as well. They have produced and still do all markets, from TV commercials and Specials to Theatrical entertainment to educational and corporate projects, comic books etc.

Disada Productions, Ltd.
P.O. Box 37009
3332 McCarthy Road
Ottawa, ON K1V 0W0
Phone: 613 247-9207
Email: disada@cyberus.ca
URL: http://www.disada.com

DKP Effects

Area(s) of Specialization: Animation, 3D Animation, Graphic Design

Number of Employees: 15+

DKP Effects, one of Canada's largest 3D animation, effects and compositing houses, with a solid team of visual and graphic artists, raising the bar in producing animation, compositing, effects and graphic design.

DKP Effects, Inc.
489 Queen St. East
Toronto, ON M5A 1V1
Phone: 416 861-9269
Fax: 416 363-3301
Email: info@dkp.com
URL: http://www.dkp.com

DKP/Dan Krech Productions, Inc.

Area(s) of Specialization: CGI, Multimedia, Animation, Film/Video, Sound

Number of Employees: 24

DKP is a fully-equipped visual-effects and animation facility whose solutions to creative problems are consistently unique and innovative. The head office and main facility are located in Toronto. Operating as a boutique, DKP has achieved international acclaim for its expertise in high-end visual effects for the commercial and feature film markets. Recent projects include a 48 minute all computer generated direct to video title, The Nuttiest Nutcracker for Columbia Tri-Star and approximately two minutes of 3D animation stereo IMAX for Siegfried and Roy "The Magic Box."

DKP/Dan Krech Productions, Inc.
489 Queen Street East
Toronto, ON M5A 3N9
Phone: 416 861-9269
Fax: 416 363-3301
Email: info@dkp.com
URL: http://www.dkp.com

Dragon Lake

Area(s) of Specialization: Traditional Animation

Number of Employees: 20+

Specializing in 2D animation and 3D animation special effects, this company offers services in all aspects of animation.

Dragon Lake
68 Jackman Dr.
Brampton, ON L6S 2M2
Phone: 416 885-3713
Fax: 905 799-3817
Email: inquiries@dragonlakeInc.com
URL: http://www.dragonlakeInc.com

Dynomight Cartoons

Area(s) of Specialization: Animation, 2D Animation

Number of Employees: 10+

Company offering 2D Animation/Traditional, Animated Objects, Clay, Cut-outs, Pixilation.

Dynomight Cartoons
205 Catherine St.
Ottawa, ON K2P 1C3
Phone: 613 231-6337
Fax: 613 233-6634
Email: dyno@storm.ca
URL: http://www.dynomight.com

Exhibita

Area(s) of Specialization: Animation

Number of Employees: 6+

Animation studio offering a wide range of services.

Exhibita
300 Richmond St. West, Suite 200
Toronto, ON M5V 1X2
Phone: 416 260-9666
Fax: 416 260-9373
Email: info@exhibita.tv
URL: http://www.exhibita.tv

Eyes Post Group

Area(s) of Specialization: Animation, Television, Post Production

Number of Employees: 50+

Initially founded over ten years ago as a single owner operation, Eyes Post Group has pushed the envelope to become one of Canada's largest and most successful post houses. With an emphasis on individual client service and satisfaction, Eyes developed a loyal following in the feature film, television series, documentary, specialty show, commercial and corporate industries. Endeavoring to provide a wider range of services with a diverse and flexible array of equipment.

Eyes Post Group
320 King St.
Toronto, ON M5A 1K6
Phone: 416 363-3073
Fax: 416 363-6335
Email: steve@eyespost.com
URL: http://www.eyespost.com

Film Effects, Inc.

Area(s) of Specialization: Traditional Animation

Number of Employees: 20+

Film Effects provides digital film services to the motion picture industry worldwide, including title design, opticals, visual effects, digital intermediates, digital-to-film transfers and film recording, in all 16mm and 35mm formats.

Film Effects, Inc.
21 Phoebe St.
Toronto, ON M5T 1A8
Phone: 416 598-3456
Fax: 416 598-7895
Email: inquire@filmeffects.com
URL: http://www.filmeffects.com

Flash To TV

Area(s) of Specialization: Animation, Television

Number of Employees: 10+

'Flash To TV' has developed webisodes, commercials and television pilots for a number of clients.

Flash To TV
Box 214
Miami, MB R0G 1H0
Phone: 204 435-2771
Email: info@flashtotv.com
URL: http://www.flashtotv.com

Fog Studio, Inc.

Area(s) of Specialization: Animation

Number of Employees: 10+

Founded in 1997 by Sylvain Lebeau, FOG Studio is set as one of the companies with upscale development potential in the province of QC for the production of CGI projects.

Fog Studio, Inc.
4000, rue St-Ambroise, #279
Montreal, QC H4C 2C7
Phone: 514 846-8994
Fax: 514 846-8994
Email: info@fogstudio.com
URL: http://www.fogstudio.com

Foresight Animation Studio

Area(s) of Specialization: Animation, Film, Television

Number of Employees: 10+

Complete creative animation services for film, television, and digital productions. From storyboards to traditional hand-drawn art, through to character voice creation, sound effects and music.

Foresight Animation Studio
P.O. Box 788
10 Norwind Rd.
Moncton, NB E1C 8N6
Phone: 506 853-3033
Fax: 506 859-1319
Email: bob@foresightanimation.com
URL: http://www.foresightanimation.com

Funbag Animation Studios

Area(s) of Specialization: Animation

Number of Employees: 20+

Full-service animation studio specializing in children's animation.

Funbag Animation Studios
55 Murray St., Suite 400
Ottawa, ON K1N 5M3
Phone: 613 562-3590
Fax: 613 562-3518
Email: laura@funbag.com
URL: http://www.funbag.com

Gajdecki Visual Effects

Area(s) of Specialization: Film/Video, Multimedia, CGI, Animation

Number of Employees: 15

GVFX is an award-winning visual effects company servicing the motion picture, commercial, television and special venue industries. Based in Toronto and Vancouver, the company offers visual effects supervision, digital compositing and animation, physical production facilities including motion control systems, a model shop, insert stage and pyro team. GVFX has created effects for over 150 major international motion picture and television productions.

Gajdecki Visual Effects
1145 West 7th Ave.
Vancouver, BC V6H 1B5
Phone: 604 736-4839
Fax: 604 736-4838
URL: http://www.gvfx.com

Genex Productions

Area(s) of Specialization: Animation, Film, Digital Media

Number of Employees: 20+

Established in 1998, Genex Productions quickly developed a solid reputation as a high-end digital media production facility.

Genex Productions
50 Gervais Dr., Suite 307b
Toronto, ON M3C 1Z3
Phone: 416 386-0028
Fax: 416 386-0025
Email: sales@genexproductions.com
URL: http://www.genexproductions.com

Ghostmilk

Area(s) of Specialization: Animation, Television Film

Number of Employees: 10+

Ghostmilk is a brand new studio with a team of award-winning designers, artists, illustrators, animators and directors that have joined forces to create fresh visuals for television, film, print and the Web.

Ghostmilk Studios
116 Spadina Ave., Suite 206
Toronto, ON M5V 2K9
Phone: 419 703-6347
Email: ghostadmin@ghostmilk.com
URL: http://www.ghostmilk.com

GhostShip Studio

Area(s) of Specialization: 3D Animation, Animation, Television

Number of Employees: 20+

GhostShip Studio takes new media and animation into the realm of fine art. The GhostShip team has created 3D animation for National Geographic Channel's THE SEA HUNTERS, animated Flash Webisodes for DreamWorks Web venture Pop.com and is presently developing a one hour animated documentary FAIRY FOLIO for CTV. FAIRY FOLIO uses fine art painted imagery in combination with Flash to deliver a rich and detailed animated experience unlike any other.

GhostShip Studio
2762 Robie St.
Halifax, NS B3K 4P2
Phone: 902 455-2300
Fax: 902 423-6226
Email: frank@ghostship.ca
URL: http://www.ghostship.ca

Grafixation

Area(s) of Specialization: Graphics, Web Design, Web Hosting

Number of Employees: 10

Grafixation provides small to medium sized companies with complete Web or e-commerce solutions.

Grafixation
6810 Simpson Pioneer Trail
Mississauga, ON L5W 1A6
Phone: 416 817-0828
Fax: 905 565-9395
URL: http://www.grafixation.com

Guru Animation Studio

Area(s) of Specialization: Animation, 3D
Animation

Number of Employees: 15+

Guru Animation Studio is a 3D
animation character animation studio
using traditional narrative techniques.

Guru Animation Studio
317 Adelaide St. West, Suite 903
Toronto, ON M5V 1P9
Phone: 416 599-4878
Fax: 416 628-6926
Email: info@gurustudio.com
URL: http://www.gurustudio.com

GVFX

Area(s) of Specialization: Animation,
Digital Media

Number of Employees: 25+

Since its inception in 1991, GVFX has
been producing award winning visual
effects, servicing the motion picture,
television, commercial and special venue
industries.

GVFX
29 Booth Ave., Suite 205
Toronto, ON M4M 2M3
Phone: 416 463-6753
Fax: 416 463-7312
Email: inquiries@gvfx.com
URL: http://www.gvfx.com

Head Gear Animation

Area(s) of Specialization: Stop-Motion,
Cel Animation, Mixed Media

Number of Employees: 3

Head Gear was launched in July, 1997,
after three years of building an extensive
reel of unique animation work at
Toronto production house Cuppa
Coffee.

Head Gear Animation
35 McCaul, Suite 301
Toronto, ON
Phone: 416 408-2020
Fax: 416 408-2011
Email: paula@headgearanimation.com
URL: http://www.headgearanimation.com

Hybride

Area(s) of Specialization: Animation, Film

Number of Employees: 25+

Hybride technologies specializes in digital visual effects for the feature, advertising and video industries. Hybride also does its own research and development to create specialized software and equipment that respond to the highest demands of the North American movie industry.

Hybride Technologies
111, ch de la Gare
Piedmont, QC J0R 1K0
Phone: 450 227-4245
Fax: 450 227-5245
Email: info@hybride.com
URL: http://www.hybride.com

JesterJester Media

Area(s) of Specialization: Animation

Number of Employees: 15+

JesterJester Media is a multifunctional animation studio created to offer a cheaper Eastern Canadian alternative to international private businesses, studios, firms and government institutions.

JesterJester Media
5252 Tobin St. #121
Halifax, NS B3H 4K2
Phone: 902 425-6775
Email: production_services@
jesterjester.com
URL: http://www.jesterjester.com

KliK Animation

Area(s) of Specialization: Traditional Animation

Number of Employees: 10+

KliK Animation is proud to count itself amongst Canadian leaders in high quality animation. Founded in 1997, KliK employs a score of people from all disciplines requested in the production of computer animation.

KliK Animation
5524, St-Patrick St., Suite 302
Montreal, QC H4E 1A8
Phone: 514 842-6602
Fax: 514 842-6603
Email: info@klikanimation.com
URL: http://www.klikanimation.com

La Raffinerie IMS

Area(s) of Specialization: Animation

Number of Employees: 6+

Studio offering 2D Animation Computer Animation, 3D Animation Computer Animation, and Digital/Visual Effects.

La Raffinerie IMS
4416 St. Laurent
Montreal, QC H2W 1Z5
Phone: 514 843-0202
Fax: 514 985-2212
Email: laraffinerie@qc.aira.com

Loop Media Inc.

Area(s) of Specialization: Computer Animation

Number of Employees: 9

Loop Media Inc. is an innovative 2D animation and 3D animation computer animation studio, offering a variety of high-end production services. Using Silicon Graphics workstations with Prisms, Houdini and Renderman software. Loop provides character and corporate animation in addition to visual effects for film and television.

Loop Media Inc.
401 Richmond St. West, Suite 243
Toronto, ON M5V 3A8
Phone: 416 595-6496
Fax: 416 595-0306
Email: admin@loopmedia.com
URL: http://www.loopmedia.com

Lost Boys Studios

Area(s) of Specialization: Design and Consulting, Video/ Film Production and Post Production

Number of Employees: 12

Lost Boys Studios was formed in the winter of 1997 through an alliance of the Vancouver based Solstice Digital Imaging and LA-based Virgin Digital Studios. Lost Boys Studios is a creative house specializing in the design and execution of the finest quality DFX that will suit clients individual budgets. They involve themselves in the entire pipeline from pre-production DFX design and budgeting consulting, on-set DFX Supervision, DFX execution, and approvals.

Lost Boys Studios
Third Floor - 395 Railway Street
Vancouver, BC V6A 1A6
Phone: 604 738-1805
Fax: 604 738-1806
Email: roula@lostboys-studios.com
URL: http://www.lostboys-studios.com

Lost Pencil Animation Studios, Inc.

Area(s) of Specialization: Animation

Number of Employees: 20+

A full-service animation company.

Lost Pencil Animation Studios, Inc.
84 Marquis Place
Airdrie, AB T4A1Z1
Phone: 403 948-6823
Email: paul@lostpencil.com
URL: http://www.lostpencil.com

Magnetic North

Area(s) of Specialization: Television

Number of Employees: 6+

A full-service animation studio.

Magnetic North
70 Richmond St. East, Suite 100
Toronto, ON M5C 1N8
Phone: 416 365-7622
Fax: 416 365-2188
Email: sales@magpost.com
URL: http://www.magpost.com

Mainframe Entertainment, Inc.

Area(s) of Specialization: 3D Animation

Number of Employees: 330

The company has evolved from a small crew of animators in 1993 to a staff of over 200 today. The company also develops and owns a number of proprietary software programs that enhance and accelerate animation production processes, and manages a highly successful Merchandising and Licensing program based on its properties.

Mainframe Entertainment, Inc.
2025 West Broadway, Suite 500
Vancouver, BC V6J 1Z6
Phone: 604 714-2600
Fax: 604 714-2641
Email: info@mainframe.ca
URL: http://www.mainframe.ca

Mercury Filmworks

Area(s) of Specialization: 3D Animation, Digital Editing

Number of Employees: 40

Located in a custom designed, leading edge, 8,000 sq. ft. facility overlooking Vancouver's Coal Harbor and the Coastal Mountains, Mercury Filmworks is a fully equipped digital animation facility. From feature quality digital paint, special effects, 3D animation, and compositing, to uncompressed digital online editing, mastering, and network packaging, Mercury Filmworks services clients world wide from the heart of Vancouver via high-speed wireless to fiber optic connection.

Mercury Filmworks
190 Alexander Street, Suite 500
Vancouver, BC V6A 1B5
Phone: 604 684-9117
Fax: 604 684 8339
Email: info@mercuryfilmworks.com
URL: http://www.mercuryfilmworks.com

Michael Mills Productions, Ltd.

Area(s) of Specialization: Animation

Number of Employees: 15+

Founded in 1974, is the oldest, established, commercial production animation house in Canada. The studio employs over 15 industry professionals providing the latest technology and expertise in creative illustration, design, and production for the Film and Advertising Industries. The company has established itself as a highly creative studio, credited with developing new projects and animation techniques. The company has an enviable record of success, with unsurpassed experience in half hour television series, specials, short films, spot commercials and interactive CD-ROMs.

Michael Mills Productions, Ltd.
4492 St. Catherine St. West
Montreal, QC H3Z1R7
Phone: 514 931-7117
Fax: 514 931-7099
Email: michael@thumbnailspots.com
URL: http://www.thumbnailanimation.com

Moovmento

Area(s) of Specialization: Animation, Digital Animation, 3D Animation

Number of Employees: 15+

Moovmento is a multidisciplinary design studio bridging print and digital media worlds. Drawing on the combined expertise of its founding partners and employees in graphic design, image synthesis, multimedia and 3D animation, the company offers integrated design services for corporate identities, brochures, packaging design, Web sites, multimedia production, video animation, and user interface design.

Moovmento, Inc.
5520 Chabot, #301
Montreal, QC H2H 2S7
Phone: 514 527-1024
Fax: 514 527-1189
Email: info@moovmento.com
URL: http://www.moovmento.com

Myotte Bellamy Productions, Inc.

Area(s) of Specialization: Animation, Film, Television

Number of Employees: 10+

This company offers the vision and experience gained from years spent on film and TV series.

Myotte Bellamy Productions, Inc.
1061 St-Alexandre #407
Montreal, QC H2Z 1P5

Phone: 514 868-9849
Fax: 514 868-9849
Email: info@myottebellamy.com
URL: http://www.myottebellamy.com

Nelvana Limited

Area(s) of Specialization: Animation
Production

Number of Employees: 700

A leading producer and distributor of
animated children's and family
entertainment, Nelvana's areas of
programming include animated
television series, specials and feature
films. Nelvana's Toronto head office
houses one of North America's largest
animation studios. The Company also
has operations in Los Angeles, London
and Paris. As an international distributor
to the global television marketplace, the
Company has licensed its programming
to more than 160 countries.

Nelvana Limited
32 Atlantic Ave.
Toronto, ON M6K 1X8
Phone: 416 588-5571
Fax: 416 588-5252
Email: Webmaster@nelvana.com
URL: http://www.nelvana.com

Northwest Imaging and FX

Area(s) of Specialization: Post
Production

Number of Employees: 40

Ten Years ago, the Northwest Imaging
and FX founders opened the doors to
Canada's first fully digital visual effects
edit suite with an enthusiastic staff of
three. Today, services include visual
effects supervision, 3D animation,
compositing, digital matte painting,
morphing, image tracking, film transfer
(35mm and 16mm), tape to tape color
correction, online picture finishing,
offline editing, and tape duplication.

Northwest Imaging and FX
2339 Columbia, Suite 100
Vancouver, BC V5Y 3Y3
Phone: 604 873-9330
Fax: 604 873-9339
Email: alex@nwfx.com
URL: http://www.nwfx.com

Nudge Productions, Inc.

Area(s) of Specialization: Traditional
Animation

Number of Employees: 6+

Nudge Productions, Inc.
200a – 1224 Hamilton St.
Vancouver, BC V6Z 2S8

Phone: 604 602-0082
Fax: 604 602-0082
Email: Samantha@nudgeproductons.com
URL: http://www.nudgeproductions.com

Optix Digital Post and FX, Inc.

Area(s) of Specialization: Animation

Number of Employees: 25+

Full-service animation studio offering a wide range of digital media services.

Optix Digital Post and FX, Inc.
157 Princess St.
Toronto, ON M5A 4M4
Phone: 416 214-9911
Fax: 416 214-9912
Email: info@optix-i.com
URL: http://www.optix-i.com

Picard Film Services, Inc.

Area(s) of Specialization: Animation, CGI

Number of Employees: 10+

Full-service animation studio offering a wide range of services.

Picard Film Services, Inc.
15 Brookbanks Dr., #1603
Toronto, ON M3A2T1
Phone: 416 447-7564
Fax: 416 446-6421
Email: deedub@deedub.ca
URL: http://www.deedub.ca

Plastic Thought Studios

Area(s) of Specialization: Animation, Sales/Marketing, Film, Television

Number of Employees: 30+

Plastic Thought Studios provides creative and production services for all sectors of enterprise.

Plastic Thought Studios
#300, 10301 - 108 St.
Edmonton, AB T5J 1L7
Phone: 780 429-5051
Email: joe@plasticthought.com
URL: http://www.plasticthought.com

The Post Group

Area(s) of Specialization: Post Production

Number of Employees: 14+

Over the past five years, The Post Group has been providing its clients with exceptional talent, time sensitivity and budgeting promises. They offer a unique blend of high-end technology under the commands of an award-winning team of artists – providing both online and offline, leading-edge editing.

The Post Group
411 Richmond Street East, Suite 205
Toronto, ON M5A 3S5
Phone: 416 363-3004

Fax: 416 363-8960
Email: johnson@thepostgroup.com
URL: http://www.thepostgroup.com

Red Rover Studios Ltd.

Area(s) of Specialization: Traditional Animation

Number of Employees: 30+

Red Rover Studios Ltd. is a fully faceted traditional/CGI commercial, TV, feature animation studio.

Red Rover Studios Ltd.
345 Adelaide St. West, Suite 5
Toronto, ON M5V 1R5
Phone: 416 591-6500
Fax: 416 591-6501
URL: http://www.redrover.net

Relic Entertainment, Inc.

Area(s) of Specialization: Game Developer

Number of Employees: 43

Relic Entertainment Inc. is a developer of electronic entertainment software. The long-term goals of the Company include other types of electronic entertainment such as online gaming, arcade, and location-based media. Relic has also developed leading edge

technologies in the area of 3D animation imagery and sound systems.

Relic Entertainment, Inc.
400-948 Homer St.
Vancouver, BC V6B 2W7
Phone: 604 801-6577
Fax: 604 801-6578
Email: contact@relic.com
URL: http://www.relic.com

Seamless Creations

Area(s) of Specialization: Animation, Digital Media

Number of Employees: 3+

Seamless Creations was established in 1997 as an identity for the visually creative works of Rob Del Ciancio. Teamed up with the audio talents of Ian Haskin, many creative independent projects were produced in-house. Seamless has worked in all media producing high quality work for film, broadcast, print and Web.

Seamless Creations
576 Kingston Rd.
Toronto, ON M4E 1P9
Phone: 416 993-7493
Fax: 720 294-3719
Email: info@seamless.org
URL: http://www.seamless.org

Sequence Productions

Area(s) of Specialization: Traditional Animation

Number of Employees: 3+

Sequence Productions houses the digital sound studios for television and film composer Angelo Oddi. Angelo composes music for television and film.

Sequence Production Studios, Ltd.
19 Mercer St., Suite 201
Toronto, ON M5V 1H2
Phone: 416 217-0505 x1
Fax: 416 217-0333
Email: info@sequenceproductions.com
URL: http://www.sequence productions.com

Singular Inversions

Area(s) of Specialization: Animation, CGI, Digital Media

Number of Employees: 100+

Founded in 1998, Singular Inversions specializes in statistical modeling of the shape and appearance of human faces, combining expertise in computer vision, statistics, and computer graphics.

Singular Inversions
1-1350 West 14th Ave.
Vancouver, BC V6H 1R1

Phone: 604 730-1727
Email: sales@singularinversions.com
URL: http://www.facegen.com

Skookum Sound

Area(s) of Specialization: Animation, Film

Number of Employees: 15+

A reputable facility within the Animation industry, Skookum Sound has worked on over 340 animated half-hour episodes. Production services have also been rendered on a variety of features, pilots, shorts and commercials.

Skookum Sound
2650 Crystal Dr.
Ct.enay, BC V9N 9K1
Phone: 250 338-2469
Fax: 250 338-2489
Email: skookumsound@telus.net
URL: http://www.skookumsound.com

Soho Post and Graphics

Area(s) of Specialization: Animation

Number of Employees: 50+

Full-service animation studio.

Soho Post and Graphics
26 Soho St.
Toronto, ON M5T 1Z7
Phone: 416 591-1400

Fax: 416 591-6854
Email: doug@26soho.com
URL: http://www.26soho.com

Squeeze Animation

Area(s) of Specialization: Animation, Film

Number of Employees: 10+

Squeeze Animation was formed in July 2002 by veteran classical 2D Animation animators Charlie Bonifacio and Chuck Gammage. The Company seeks to develop and produce a broad range of programming for the television networks, first run domestic syndication and international markets with an emphasis on development and production of theatrical release feature animation for both proprietary and fee for service basis.

Squeeze Animation
317 Adelaide St. West, Suite 910
Toronto, ON M5V 1P9
Phone: 416 593 9627
Email: charlie@squeezeanimation.com
URL: http://www.squeezeanimation.com

The Studio Upstairs

Area(s) of Specialization: Animation, Digital Media

Number of Employees: 100+

Full-service creative company offering many multimedia services.

The Studio Upstairs
510 Front St. West, Suite 103
Toronto, ON M5V 1B8
Phone: 416 979-8983
Fax: 416 979-8246
Email: info@thestudioupstairs.com
URL: http://www.thestudioupstairs.com

Sub Atomic Productions, Inc.

Area(s) of Specialization: Animation, Video, Digital Media, Graphic Design

Number of Employees: 30+

Corporate communication specialists providing leading edge creative in a variety of media including print, animation, video, multimedia. They work with blue chip and Fortune 500 companies as well as medium and small size firms.

Sub Atomic Productions, Inc.
90C Centurian Dr., Unit 1
Markham, ON L3R 8C5
Phone: 905 474-9393
Fax: 905 474-0209
Email: todd@subatomicproductions.com
URL: http://www.subatomic
productions.com

Sullivan Entertainment, Inc.

Area(s) of Specialization: Animation, Film, Digital Media, Television

Number of Employees: 200+

Sullivan Entertainment has been entertaining audiences in Canada and around the world for the past 20 years. Through Sullivan Entertainment International, the company has established a presence in the world marketplace as a producer and distributor of quality films and television series.

Sullivan Entertainment, Inc.
110 Davenport Rd.
Toronto, ON M5R 3R3
Phone: 416 921-7177
Fax: 416 921-7538
Email: inquire@sullivan-ent.com
URL: http://www.sullivan-ent.com

Sundog Films

Area(s) of Specialization: Animation

Number of Employees: 40+

Sundog Films provides post production services for feature films and television programming. Sundog is committed from the initial stages of pre production, lending on set supervision right through to the finished master product outputted to film or HD tape. In its creation of 3D animation and 2D animation visual effects, Sundog Films places the focus of its business on artistry and a "pushing the envelope" approach to its creations. Sundog artists have established an esteemed track record within the television, film, and commercial industries.

Sundog Films
530 Richmond St. West
Toronto, ON M5V 1Y4
Phone: 416 504-2555
Fax: 416 504-4545
Email: robin@sundogfilms.ca
URL: http://www.sundogfilms.ca

Sweet Thing Productions

Area(s) of Specialization: Animation, Digital Media

Number of Employees: 20+

Sweet Thing Productions is a microstudio specializing in creative stop-motion productions in 35mm or digital.

Sweet Thing Productions
2 Second St. Ward's Island
Toronto, ON M5J 2A8
Phone: 416 203-3730
Fax: 416 203-3775
Email: sweetthing@rogers.com

Talltree Studios

Area(s) of Specialization: Animation, 2D Animation, 3D Animation, Digital

Number of Employees: 15+

From script to screen, Talltree does 2D animation and 3D animation digital animation, motion graphics, visual effects, and broadcast design.

Talltree Studios
545 Ouellette Ave., Suite 202
Windsor, ON N9A 4J3
Phone: 519 258-3717
Fax: 519 256-0243
Email: info@talltreestudios.com
URL: http://www.talltreestudios.com

Topix/Mad Dog

Area(s) of Specialization: Special Effects

Number of Employees: 20

Founded in September 1987, Toronto-based TOPIX has become Canada's premiere computer graphics and animation facility. They are specialists in character animation, special effects, film titling, type and broadcast design, the company creates superior photo-realistic, computer-generated animation for the advertising, feature film, broadcast and music video industries. Clients include: Coca Cola, Kraft Foods, Chrysler, Budweiser, Playtex, Discover Card and Post Cereals, among others; international campaigns for Alka Seltzer, Pepsi Cola and Honda, McDonald's, Nescafe, Ford, Molson's, and Labatt's. They have collaborated on ground breaking rock videos including David Bowie's "Little Wonder," Sheryl Crow's "Anything But Down," Sarah McLachlan's "Sweet Surrender," The Tragically Hip's "Ahead by a Century," The Barenaked Ladies' "Brian Wilson," Amel Larrieux "Get Up," and Mary J. Blige "All That I Can Say." another TOPIX · Mad Dog co-venture: Red Giant, a television production company that has co-created the magazine-style television series, "Splat."

Topix/Mad Dog
35 McCaul St., Suite 200
Toronto, ON M5T 1V7
Phone: 416 971-7711
Fax: 416 971-9277
Email: info@topix.com
URL: http://www.topix.com

Toybox Toronto

Area(s) of Specialization: Animation, Post Production, Digital Media

Number of Employees: 100+

A studio offering all data, standard & high definition formats, and provides a full range of visual effects, Post Production, scanning, recording and pre-press services for feature films, long form television and commercials. A division of the Command Post & Transfer Corporation with sister companies in Vancouver, Toronto and LA.

Toybox
179 John St., 8th Fl.
Toronto, ON M5T 1X4
Phone: 416 585-9995
Fax: 416 979-0428
URL: http://www.compt.com

Trainingscape Studios

Area(s) of Specialization: Animation

Number of Employees: 20+

Studio offering services that include: Animated Characters, Animated Web Graphics, Commercials, Educational/ Industrial Films, Feature Films, Music Videos, Short Films, Television Series, Television Specials, Title Sequences, Webisodes.

Trainingscape Studios
5161 George St.
Halifax, NS B3J 1M7
URL: http://www.trainingscape.com

Vivid Group Inc.

Area(s) of Specialization: Multimedia, CGI, Film/Video, Animation

Number of Employees: 20

Vivid Group creates and develops interactive arenas used primarily in the Museum, Science Center and Hall of Fame Industry. The company's patented Gesture Xtreme technology allows for custom programming of Corporate Communication packages using the clients' logo and/or theme objective. Originally created for use as a performance medium, GX(r) technology branched out and quickly caught on as a powerful education and entertainment instrument.

Vivid Group Inc.
317 Adelaide Street West, Suite 302
Toronto, ON M5V 1P9
Phone: 416 340-9290
Fax: 416 348-1189
Email: info@vividgroup.com
URL: http://www.vividgroup.com

Wave Generation

Area(s) of Specialization: Animation, Film, Television

Number of Employees: 10+

Specializing in everything from music licensing, music composition, sound effects, audio design, casting, arrangements, studio recording, voice recording, postproduction, and editing, Wave Generation's audio production expertise serves them well by enabling them to fill a critical niche in TV, animation and interactive entertainment.

Wave Generation
6300 Parc Ave., Suite 200
Montreal, QC H2V 4H8
Phone: 514 272-3535
Fax: 514 272-1321
Email: info@wavegeneration.ca
URL: http://www.wavegeneration.ca

Whitehouse Animation, Inc.

Area(s) of Specialization: Animation

Number of Employees: 100+

A full-service animation company offering a wide range of animation and media services including animation and post production services.

Whitehouse Animation, Inc.
225 Clinton St.
Toronto, ON
Email: whitehouse@halfempty.com
URL: http://www.whitehouseanimation
Inc.com

Xenos

Area(s) of Specialization: Animation

Number of Employees: 2+

Small animation studio.

Xenos
#373 - 1755 Robson St.
Vancouver, BC V6G 3B7
Phone: 604 421-5046
Fax: 604 421-5046
Email: sarthur@look.ca
URL: http://mypage.direct.ca/w/writer/xenos.html

XYZ RGB

Area(s) of Specialization: Animation

Number of Employees: 25+

XYZ RGB is a 3D animation scanning bureau and content creation company located within the IPF.

XYZ RGB
1200 Montreal Rd.
Bldg. M-50, IPF Room E-195
Ottawa, ON K1A 0R6
Phone: 613 748-9596
Fax: 613 748-8054
Email: info@xyzrgb.com
URL: http://www.xyzrgb.com

Zebra Creative Group, Inc.

Area(s) of Specialization: Animation, Television

Number of Employees: 6+

Since the animation studio was opened in August of 2000, they have filled their slate with everything from shorts to bumpers to their own television series. They have produced "Olliver's Under the Bed Adventures," their own animated series for Teletoon.

Zebra Creative Group, Inc.
5275 Wellburn Dr.
Delta, BC V4K 4H9
Phone: 604 946-0967
Fax: 604 946-1615
Email: design@zebracreative.com
URL: http://www.zebracreative.com

Zodiac Media Inc.

Area(s) of Specialization: Animation, Graphic Design, Digital Media

Number of Employees: 15+

Zodiac Media Inc. is a design, development and animation studio that produces original programming and update existing character brands.

Zodiac Media Inc.
444 Dundas St. West, 2nd Fl.
Toronto, ON M5T 1G7
Phone: 416 977-0002
Fax: 416 977-8404
Email: info@zodiacmedia.com
URL: http://www.zodiacmedia.com

International

Anidini & Associate

Rm.16, 10/F., Tower B, Proficient Ind.
Rm.3306, Ka Wing House, Ka Tin
Ct., Tai Wai
Hong Kong, Hong Kong
Phone: 852 2189 7366
Fax: 852 2189 7273
Email: anidini88@yahoo.com.hk
URL: http://www.animdini.com

Aniever, Inc.

4F Daekwang Bldg., 376-5
Seokyo-Dong Mapo-Gu
Seoul, South Korea
Phone: 82 2 336-5432
Fax: 82 2 336-5433
Email: aniever@aniever.com
URL: http://www.aniever.com

Anikino Inc.

1337-3 Seocho-Dong
Seocho-Gu
Seoul, South Korea
Phone: 82 2 6257-6000
Fax: 82 2 581-7234
Email: anikino@anikino.co.kr
URL: http://www.anikino.co.kr

Anima, Karekare Film Yapim A.S.

100. Yil Sanayi Sitesi Girisi No.4
Maslak
Istanbul, 80670
Turkey
Phone: 90 212 286 2046
Fax: 90 212 286 2045
Email: anima@anima.gen.tr
URL: http://www.anima.gen.tr
AniMagic Productions, LLC

Animagic Studio

Avda. Fuente Nueva, 6
San Sebasti·n de los ReyesMadrid, 28700
Spain
Phone: 34 91 6592036
Fax: 34 91 6639645
Email: recepcion@animagicstudio.com
URL: http://www.animagicstudio.com

AnimagicNet AS

Storgata 51
Oslo, 0183
Norway
Phone: 47 22 99 76 10
Fax: 47 22 99 76 11
Email: info@animagicnet.no
URL: http://www.animagicnet.no

Animagix Media

Hamburger Strasse 205
Hamburg, 22083
Germany
Phone: 49 40 2994611
Fax: 49 40 2994656
Email: infoanimagix@animagix.com
URL: http://www.animagix.com

Animago, Lda

Rua Guerra Junqueiro, 495, 1° Sala J
Porto, 4150-389
Portugal
Phone: 351 22 5432070
Fax: 351 22 5432071
Email: info@animago.pt
URL: http://www.animago.pt

Animal, Inc.

711 Hyundai Dream Tower
923-14 Mok-dong
Yancheon-gu
Seoul, South Korea
Phone: 82 2 2166-2315
Fax: 82 2 2166-2315
Email: jango-25@hanmail.net
URL: http://www.studioanimal.co.kr

Animalada

Camacho Av. and Burnett
Tower 2 Suite 303
Punta del Este, Maldonado 20000
Uruguay

Phone: 598 42 233345
Fax: 598 42 251693
Email: info@animalada.com
URL: http://www.animalada.com

Animantics

10B Fernwood Ct.
Newlands
Wellington, New Zealand
Phone: 64 4 9399009
Email: ross@paynemail.com
URL: http://www.animantics.co.nz

Animart

II.Makariopolski N2
Sofia, 1301
Bulgaria
Phone: 359 2 317 902
Email: kokosarkisian@hotmail.com

AnimaThorFilm

Krokveien 10
Inderoy, 7670
Norway
Phone: 47 74 153724
Fax: 47 74 153067
Email: animatho@online.no
home.online.no/~animatho

Animation & Special Effects

612 Telok Blangah Rd. #06-08
Singapore, 109026
Singapore

URL: http://www.geocities.
comnatashayong

Animation India

1311, 2nd Fl.,Saptagiri, 11th Main Rd.,
Vijayanagar, Bangalore.
Bangalore, Karnataka 560040
India
Phone: 91 80 3357580
Fax: 91 80 3357580
Email: animationindia@yahoo.com
URL: http://www.mandy.comhome.
cfm?c=ani064

Animation Unlimited

Pinhas Levon 23
Netanya
Israel
Phone: 97 253 413804
Email: sharon_a@012.net.il
http://go.to/animation-unlimited

Animatographo

Rua Duilio Calderari, 63 - lj. 3
Curitiba, Parana 80040-250
Brazil
Phone: 55 41 362-8600
Email: animatographo@animato-
grapho.com
URL: http://www.animatographo.com

Animax

Kosmicka 537
Prague, 14900
Czech Republic
Phone: 420 2 67914208
Fax: 420 2 67913699
Email: et@animax-studio.com
URL: http://www.animax-studio.com

Animedia

65, Skylon
Opp.Agarwal Hall
University Road
Ahmedabad, Gujarat 380015
India
Phone: 91 79 6304711
Email: admin@animediaindia.com
URL: http://www.animediaindia.com

Animega

Box 3113
Brahegatan, 7
Jonkoping, 55003
Sweden
Phone: 46 36 125 521
Fax: 46 36 712 001
Email: info@animega.com
URL: http://www.animega.com

Animier Co., Ltd.

Ansan S.W. Center Blvd.643-7
Won-Gok Dong
Ansan-Si

Kyounggi-Do,
South Korea
Phone: 82 31 495-2545
Fax: 82 31 495-2545
animier@hanmail.net
URL: http://www.animier.com

Animoke Limited

GFF 2 Chatham Place
Brighton, BN1 3TP
United Kingdom
Phone: 44 775 9679384
Email: tim@animoke.com
URL: http://www.animoke.com

Anitong, Inc.

#812 Hyundai Dream Tower
923-14 Yangcheon-Gu
Seoul
South Korea
Phone: 82 2 2166-2515
Fax: 82 2 2166-2516
Email: pouru07@hanmail.net

Aniway Co., Ltd.

116 Yangjae-Dong
Seocho-Gu
Seoul
South Korea
Phone: 82 2 571-1478
Fax: 82 2 571-1427
Email: george@ani-way.com
URL: http://www. ani-way.com

Another World Productions

Lismore House
23 Church St.
Portadown, Co Armagh
Portadown, Northern Ireland BT63
3LN
United Kingdom
Phone: 44 283 833 2933
Fax: 44 283 839 6941
Email: info@awproductions.com
URL: http://www.awproductions.com

AnteFilms (Levallois)

3, rue Collagne
Levallois, 92300
France
Phone: 33 1 55 21 99 40
Fax: 33 1 55 21 99 41
URL: http://www.antefilms.com

Antefilms International

103 rue de Miromesnil
Paris, 75008
France
Phone: 33 1 53 53 06 30
Fax: 33 1 53 53 06 29
Email: production@antefilms.com
URL: http://www.antefilms.com

Antefilms Studio

31, rue Marengo
Angouleme, 16000

France
Phone: 33 5 45 22 95 00
Fax: 33 5 45 22 95 01
URL: http://www.antefilms.com

Antenna Men

Lloydstraat 9c
3024 EA
Rotterdam,
Netherlands
Email: info@antenna-men.com
URL: http://www.antenna-men.com

Anthropics Technology, Ltd.

Ealing Studios
Ealing Green
London, W5 5EP
United Kingdom
Phone: 44 208 758 8619
Fax: 44 208 758 8619
Email: info@anthropics.com
URL: http://www.anthropics.com

Argon Animation Inc.

9094 Banuyo St.
San Antonio Village
Makati, Manila, 1203
Philippines
Phone: 63 2 896 5494
Fax: 63 2 896 5494
Email: tim_bennett_laser@yahoo.co.uk

Art In Motion

49 Borrowdale Rd.
Riverclub
Johannesburg, Gauteng 2049
South Africa
Phone: 27 11 7064992
Fax: 27 11 7064991
Email: artinmotion@mWeb.co.za

Archisoft Technologies Pvt.Ltd.

501, Bhaveshwar Complex
Vidyavihar (West)
Mumbai, Maharashtra 400 086
India
Phone: 91 22 5147017
Fax: 91 22 5988615
Email: info@archisofttechnologies.com
URL: http://www.archisoft
technologies.com

Arena Multimedia

Kohinoor # 6
105 Park St.
Kolkata, West Bengal 700016
India
Phone: 91 33 249-2300
Fax: 91 33 246-6784
Email: arenaps@vsnl.com
URL: http://www.arena-multimedia.com

Artepict Studio

16 cours Sablon
Clermont-Ferrand, 6300
France
Phone: 33 4 73 14 16 31
Fax: 33 4 73 93 12 57
Email: info@artepict.net
URL: http://www.artepictstudio.com

Artimagen Digital

Av. Romulo Gallegos, Edif. Park Ave.
piso 12, Apto 128, Urb. Horizonte
Caracas, Miranda 1060
Venezuela
Phone: 58 212 2388571
Fax: 58 212 2388571
Email: informacion@artimagendigital.com
URL: http://www.artimagendigital.com

Asset Media International AG

Asset Media Ring 17
Munich, 80807
Germany
Phone: 49 89 354990
Fax: 49 89 35499500
Email: office@asset.media.com
URL: http://www.asset-media.com

Asterisk* Productions

58 Belford Dr., Wellington Point
Brisbane, Queensland 4160
Australia
Phone: 61 7 3822 5738
Fax: 61 7 3822 1821
Email: asterisk@iprimus.com.au

Attitude Studio France

100, Av du General Lederc
Pantin, 93692
France
Phone: 33 1 41 71 70 78
Fax: 33 1 41 71 01 68
URL: http://www.attitude-studio.com

AudioMotion

Beaumont Rd.
Banbury, Oxon ox17 1rh
United Kingdom
Phone: 44 1295 266 622
Fax: 44 1295 266 622
Email: info@audiomotion.com
URL: http://www.audiomotion.com

Audiovisuales de Valdes

Animacion 3D Animation
Luz Savinon 13-902
Colonia Del Valle, 03100
Mexico
Phone: 52 55 5543-4743
Email: ventas@avv.com.mx
URL: http://www.animacion3D
Animation.com.mx

Aum Creations

1-b, Laxmi Industrial Estate, andheri(w)
Mumbai, Maharashtra 400058
India
Phone: 91 22 6350953
Fax: 91 22 6359974
aumcreation@hotmail.com

AWAFI

Av. Santa Fe 1460, piso 2
Buenos Aires, C1060ABN
Argentina
Phone: 54 11 4812-1222
Fax: 54 11 4812-6001
Email: jserna@fibertel.com.ar
URL: http://www.awafisa.com

AXIS Animation

Pentagon Buisness Center, 36
Washington St.
Glasgow, G3 8AZ
United Kingdom
Phone: 44 141 572 2802
Fax: 44 141 572 2809
Email: enquiries@axisanimation.com
URL: http://www.axisanimation.com

B-cosmos

Av. Nestle 34
Vevey, 1800
Switzerland
Phone: 41 21 922 61 96
Fax: 41 21 922 61 96
Email: info@b-cosmos.com
URL: http://www.b-cosmos.com

b.toons

1051 GG
Amsterdam,
Netherlands
Phone: 31 20 682 85 87
Fax: 31
Email: b.toons@Web.de

Bailey Bros.

Heaton
Newcastle upon Tyne,
United Kingdom
Phone: 44 191 209 9314
Email: baileybros@cwcom.net
URL: http://www.the-ministry.tv

Banjax

Suite 407, Curtain House,
134-146 Curtain Road
London, EC2A 3AR
United Kingdom
Phone: 44 207 739 8118
Fax: 44 207 739 3890
Email: richard@banjax.com
URL: http://www.banjax.com

Base 77

D-77 Defense Colony
New Delhi, 110024, India
Phone: 91 11 4625330
Email: marketing@base77.com
URL: http://www.base77.com

Baumhaus Medien AG

Juliusstrasse 12
Frankfurt, 60487
Germany
Phone: 49 69 97 77 67-0
Fax: 49 69 97 77 67-67
Email: mailbox@baumhaus-medien.de
URL: http://www.baumhaus-medien.de

Bazley Films

Corsham Media Park, Spring Quarry
West Wells Road
Corsham, Wiltshire SN13 9GB
United Kingdom
Phone: 44 1225 816 210
Fax: 44 1225 816 211
Email: richard@bazleyfilms.com
URL: http://www.bazleyfilms.com

BBC MediaArc's 3D Animation

CharacterShop
Birmingham, B7 5QQ
United Kingdom
Phone: 44 121 432 9636
URL: http://www.bbcmediaarc.com

Benz Infotech

Benz Towers
Edappally
Cochin, Kerala 682024, India
Phone: 91 484 342226
Fax: 91 484 342226
URL: http://www.benzinfotech.com

Bergani Films, Ltd.

Aurakatu 14 C
Turku, 20100
Finland
Phone: 358 2 2503630
Fax: 358 2 2503620
Email: animation@bergani.com
URL: http://www.bergani.com

Bergen Animation

Georgernes Verft 12
Bergen, 5011
Norway
Phone: 47 55 96 24 20
Fax: 47 55 96 24 20
Email: post@bergenanimasjon.no
URL: http://www.bergenanimasjon.no

Big Al Limited

Production
24 Cornwall Rd.
London, SE1 8TW
United Kingdom
Phone: 44 207 922 1314
Fax: 44 207 922 1394

Big I Entertainment

Rm 501 Hansung B/D
590-19 Shinsa-dong Kangnam-Gu
Seoul
South Korea
Phone: 82 2 518-0975
Fax: 82 2 3442-4351
Email: bigi@bigient.com
URL: http://www.bigient.com

Big Time Pictures

Hillside Studios
Merry Hill Road
Bushey, Hertfordshire WD23
1DR
United Kingdom
Phone: 44 208 950 7919
Fax: 44 208 950 1437
Email: info@bigtimepictures.co.uk
URL: http://www.bigtimepictures.co.uk

Bionatics

12, Ave. Raspail
Gentilly, 94250
France
Phone: 33 1 49 69 12 20
Fax: 33 1 49 69 12 29
Email: info@bionatics.com
URL: http://www.bionatics.com

Bionic Informatics Pvt, Ltd.

524, 5th Cross
Mahalakshmi Layout
Bangalore, Karnataka 560086
India
Phone: 91 80 3592919
Fax: 91 80 3593110
Email: info@bionicinformatics.com
URL: http://www.bionicinformatics.com

BIT&MINA

C/Pasai San Pedro 19
San Sebastian, Gipuzkoa 20017
Spain
Phone: 34 9 43448239
Email: info@bitymina.com
URL: http://www.bitymina.com

Bitart Infografaa

Tivoli, 24
Bilbao, 48007
Spain
Phone: 34 94 4130385
Fax: 34 94 4459263
Email: bitart@bitart.info
URL: http://www.bitart.info

Black Maria Studios

P.O. Box 12304
Valencia, 46020
Spain
Phone: 34 96 3891010
Fax: 34 96 3891010
Email: studio@blackmaria.es
URL: http://www.blackmaria.es

Blue Dahlia Films

Melbourne, Victoria
Australia
Phone: 61 3 9557 6957
Fax: 61 3 9557 6957
Email: dahlia@bigpond.net.au
URL: http://www.bluedahliafilms.com

Blunt Pictures

3, Mount Stuart Square
Butetown
Cardiff, Wales CF10 5EE
United Kingdom
Phone: 44 292 048 8400
Fax: 44 292 048 5962
Email: lynne.stockford@siriol.co.uk
URL: http://www.bluntpictures.com

Bluue

Rudolf-Breitscheid Strasse 162
14482 Potsdam
Babelsberg, Berlin
Germany
Phone: 49 33 1 7044700
Fax: 49 33 17044710
URL: http://www.bluue.com

Bo Nordin Animation

Brahegatan, 7
Jonkoping, 55334
Sweden
Phone: 46 36 186476
Email: info@bonordin.se
URL: http://www.bonordin.se

Boing Productions

10/201 Franklin St.
Melbourne, Victoria 3000
Australia
Phone: 61 3 9602 1403
Fax: 61 3 9760 0211
Email: neil@boingproductions.com
boingproductions.com

Boulder Media, Ltd.

Unit 77
Guinness Enterprise Centre
Taylors Lane
Dublin, D6
Ireland
Phone: 353 1 4100653
Fax: 353 1 4100985
Email: info@bouldermedia.tv
URL: http://www.bouldermedia.tv

Box

121 Princess St., 5th Fl.
Manchester, M1 7AD
United Kingdom
Phone: 44 161 228 2399
Fax: 44 161 228 2399
Email: mail@the-box.co.uk
URL: http://www.the-box.co.uk

Brass Cat Creative

63 Felix St.
Wooloowin
Brisbane, Queensland 4030

Australia
Phone: 61 7 3857 2728
Email: brasscat@furtales.com
URL: http://brasscat.furtales.com

Brown Bag Film

28 North Lotts
Dublin, 1
Ireland
Phone: 353 1 1872 1608
Fax: 353 1 1872 3834
Email: studio@brownbagfilm.com
URL: http://www.brownbagfilms.com

Bubble & Squeak

Suite 325 Princess House
50-60 Eastcastle St.
London, W1W 8EA
United Kingdom
Phone: 44 20 7636 0781
Fax: 44 20 7636 0262
Email: sadie@bubblesqueak.com
URL: http://www.bubblesqueak.com

Bunch

88-90 Gray's Inn Rd.
London, IC1X 8AA
United Kingdom
Phone: 44 (0)78 33196122
Email: carlos.santos@bunchdesign.com
URL: http://www.bunchdesign.com

Burst Video Professional

Periferico Sur # 5472
Planta Baja, Col. Olimpica
Delegacion
Coyoacan, Mexico
Phone: 52 55 5424 1423
Fax: 52 55 5665 0970
Email: produccion@burst.com.mx
URL: http://www.burstproduccion.com.mx

CAOZ

Aegisgata 7
Reykjavik, IS 101
Iceland
Phone: 354 511 3550
Fax: 354 511 3551
Email: info@caoz.is
URL: http://www.caoz.com

Carbon Digital, Ltd.

12 Maliston Rd.
Great Sankey
Warrington, WA5 1JR
United Kingdom
Phone: 44 192 547 0838
Email: info@carbondigital.co.uk
URL: http://www.carbondigital.co.uk

Caribara France

36 boulevard de la bastille
Paris, 75012
France

Phone: 33 1 44 74 32 32
Fax: 33 1 44 74 32 21
URL: http://www.caribara.com

Carico Estudio

Galicia 1415, Conjunto urbano
Esperanza
Mexicali, Baja California 21350
Mexico
Phone: 52 686 556 8433
Email: carico@yahoo.com
URL: http://www.geocities.comcarico

Carrasco

Av. Ordoñez Lazo condominio la
Laguna
Dep. 701
Cuenca, Azuay 000000
Ecuador
Phone: 593 7 824397
Fax: 593 7 881224
Email: carrasco@cine.com
URL: http://www.animados.net

Cartoon Network Europe

Turner House
16 Great Marlborough St.
London, W1F 7HS
United Kingdom
Phone: 44 207 693 1000
Fax: 44 207 693 1001
Email: Paloma.eyre@turner.com
URL: http://cartoonnetwork.co.uk

Cartoon Webworks

H1123
Budapest
Csorsz u. 13
Hungary
Phone: 36 1 2250170
Fax: 36 1 2129184
Email: info@cartoonWebworks.com
URL: http://www.cartoonWebworks.com

Cartoonia

Via cesare battisti, 15
Torino, 10123
Italy
Phone: 39 11 8122681
Fax: 39 11 8394179
Email: cartonia@tin.it

Casanimada

SHIN CA 07 BLOCO L LOTE 12
Brasilia, DF 71505000
Brazil
Phone: 55 61 4684816
Fax: 55 61 4684816
Email: casanimada@asacine.com.br

Catalyst Pictures

34 Chester Square
Ashton-Under-Lyne
Lancs, OL67TW
United Kingdom
Phone: 44 161 339 3353

Email: upstairs@catalystpics.co.uk
URL: http://www.catalystpics.co.uk

Catflap Animation

356 Darling St.
Balmain
Sydney, New South Wales 2041
Australia
Phone: 61 2 9818 66 99
Fax: 61 2 9818 63 44
Email: studio@catflap.com.au
URL: http://www.catflap.com.au

CCG/ZGDV Center of Computer

Graphics
Rua Teixeira Pascoasis 596
Guimaraes, 4800-073
Portugal
Phone: 351 25 3 439 300
Fax: 351 25 3 439 348
URL: http://www.ccg.pt

CeMedia - Central European

Media Workshop
Szent Istvan Park 14
Budapest, 1137
Hungary
Phone: 36 1 2392538
Fax: 36 1 3498234
Email: info@cemedia.co.hu
URL: http://www.cemedia.co.hu

Centro Integral de Cursos

Especializados
Maldonado 48
Madrid, 28006
Spain
Phone: 34 91 4010702
Fax: 34 91 3091894
Email: cice@cicesa.com
URL: http://www.cicesa.com

CGCG, Inc.

12F, 65 Sung Teh Rd.
Taipei, 110
Taiwan
Phone: 886 2 2759 8899
Fax: 886 2 2727 8592
Email: Webmaster@cgcg.com.tw
URL: http://www.cgcg.com.tw

Channimation Productions

Limited
Saramar East
La Grande Route Des Sablons
Grouville, Jersey JE3 9BB
United Kingdom
Phone: 44 153 451 1924
Email: tbarnes@netcomuk.co.uk

Character Republic

Blk 737 Pasir Ris Dr. 10, #07-39
Singapore, 510737
Singapore

Phone: 65 65842638
Email: michael@characterrepublic.com
URL: http://www.character-republic.com

Charamel GmbH

Richard-Wagner str.39
Cologne, 50674
Germany
Phone: 49 22 1336640
Fax: 49 22 13366419
Email: contact@charamel.com
URL: http://www.charamel.com

Chicop Animation Arts

Nic. Baurstraat 26
Harlingen, Friesland 8861 JA
Netherlands
Phone: 31 65 3668437
Email: info@chicop-animation.com
URL: http://www.chicop-animation.com

Chivydog Productions

13 Griffin Rd.
North Curl Curl, New South Wales 2099
Australia
Phone: 61 2 99059955
Fax: 61 2 99056877
Email: chivydog@bigpond.com
URL: http://www.chivydog.com

cHmAn

81, rue du Pré Catelan
La Madeleine, 59110
France
Phone: 33 3 28 52 39 90
Fax: 33 3 28 52 69 21
Email: team@chman.com
URL: http://www.chman.com

Ciberfilms

Pachuca 1-202
Colonia Condesa, 06140
Mexico
Phone: 52 55 5286-1960
Email: contacto@ciberfilms.com
URL: http://www.ciberfilms.com

Clair Obscur

72, rue Amelot
Paris, 75011
France
Phone: 33 1 49 23 00 01
Fax: 33 1 49 23 00 02
Email: info@clairobscur.fr
URL: http://www.clairobscur.fr

ClapTrap Music

Breisacher Strasse 21
Munich, Bavaria 81667
Germany
Phone: 49 89 48 95 38 81
Fax: 49 89 44 14 18 54
Email: info@claptrapmusic.com

Clasticon Solutions

Brand Building
Wood Head Centre, 1st Fl.
23 Sivaganga Road,
Nungambakkam
Chennai, Tamil Nadu 600034
India
Phone: 91 44 8201527
Email: everyone@clasticon.com
URL: http://www.clasticon.com

StudioSiggi/Desert Island

Animation
V–nnu 2
Haapsalu, 90503
Estonia
Phone: 372 514 1716
Fax: 372 650 0734
Email: siggi@hot.ee

Supermodels

Double Bay
Sydney, New South Wales 2028
Australia
Phone: 61 4 1620 3012
Email: therealmisssteen@hotmail.com
URL: http://www.materias.com.au/
supermodels

Synthetique

6 Ave. Henri Polnc.aré
Bondues, Nord 59910

France
Phone: 33 3 28 23 51 80
Fax: 33 3 20 28 31 03
Email: info@synthetique.com
URL: http://www.synthetique.com

The Animation Workshop

Ll. Sct. Hans Gade 7 - 9
Viborg, 8800
Denmark
Phone: 45 87 25 54 00
Fax: 45 87 25 54 11
Email: info@animwork.dk
URL: http://www.animwork.dk

The Ministry of Toons

6 - 7 Pavilion House
Brighton, East Sussex BN1 1EJ
United Kingdom
Phone: 44 127 369 652
Fax: 44 127 360 670
URL: http://www.ministryoftoons.co.uk

The Odd Squad

15 Mortain Dr.
Berkhamsted, Hertfordshire HP4
1JZ
United Kingdom
Phone: 44 144 287 0267
Fax: 44 144 287 7314
Email: allan@plendy.freeserve.co.uk
URL: http://www.theoddsquad.co.uk

The Postoffice

ABRAJ Center Block B, 6th Fl.
Furnel Chebback
P.O. Box 50-266
Beirut, 10112030
Lebanon
Phone: 961 1 291892
Fax: 961 1 291893
Email: posto@cyberia.net.lb

Toonz Animation India Pvt., Ltd.

731-739 Nila Bldg, Technopark
Pin - 695 581
Trivandrum, Kerala 695581
India
Phone: 91 47 1700 929
Fax: 91 47 1700 954
Email: toonz@toonzanimationindia.com
URL: http://
www.toonzanimationindia.com

Touchtoons Animation Studio

151 N. Buona Vista Rd
PhaseZ.Ro Technopreneur Park
Blk C #02-07 The Connection
Singapore, 139347
Singapore
Phone: 65 6773 6572
Fax: 65 6773 6573
Email: info@touchtoons.com
URL: http://www.touchtoons.com

TOUGH EYE - International

Turku Animated Film Festival
Linnankatu 54
Turku, 20100
Finland
Phone: 358 40 539 7434
Email: info@tough-eye.com
URL: http://www.tough-eye.com

Toutenkartoon Paris

19, rue Valette
Paris, 75005
France
Phone: 33 1 40 46 41 20
Email: pcharlet@toutenkartoon.com
URL: http://www.toutenkartoon.com

Visual Myriad Pty, Ltd.

18 Kentlyn St.
Brisbane, Queensland 4113
Australia
Phone: 61 7 3341 5996
Fax: 61 7 3341 5996
Email: daniel@visualmyriad.com.au
URL: http://www.visualmyriad.com.au

Viz-fx

150 Great Portland St.
London, W1W 6QD
United Kingdom
Phone: 44 207 636 0456
Fax: 44 207 636 0459

Email: info@viz-fx.com
URL: http://www.viz-fx.com

Why Not Animation

7. rue de Charmoisy
Annecy, 74000
France
Phone: 33 4 5045 2270
Fax: 33 4 5045 6198
Email: wna@wanadoo.fr
URL: http://www.whynotanimation.com

Wild Brain UK

11 Grosvenor Crescent
London, SW1X 7EE
United Kingdom
Phone: 44 207 245 6864
Fax: 44 207 245 1278
Email: info@wildbrain.com
URL: http://www.wildbrain.com

XTV

157 Wardour St.
London, W1F 8WQ
United Kingdom
Phone: 44 207 208 1500
Fax: 44 207 208 1510
Email: richard.markell@xtv.co.uk
URL: http://www.xtv.co.uk

STVDIO Media Animation

P.O. Box 5263

Hong Kong, Hong Kong
Phone: 852 2984 8807
Fax: 852 2984 8987
Email: info@stvdio.com
URL: http://www.stvdio.com

Tandem Films

26 Cross Str.
London, N1 2B9
United Kingdom
Phone: 44 207 688 1717
Email: info@tandemfilms.com
URL: http://www.tandemfilms.com

TBC Media ApS

Vejdammen 90
Gl. Holte
Holte, 2840
Denmark
Phone: 45 7022 02 01
Fax: 45 7022 02 71
Email: info@tbcrecords.com
URL: http://www.tbcrecords.com

The Brothers Dimm, Ltd.

1/1, 16 Ruthven St.
Glasgow, Scotland G12 9BS
United Kingdom
Email: thebrothersdimm@ntlworld.com
URL: http://www.thebrothersdimm.com

The Canning Factory

11b Albert Place
London, W8 5PD
United Kingdom
Phone: 44 207 937 1136
Fax: 44 207 938 1896
Email: all@canningfactory.co.uk
URL: http://www.canningfactory.co.uk

The Cartoon Saloon

St. Josephs Studios
Waterford Rd.
Kilkenny, Ireland
Phone: 353 5 664481
Fax: 353 5 620089
Email: info@cartoonsaloon.ie
URL: http://www.cartoonsaloon.ie

The Chimney Pot

CGI Department
Sturegatan 58
Stockholm, 114 36
Sweden
Phone: 46 8 587 50 500
Fax: 46 8 587 50 501
Email: info@chimney.se
URL: http://www.chimney.se

The Video Lab

Cnr Eileen & Geneva Rd.
Blairgowrie
P.O. Box 1854 Pinegowrie
Johannesburg, Gauteng 2123

South Africa
Phone: 27 11 293 3000
Fax: 27 11 293 3090
Email: info@videolab.co.za
URL: http://www.videolab.co.za

Top Draw Animation, Inc.

3rd Fl. JEMCO Bldg.
C. Raymundo Ave. cor.
Bernal St., Rosario
Pasig City, 1600
Philippines
Phone: 63 2 640 1512
Fax: 63 2 640 1623
Email: wayned@topdraw.com.ph
URL: http://www.topdraw.com.ph

TRIBU

225, Chemin de Cazals
Valergues, MONTPELLIER 34130
France
Phone: 1 00 33 04 67 1
Fax: 1 00 33 04 67 1
Email: tribu@tribu.tm.fr
URL: http://www.tribu.tm.fr

Trickfilmerei

Zur Sch—nen Gelegenheit 14
Regensburg, 93047
Germany
Phone: 49 94 1567934
Email: post@trickfilmerei.de
URL: http://www.trickfilmerei.de

Triggerfish Animation

P.O. Box 64
Woodstock
Cape Town, W. Cape 7915
South Africa
Phone: 27 21 448 0973
Fax: 27 21 447 2813
Email: emma@triggerfish.co.za
http://triggerfish.co.za

Trixter Film

Oberfohringerstr. 186
Munich, 81925
Germany
Phone: 49 89 95 99 55 90
Fax: 49 89 95 99 55 99
Email: info@trixter.de
URL: http://www.trixter.de

Wacky Toon TV

Via Tirso, 4 Milano
Milan, Lombardia 20141
Italy
Phone: 39 33 88104224
Fax: 39 2 55230267
Email: paul@wackytoon.tv
URL: http://www.wackytoon.co.uk

Wildlight Studios

St. Michalesgrand 11B
Visby, 621 57
Sweden
Phone: 46 70 215 09 70

Fax: 46 70 258 31 92
Email: info@wildlight.se
URL: http://www.wildlight.se

Yolanda Productions

Stop Motion
15 Donald St, Roath
Cardiff, Wales CF24 4TJ
United Kingdom
Phone: 44 292 046 1077
Email: alundy01@hotmail.com

Yukfoo Animation Studios

39A Woodside Ave.
P.O. Box 36644
Northcote
Auckland,
New Zealand
Phone: 64 9 480 0093
Fax: 64 9 480 0094
Email: info@yukfoo.net
URL: http://www.yukfoo.net

Z-A Production

64, rue de la Folie
MeriCt.
Paris, 75011
France
Phone: 33 1 48066566
Fax: 33 1 48064875
Email: info@z-a.net
URL: http://www.z-a.net

z.e.r.o.n.e Animation|Visual FX

Taman Kedoya Elok
Blok A1 No. 21
Jakarta, DKI
Indonesia
Phone: 62 21 5312203
Fax: 62 21 6612578
Email: hgunags@hotmail.com

Zigzag Animation

Bondegatan 46
Stockholm, 11633
Sweden
Phone: 46 8 6150882
Fax: 46 8 6150883
Email: animation@zigzag.se
URL: http://www.zigzag.se

Sunwoo Entertainment Group

Seoul
South Korea
Phone: 82 2 2188 3015
Fax: 82 2 2188 3024
URL: http://www.sunwoo.com

TeamcHmAn

81, rue du Pre Catelan
La Madeleine, 59110
France
Phone: 1 33 3 28 52 39 90

Fax: 1 33 3 28 52 69 21
Email: team@teamchman.com
URL: http://www.teamchman.com

Tectoon S.L.

C/Obdulio Lopez de Uralde N°18
oficinas 1° Izq
Vitoria-Gasteiz, Alava 01008
Spain
Phone: 34 945 249986
Fax: 34 945 249986
Email: info@tectoon.com
URL: http://www.tectoon.com

Telemagination, Ltd.

Royalty House
72 -74 Dean St.
London, W1V 6AE
United Kingdom
Phone: 44 207 434 1551
Fax: 44 207 434 3344
Email: mail@tmation.co.uk
URL: http://www.telemagination.co.uk

The Consortium of Gentlemen

27 Beethoven St.
London, W10 4LG
United Kingdom
Phone: 44 208 964 02
Fax: 44 208 968 77
Email: mail@cogonline.co.uk
URL: http://www.cogonline.co.uk

The Funny Farm Pty Ltd.

3 Lefevre St.
Spotswood, Victoria 3015
Australia
Phone: 61 3 9399 2900
Fax: 61 3 9399 2900
Email: funnyfarm@bigpond.com

The Halas & Batchelor Collection

67 Southwood Lane
London, N6 5EG
United Kingdom
Phone: 44 208 34896
Fax: 44 208 3483
Email: vivien@haba.demon.co.uk
http://halasandbatchelor.com

Titalee Digital Studios

9, Seshadri Rd.,
Alwarpet
Chennai, Tamil Nadu 600018
India
Phone: 91 44 498 66 22
Fax: 91 44 498 66 22
Email: martintitalee@hotmail.com
URL: http://www.titalee.com

TMS Entertainment, Ltd.

5-39-1 Kamitakada, Nakano-ku
Tokyo, 164-0002
Japan
Phone: 81 3 3319 1132

Fax: 81 3 3319 1146
Email: takeuchi@tms-e.co.jp
URL: http://www.tms-e.com

Top Peg Animation & Creative Studio, Inc.

314 Apt. A, 2nd Fl.
Antipolo St., Baranggay Mauway
Mandaluyong City
Manila, 1553
Philippines
Phone: 63 2 8711590
Fax: 63 2 5311491
Email: toppeg@nsclub.net
http://toppeg.freeservers.com
URL: http://www.turtlerock.com

TV Animation

Landskronagade 66, 4
Copenhagen, 2100
Denmark
Phone: 45 7023 8008
Fax: 45 7023 9009
Email: sales@tv-animation.com
URL: http://www.tv-animation.com

TV Loonland

Royalty House
72-74 Dean St.
London, W1V 6AE
United Kingdom
Phone: 44 207 434 2377

Fax: 44 207 434 1578
Email: info@loonland.com
URL: http://www.tvloonland.com

Washton

Gran Avenida 13556 Block A depto. 22
San Bernardino, Santiago 7860923
Chile
Phone: 56 2 5289840
Fax: 56 2 5289840
Email: washton_@hotmail.com
URL: http://www.fragmentaria.cl/washton/
banchi.htm

Web Animation Studio

14 Fair View, 5th Rd., Chembur
Mumbai, Maharashtra 400071
India
Phone: 91 22 5570270
Email: yogi@wasindia.com
URL: http://
www.Webanimationstudio.com

Wip:On Animation

121, rue Chanzy
Lille-Hellemmes, 59260
France
Phone: 33 3 20675954
Fax: 33 3 20675950
Email: contact@wipon.fr
URL: http://www.wipon.fr

Zagreb Film

Vlaska 70
Zagreb, 10000
Croatia
Phone: 385 1 46 13 689
Fax: 385 1 45 57 068
Email: zagreb-film@zg.tel.hr
URL: http://www.zagrebfilm.hr

Zanita Films

Ardmore Studios
Herbert Road, Bray
Co. Wicklow,
Ireland
Phone: 353 1 286 2971
Fax: 353 1 276 0020
Email: Production@zanita.ie
URL: http://www.zanitafilms.com

ZDF Enterprises

Spichernstrasse 75-77
Cologne, 50672
Germany
Phone: 49 221 9488850
Fax: 49 221 9488851
Email: westphal.s@zdf.de
URL: http://www.zdf-enterprises.zdf.de

Zoomorphix Systems

P.O. Box 208
Melbourne, Victoria 3163
Australia

Phone: 61 3 9543 6610
Email: enquiries@zoomorphix.com.au
URL: http://www.zoomorphix.com.au

Terabyte, Inc.

3F Daimex Bldg. Minami 2JO
Nishi 10Choume, Chuo-ku
Sapporo, Hokkaido 060-0062
Japan
Phone: 81 11 280-2180
Fax: 81 11 280-2181
Email: roy@tera-byte.co.jp
URL: http://www.tera-byte.co.jp

The Juice Design

Scarsdale House
Derbyshire Lane
Sheffield, S8 8SE
United Kingdom
Phone: 44 114 249 6400
Fax: 44 114 249 6404
Email: info@thejuice.co.uk
URL: http://www.thejuice.co.uk

The Mill

40-41 Great Marlborough St.
London,
United Kingdom
Phone: 44 207 287 4041
Email: info@mill.co.uk
URL: http://www.mill.co.uk

Tomavistas

Gracia 1 Principal 2
Barcelona, 08012
Spain
Phone: 34 93 2177025
Fax: 34 93 4160799
Email: info@tomavistas.com
URL: http://www.tomavistas.com

Toonbase Alfa

Rosenorns alle 57 1 th
Copenhagen, Frederiksberg 1970
Denmark
Phone: 1 45 35363699
Fax: 1 44 870-138-5478
Email: hatukah@city.dk
URL: http://www.hatukah.com

Toontime Animation Studio

Unit 341 Union Square Condo.
15th Ave. Cubao,
Quezon City, 1109
Philippines
Phone: 63 2421 37 34
Fax: 63 2421 37 34
Email: toontime_26@yahoo.com

Totem S.D.I. Ltda.

Calle 13 # 8-19
Chia, Cundinamarca 00001
Colombia
Phone: 57 1 8631030
Email: pacor_b@hotmail.com

Touchtoon Cartoon Company

45 Lochaven Dr.
Nowra, New South Wales 2541
Australia
Phone: 61 2 4423 5049
Fax: 61 2 9310 2235
Email: info@touchtoon.com.au
URL: http://www.touchtoon.com.au

TV Loonland AG

16 Munchener Strasse
Unterfohring, 85774
Germany
Phone: 49 89 205 080
Fax: 49 89 205 08199
Email: gpitt@loonland.com
URL: http://www.tvloonland.de/

Virtual Clones

418 Boyd Orr Bldg.
University Ave.
Glasgow, Scotland G12 8QR
United Kingdom
Phone: 44 141 330 3118
Fax: 44 141 330 3119
Email: info@virtualclones.com
URL: http://www.virtualclones.com

Webdesign-Factory

8, rue Emile Pehant
Nantes, 44000
France

Phone: 33 2 40 20 32 72
Fax: 33 2 40 20 24 56
Email: info@Webdesign-factory.com
URL: http://www.Webdesign-factory.fr

Wellpig Co., Ltd.

401 Medicine Venture Tower Annex 997
10
Dae-Chi Dong, Gwang Nam-Gu
Seoul
South Korea
Phone: 82 2 3452-9281
Fax: 82 2 2194-3994
Email: ceo@wellpig.com
URL: http://www.wellpig.com

Zentropa Production

Filmbyen Postbox 505
Avedore Tvúrvej 10
Hvidovre, 2650
Denmark
Phone: 45 36 78 00 55
Fax: 45 36 78 00 77
URL: http://www.zentropa-film.com

Zeon Designs

145/44 Mantana V.
SoiSiamtoranee
Kubon Rd. Bangkhen
Bangkok, 10220
Thailand
Phone: 66 2 945 3188
Fax: 66 2 945 3616

Zeppelin Filmes, Lda.

Av. de Portugal, 66 - 1° Dto.
Carnaxide, Oeiras 2795-554
Portugal
Phone: 351 21 4251980
Fax: 351 21 4251989
Email: zeppelin_filmes@yahoo.com
URL: http://www.zeppelin-filmes.com

Zootrope

Passatge Ajuntament 19
Cerdanyola
Barcelona, Catalonia 08290
Spain
URL: http://www.zootrope.com

10pTV

2 Rosemary Cottages
Burcot, Abingdon
Oxford, Oxon 408 135
United Kingdom
Phone: 44 186 5408 135
Email: info@10p.tv
URL: http://www.10p.tv/About/about.html

2 Minutes

9, rue Biscornet
Paris, 75012
France
Phone: 33 1 53 17 37 00
Fax: 33 1 53 17 07 37
URL: http://www.2minutes.fr

422 Studios

St. John's Ct.
Whiteladies Road
Bristol, BS8 2QY
United Kingdom
Phone: 44 117 946 7222
Fax: 44 117 946 7722
Email: bristol@422.com
URL: http://www.422.com

A Film Estonia, Ltd.

Kaare 15
Tallinn, 11618
Estonia
Phone: 372 6706485
Fax: 372 6706433
Email: afilm@afilm.ee
URL: http://www.afilm.ee

Clayman's Funhouse 3D Animation

Cartoons & Animation
696-185-911 Yates St.
Victoria, BC V8V 4Y9
Phone: 1 250 382-8780
Email: paul@theman.com
URL: http://www.theclayman.com

CMC Digimage

15, rue Benjamin Raspail
B.P. 60
Malakoff, 92242
France

Phone: 33 1 46 12 19 19
Fax: 33 1 46 12 19 20
Email: information@cmc-video.fr
URL: http://www.cmc-video.fr
URL: http://www.collideascope.com

2D Animation 3D Animations

72, rue Fontaine du Lizier
Angouleme, 16000
France
Phone: 33 5 45 90 12 88
Fax: 33 5 45 90 12 89
Email: info@2D Animation3D Animation -
animations.com
URL: http://www.2D Animation3D
Animation -animations.com

2nd Nature

P.O. Box 56-402
Auckland
New Zealand
Phone: 64 9 308 9883
Fax: 64 9 336 1002
Email: info@2ndnature.co.nz
URL: http://www.2ndnature.co.nz

2nz Animation Co.

287, 2- SURBALA, S.V. Rd.
Bandra (W)
Mumbai, Maharashtra 400050
India
Phone: 91 22 6511026
Fax: 91 22 6459669

Email: info@2nz.com
URL: http://www.2nz.com

3 Bear Animations

Unit 45, Hartley Fold
Kirkby Stephen, Cumb CA17 4JH
United Kingdom
Phone: 44 176 837 1114
Fax: 44 176 837 1118
Email: doodi@3bears.co.uk
URL: http://www.3bears.co.uk

A Film Latvia

Volguntes str.7
Riga, 1046
Latvia
Phone: 371 7610 231
Fax: 371 7807 238
Email: afilm@afilm.apollo.lv
URL: http://www.afilm.dk

A Productions

52 Old Market St.
Bristol, BS2 0ER
United Kingdom
Phone: 44 117 929 9005
Fax: 44 117 929 9004
Email: info@aproductions.co.uk
URL: http://www.aproductions.co.uk

A Steen Production

Hedgardarna 12
Borlange, 78196

Sweden
Phone: 46 243 793350
Email: a.steen.prod@telia.com

Collingwood O'Hare

Entertainment, Ltd.
10-14 Crown St.
London, W3 8SB
United Kingdom
Phone: 44 208 993 3666
Fax: 44 208 993 9595
Email: info@crownSt.co.uk
URL: http://www.collingwoodohare.com

Color Chips India

Plot No.16
Road No.5
Jubilee Hills
Hyderabad, PIN 500-033
India
Phone: 91 49 3550268
Email: info@colorchipsindia.com
URL: http://www.colorchipsindia.com

Colorland Animation

Productions, Ltd.
909 Austin Tower
22-26 Austin Ave.
Tsimshatsui, Kowloon
Hong Kong, China
Phone: 852 23669013
Fax: 852 23679087
Email: col@colorland.com.hk
URL: http://www.colorland-animation.com

3D Animation Animagics Inc.

1003 Anam Tower, 702-10
Yuksam 1 - Dong
Kangnam-Gu
Seoul, South Korea
Phone: 82 2 2009-3363
Fax: 82 2 2009-3365
Email: support@3D Animation
animagics.com
URL: http://www.3D Animation
animagics.com

422 Studios

Battersea Rd.
Heaton Mersey
Stockport, Cheshire SK4 3EA
United Kingdom
Phone: 44 161 432 9000
Fax: 44 161 443 1325
Email: studios@422.com
URL: http://www.422.com

A. Film A/S

Tagensvej 85 F
Copenhagen, 2200
Denmark
Phone: 45 35827060
Fax: 45 35827061
Email: info@afilm.dk
URL: http://www.afilm.dk

a.n.a.r.c.h.i.t.e.c.t.o.n

Rua dos Arneiros 92 2!A
Lisbon, 1500-060
Portugal
Phone: 351 917447711
Email: anarchitecton@hotmail.com
URL: http://www.anarchitecton.com

Comic House

Stationsweg 20
Oosterbeek, 6861 EH
Netherlands
Phone: 32 26 32 100 32
Fax: 32 26 32 100 36
Email: mail@comichouse.nl
URL: http://www.comichouse.nl

Concept Interactive

101 The Waverley Office Business Park
Suite 17, Wyecroft Road
Mowbray, Western Cape 7700
South Africa
Phone: 27 21 448 8451
Fax: 27 21 448 8418
Email: info@icon.co.za
URL: http://www.conceptinteractive.net

3D Animation Imaging

12 Woodside Rd.
Simonstone
Burnley, Lancashire BB12 7JG
United Kingdom

Phone: 44 870 7409016
Fax: 44 870 131 5997
Email: info@3D Animation -imaging.co.uk
URL: http://www.3D Animation -
imaging.co.uk

3D Animation Jamie

Number 1 Neal's Yard
Covent Garden
London, WC2H 9DP
United Kingdom
Phone: 44 207 379 0105
Email: info@3D Animation jamie.com
URL: http://www.3D Animation jamie.com

422 Studios

4th Fl. South Central
11 Peter St.
Manchester, M2 5QR
United Kingdom
Phone: 44 161 839 6080
Fax: 44 161 839 6081
Email: manchester@422.com

Aardman Animations, Ltd.

7 Gasferry Rd.
Bristol, BS1 6UN
United Kingdom
Phone: 44 117 984 8485
Fax: 44 117 984 8486
URL: http://www.aardman.com

AB Productions

132 Ave. du President Wilson
La Plaine Saint Deni, 93213
France
Phone: 33 1 49 22 20 01
Fax: 33 1 49 22 22 16
Email: ventes@groupe-ab.fr
URL: http://www.ab-international.com

Abrakam Estudio

Luzarra 18
Bilbao, 48014
Spain
Phone: 34 94 4 761 607
Fax: 34 94 4 757 421
Email: wolfeimer@abrakam
estudio.com
URL: http://www.abrakam-estudio.com

Conkerco, Ltd.

Studio One
2-4 Corbet Place
London, E1 6NH
United Kingdom
Phone: 44 207 2475552
Fax: 44 207 2475768
Email: studio@conkerco.com
URL: http://www.conkerco.com

Connoiseur Media

No. 165, 1st'C' Cross, 18th'A' Main,
HAL II Stage, Indiranagar
Bangalore, Karnataka 560038
India
Phone: 91 80 5272345
Fax: 91 80 5272346
Email: Info@connoiseur.com
URL: http://www.connoiseur.com

Corps Business

2 Old Queen St.
St. James' Park
London, SW1H 9HP
United Kingdom
Phone: 44 207 222 8484
Fax: 44 207 222 8338
Email: recruit@corps.co.uk
URL: http://www.corps.co.uk

Cosgrove Hall Films

8 Albany Rd.
Chorlton-cum-Hardy
Manchester, M21 0AW
United Kingdom
Phone: 44 161 882 2500
Fax: 44 161 882 2556
Email: animation@chf.co.uk
URL: http://www.chf.co.uk

Crackartoons Studios

C.so Magenta 52
Milan, 20123
Italy
Phone: 39 2 43982507
Email: crackartoons@tiscalinet.it
URL: http://www.crackartoons.com

Demen Animation Studio

38AE cx Binh Hung, QL50, Binh Chanh
HoChiMinh
Vietnam
Phone: 84 8 758 2118
Email: demenfilm@hcm.vnn.vn

Denman Productions

5 Holly Rd.
Twickenham, Middlesex TW1 4EA
United Kingdom
Phone: 44 208 891 3461
Fax: 44 208 891 6413
Email: info@denman.co.uk
URL: http://www.denman.co.uk

Depth Studios

263 Oak Ave.
Randburg
Johannesburg, Gauteng 2125
South Africa
Phone: 27 11 886 86 29
Fax: 27 11 886 86 29
Email: kirsten@depthanimation.com
URL: http://www.depthanimation.com

Design & Motion

Wehrneckarstrasse 10
Esslingen, 73728
Germany
Phone: 49 71 1396930 0
Fax: 49 71 1396930 13

Email: design-motion@t-online.de
URL: http://www.design-motion.de

Digital Magic Limited

Shop 68, Ground Fl., Victoria Centre
15 Watson Road, Causeway Bay
Hong Kong,
Hong Kong
Phone: 852 25709016
Fax: 852 28073619
Email: sales@digitalmagic.com.hk
URL: http://www.digitalmagic.com.hk

Dotfx Design Studio

201 E. Seapark Apt. Jln21/13
Petaling Jaya, Selangor 46300
Malaysia
Phone: 60 3 78776229
Email: fei2992@hotmail.com
URL: http://www.dotfxstudio.com

E-3D Animation imensions Pvt., Ltd.

602, Barton Centre
M.G. Road
Bangalore, Karnataka 560001
India
Phone: 91 80 5091256
Fax: 91 80 5320381
Email: e3D Animation @vsnl.net
URL: http://www.e-3D Animation
imensions.com

Eallin Animation

Nad Slavii 1669
Prague, 101 00
Czech Republic
Phone: 420 6 03820631
Email: animation@eallin.com
URL: http://www.eallin.com

Escape Studios

126 Westbourne Studios
242 Acklam Road
London, W10 5JJ
United Kingdom
Email: info@escapestudios.co.uk
URL: http://www.escapestudios.co.uk

Escotoonz Animation Studio

A-36 Mohan Co-operative Ind Estate,
Mathura Rd.
New Delhi, 110044
India
Phone: 91 11 6959981
Email: escotoonz@escotoonz.com

Film Factory, Inc.

Chopina 7
Bielsko-Biala, 43-300
Poland
Phone: 48 33 8125698
Fax: 48 33 8125704
Email: factor@nask.katowice.pl

Film Magic Limited

Room 802, Block A, Seaview Estate,
2-8 Watson Road, North Point
Hong Kong,
Hong Kong
Phone: 852 25715432
Fax: 852 28073619
Email: sales@filmmagic.com.hk
URL: http://www.filmmagic.com.hk

Filmax International

C/MIGUEL HERNANDEZ
81-87 Poligino Pedrosa
L'Hospitalet de Llobregat
Barcelona, 08908
Spain
Phone: 34 93 336 85 55
Fax: 34 93 263 08 24
Email: filmaxint@filmax.com
URL: http://www.filmaxinternational.com

Filmforderung Hamburg

Friedensalle 14-16
Hamburg, 22765
Germany
Phone: 49 40 398 37 0
Fax: 49 40 398 37 0
URL: http://www.ffhh.de

Films De La Perrine (Les)

6, Cité Paradis
Paris, 75010

France
Phone: 33 1 56 03 90 29
Fax: 33 1 56 03 90 38
Email: studio@laperrine.com
URL: http://www.laperrine.com

Flux Animation Studio, Ltd.

33 George St.
Newmarket MBE P280
Auckland
New Zealand
Phone: 64 9 368 1506
Fax: 64 9 368 1507
Email: flux@fluxmedia.co.nz
URL: http://www.fluxmedia.co.nz

Folkets Bio

(Stora Nygatan 21)
Box 2068
Stockholm, 103 12
Sweden
Phone: 46 8 545 27520
Fax: 46 8 545 27527
Email: info@folketsbio.se
URL: http://www.folketsbio.se

FudgePuppy Productions

Suite 180, 353 King St. Newtown
Sydney, New South Wales 2042
Australia
Phone: 61 2 415364944
Fax: 61 2 48723762
Email: walkies@fudgepuppy.com.au
URL: http://www.fudgepuppy.com.au

Glasgow Animation

Lovat House Gavell Rd.
Glasgow, G65 9BS
United Kingdom
Phone: 44 1236 826555
Fax: 44 1236 825560
Email: info@glasgowanimation.com
URL: http://www.glasgowanimation.com

Gum Studios

Neusserstrasse 772
Cologne, 50737
Germany
Phone: 49 22 1 974 524
Fax: 49 22 1 974 524
Email: info@gum-studios.de
URL: http://www.gum-studios.de

Hahn Film AG

Schwedterstrasse 36 A
Berlin, 10435
Germany
Phone: 49 30 44 35 49 0
Fax: 49 30 44 35 49 253
Email: info@hahnfilm.de
URL: http://www.hahnfilm.de

Hibbert Ralph Animation

10 D'Arblay St.
London, W1F 8DS
United Kingdom
Phone: 44 207 494 3011

Fax: 44 207 494 0383
Email: info@hra-online.com
URL: http://www.hra-online.com

High Video

Seneca 413 Planta Baja
Colonia Polanco,
Mexico
Phone: 52 55 5282-1837
Email: video@highvideo.com.mx
URL: http://www.highvideo.com.mx

HIT Entertainment

Maple House 5th Fl.
149 Tottenham Ct. Road
London, W1T 7NF
United Kingdom
Phone: 44 207 554 2500
Fax: 44 207 388 9321
Email: consumer@hitentertainment.com
URL: http://www.hitentertainment.com

Hybrid Graphics, Ltd.

Eteliinen Makasiinikatu 4
Helsinki, 00130
Finland
Phone: 358 9 686 6380
Fax: 358 9 685 2030
Email: info@hybrid.fi
URL: http://www.hybrid.fi

HYPOLUX Film

L‚becker Str. 126
Schwerin, 19059
Germany
Phone: 49 385 5572257
Fax: 49 385 5936975
Email: info@hypolux.de
URL: http://www.hypolux.de

Image Campus

Salta 239
Buenos Aires, Capital Federal
C1074AAE
Argentina
Phone: 54 11 4383-2244
Fax: 54 11 4383-2992
Email: info@imagecampus.com.ar
URL: http://www.imagecampus.com.ar

Image Infotainment Limited

32, T.T.K Rd., Alwarpet
Chennai, Tamil Nadu 600018
India
Phone: 91 44 4671542
Fax: 91 44 4671543
Email: projects@imageil.com
URL: http://www.imageil.com

Imagehouse

27-1 nonhyun-dong,
Seoul Kangnam-gu 135-010
South Korea

Phone: 82 2 540-2330
Fax: 82 2 540-4512
Email: babi6611@yahoo.co.kr

Imagenes

Maldonado 1792
Montevideo, 11218
Uruguay
Phone: 598 2 418 7998
Fax: 598 2 418 7998
Email: info@imagenes.org
imagenes.org

Imagination Computer Services

Donau-City-Strasse 1/OG 3
Vienna, 1220
Austria
Phone: 43 1 20501 33 0
Fax: 43 1 20501 33 900
URL: http://www.imagination.at

Innovatives

58, Narayan Peth
Pune, Maharashtra 411030
India
Phone: 91 20 4457455
Fax: 91
Email: innovatives@vsnl.net
URL: http://www.innovativesgroup.com

Inspidea Animation

12G Jalan Dungun
Damansara Heights
Kuala Lumpur, 50490
Malaysia
Phone: 60 13 3624361
Fax: 60 3 62034981
Email: findoutmore@inspidea.com
URL: http://www.inspidea.com

ITE - Interactive Television

Entertainment
ITE ApS
Nattergalevej 6
Copenhagen, NV 2400
Denmark
Phone: 45 70 210 200
Fax: 45 70 210 201
Email: info@ite.dk
URL: http://www.ite.dk

Just Group, PLC

74 Shepherd's Bush Green
Just House
London, W12 8QE
United Kingdom
Phone: 44 208 746 9300
Fax: 44 208 746 9333
Email: info@justgroup.com
URL: http://www.justgroup.com

K-Effects

Gartengasse 21
Vienna, 1050
Austria
Phone: 43 15 86 30 40
Email: office@k-effects.com
URL: http://www.k-effects.com

Katuns Entertainment

XL/5887, AVS Building
Near Padma Junction
MG Road
Cochin, Kerala 682035
India
Phone: 91 48 4366378
Email: info@katuns.com
URL: http://www.katuns.com

Kavaleer Productions, Ltd.

47 Capel St.
Dublin
Ireland
Email: kavaleerproductions@yahoo.com
URL: http://www.kavaleerproductions.com

Kayenta Production

2 Impasse Mousset
Paris, 75012
France
Phone: 33 1 43 45 55 44
Fax: 33 1 43 40 69 55

Email: contact@kayenta.com
URL: http://www.kayenta.com

KCS Production

34, rue Sebastien Gryphe
Lyon, Rhone-Alpes 69007
France
Phone: 33 4 72 76 98 61
Fax: 33 4 72 76 98 61
Email: info@kcs-production.com
URL: http://www.kcs-production.com

Krogh Mortensen Animation a/s

Store Kongensgade 61B
Copenhagen, 1264
Denmark
Phone: 45 70 252 454
Email: kma@km-animation.dk
URL: http://www.km-animation.dk

Kuratorium Junger Deustcher Film

Schloss Biebrich
Rheingaustrasse 140
Wiesbaden, 65203
Germany
Phone: 49 61 160 23 12
Fax: 49 61 169 24 09
Email: Kuratorium@t-online.de
URL: http://www.kuratorium-junger film.de

Lights & Shadows Pte, Ltd.

53 Amoy St.
Singapore, 069879
Singapore
Phone: 65 62209980
Fax: 65 62209983
Email: calvin@LNS.com.sg
URL: http://www.LNS.com.sg

Lion Toons

Calabria, 16
Barcelona, Catalonia 08015
Spain
Phone: 34 93 423 0362
Fax: 34 93 424 3682
Email: info@liontoons.com
URL: http://www.liontoons.com

LukaFilm

Studio Grafiki Animowanej
Wawrzynca 38 apr 10
Krakow, Malopolska 30 052
Poland
Phone: 48 12 4217553
Fax: 48 12 4217553
Email: lukafilm@mps.krakow.pl
URL: http://www.lukafilm.com

Luma Animation

Cnr Eileen and Geneva
Blairgowrie
Randburg
Johannesburg, Gauteng 2123

South Africa
Phone: 27 11 2933376
Fax: 27 11 2933090
Email: jason@lumastudios.com
URL: http://www.lumastudios.com

MB

Venneborglaan 25
Deurne, 2100
Belgium
Fax: 32 3 272 42 44
Email: info@MB.be
URL: http://www.MB.be

Marathon International

74, rue Bonaparte
Paris, 75006
France
Phone: 33 1 53 10 91 00
Fax: 33 1 43 25 04 66
Email: marathon@marathon.fr
URL: http://www.marathon.fr

Media Brains Oy

Puikkotie 3
Helsinki, 00750
Finland
Phone: 358 50 5260034
Email: info@mediabrains.fi
URL: http://www.mediabrains.fi

Media Mutant

Adalbertstrasse 6
Berlin, 10999
Germany
Phone: 49 30 611 019-0
Fax: 49 30 611 019-19
Email: allstars@mediamutant.de
URL: http://www.mediamutant.de

MFA+ Film Distribution

Fñhringer Allee 17
Unterfohring, 85774
Germany
Phone: 49 89 958438-0
Fax: 49 89 958438-38
Email: christian.meinke@mfa-film.de
URL: http://www.mfa-film.de

Michael Algar

10 Crosthwaite Park East
Dun Laoghaire
Dublin,
Ireland
Phone: 353 1 284 3426
Fax: 353 1 230 2787
Email: algar@ireland.com

Morpheus Animation, Inc.

Plaza 66, Suite 3937
1266 Nanjing Xi Lu
Shanghai, 200040
China
Phone: 86 21 62881882
Fax: 86 21 62880052
Email: info@morpheusanimation.com
URL: http://www.morpheusanimation.com

MOTEK B.V.

Nieuwe Hemweg 6A
Amsterdam, 1013 BG
Netherlands
Phone: 31 20 419-1111
Fax: 31 20 419-2222
Email: info@e-motek.com
URL: http://www.e-motek.com

Music To Picture

74 Berwick St.
London, W1F 8TF
United Kingdom
Phone: 44 207 287 0027
Fax: 44 207 287 0158
Email: music2pic@aol.com
URL: http://members.aol.commusic2pic

MusicHouse

127 Charing Cross Rd.
London, WC2H 0QY
United Kingdom
Phone: 44 207 434 9678
Email: enquiries@musichouse.co.uk
URL: http://www.musichouse.co.uk

MUV TechnologiesLtd.

3rd Fl., Taas Mahal
10 Montieth Road
Chennai, Tamil Nadu 600008
India
Phone: 91 44 5018111
Fax: 91 44 8523521
Email: muvahead@yahoo.com
URL: http://www.muvtech.com

N1

Vlaamsekaai 73
Antwerp, 2000
Belgium
Phone: 32 477 881337
Fax: 32 477 881337
Email: karel@n1x.com
URL: http://www.n1x.com

Nexus Animation

3, rue de duras
Paris, 75003
France
Phone: 33 1 48 88 05 30
Email: etoilesprod@free.fr

Odeon Film AG

Bavariafilmplatz 7
Geiselgasteig, 82031
Germany
Phone: 49 89 64958 0
Fax: 49 89 64958 103

Email: mail@odeonfilm.de
URL: http://www.odeonfilm.de

Oeil pour Oeil Productions

66 rue d'Angleterre
Lille, Nord 59800
France
Phone: 33 3 28 36 25 25
Fax: 33 3 20 13 06 04
Email: contact@oeilpouroeil.fr
URL: http://www.oeilpouroeil.fr

Oelli S.A. de C.V.

Insurgentes Sur 1188-1107
Colonia Tlacoquemeca,
Mexico
Phone: 52 55 5563 8686
Fax: 52 55 5611 5086
Email: jlizarraga@oelli.com
URL: http://www.oelli.com

Padmalaya Telefilms, Ltd.

A-33 Rd #2 Film Nagar
Jublee Hills
Hyderabad, Andhra Pradesh
500033
India
Phone: 91 40 355 4676
Fax: 91 40 355 4682
Email: gvnrao88@yahoo.com
URL: http://www.padmalaya.com

Paprikaas Animation Studios

101-4, Citicenter
28, Church St.
Bangalore, Karnataka 560001
India
Phone: 91 80 5091771
Fax: 91 80 5585597
Email: nandish@paprikaas.com
URL: http://www.paprikaas.com

Pesky

3 Northington St.
London, WC1N 2JE
United Kingdom
Phone: 44 207 4300200
Fax: 44 207 4302020
Email: claire@pesky.com
URL: http://www.pesky.com

Philippine Animation Studio, Inc.

2100 Pasong Tamo Extension
Makati City, 1231
Philippines
Phone: 1 310 230-0535
Fax: 1 310 230-0306
Email: frank@pasi.com.ph
URL: http://www.pasi.com.ph

PICTO Co., Ltd.

4F Seokchon Bldg. 226-1
Seokchon-dong
Songpa-Gu

Seoul 135-100
South Korea
Phone: 82 2 3442 6459
Fax: 82 2 3444 6452
Email: picto@picto.co.kr
URL: http://www.picto.co.kr

Plowman Craven & Associates

141 Lower Luton Rd.
Harpenden, Hertfordshire AL5 5EQ
United Kingdom
Phone: 44 1582 765566
Fax: 44 1582 765370
Email: post@plowmancraven.co.uk
URL: http://www.plowmancraven.co.uk

Plus One Animation, Inc.

1303-3 Seocho Dong, Seocho Gu
Seoul 137-074
South Korea
Phone: 82 2 3478-1010
Fax: 82 2 3478-0909
Email: info@plusoneani.com
URL: http://www.plusoneani.com

Plutoplastik

P.O. Box 327
Flekkefjord, 4403
Norway
Phone: 47 90 761037
Email: jablom@online.no
URL: http://www.plutoplastik.com

Pyramedia-itv

P.O. Box 2373
Jerusalem, 91023
Israel
Phone: 972 2 625 4513
Fax: 972 2 625 4578
Email: ingridv@pyramedia-itv.com
URL: http://www.pyramedia-itv.com

Qanaty

Salahudin Rd., Abduli Bldg.
Dubai, Deira 35924
United Arab Emirates
Phone: 971 4 2653 844
Fax: 971 4 2653 780
Email: info@qanaty.com
URL: http://www.qanaty.com

Red Goat

G. van Ledenberchstraat 31-1
Amsterdam, 1052TZ
Netherlands
Phone: 31 6 502153503
Email: info@redgoat.nl
URL: http://www.redgoat.nl

Red Kite Productions, Ltd.

89 Giles St.
Edinburgh, EH6 6BZ
United Kingdom
Phone: 44 131 554 0060
Fax: 44 131 553 6007

Email: info@redkite-animation.com
URL: http://www.redkite-animation.com

Red Mouse Factory

C/ Aribau 168, Bajos
Barcelona, 08036
Spain
Phone: 34 93 238 63 70
Fax: 34 93 238 64 41
Email: info@redmousefactory.com
URL: http://www.redmousefactory.com

Red Rocket Animation

Jl. Wijaya II/56
Jakarta, 12160
Indonesia
Phone: 62 21 7208 003
Fax: 62 21 7243 833
Email: marketing@rocketeer.com
URL: http://www.redrocketanimation.com

RKA-the Animation Studio Pty, Ltd.

42 Clovelly Rd.
Sydney, New South Wales 2031
Australia
Phone: 61 2 93263388
Fax: 61 2 93264192
Email: info@rka-animation.com.au
URL: http://www.rka-animation.com.au

Sam-G Animation Studio

6F, Jae-Kwang Bld.
#1002-15 Bang Bae Dong
Seacho-Gu
Seoul
South Korea
Phone: 82 2 535-6773
Fax: 82 2 523-4573
URL: http://www.sam-g.com

Samsa Film

238 C, rue de Luxembourg
Bertrange, 8077
Luxembourg
Phone: 352 45 19 60 1
Fax: 352 44 24 29
Email: samsa.film@filmnet.lu
URL: http://www.samsa-film.com

Secrets Of

5 Cranbrook St.
Clarksfield
Oldham
Manchester, Lancashire OL4 1NY
United Kingdom
Phone: 44 161 345 0788
Fax: 44 161 345 0788
Email: info@secretsof.co.uk
URL: http://www.secretsof.co.uk

Selling Dreams

Zionskirchstrasse 66
Berlin, 10245
Germany
Phone: 49 30 486 256 59
Email: g@sellingdreams.de
URL: http://www.sellingdreams.de

Skryptonite, Ltd.

89 Giles St.
Edinburgh, EH6 6BZ
United Kingdom
Phone: 44 131 554 0060
Fax: 44 131 554 6007
Email: info@skryptonite.com
URL: http://www.skryptonite.com

Skyscraper TV & Web

21 8th St.
Melville
Johannesburg, Gauteng 2092
South Africa
Phone: 27 11 482 7175
Fax: 27 11 726 8555
Email: nick@skyscraper.co.za
URL: http://www.skyscraper.co.za

Some Entermedia Co., Ltd.

1544-2 Dae Kyung Bldg 1F
Seo Cho-dong Seo Cho-Gu
Seoul, South Korea
Phone: 82 2 598-951
Fax: 82 2 598-9512
Email: some@someworld.co.kr
URL: http://www.someworld.co.kr

Spans & Partner GmbH

Muhlenkamp 59
Hamburg, 22303
Germany
Phone: 49 40 40 27 81 88
Fax: 49 40 40 27 81 88
Email: spans@spans.de
URL: http://www.spans.de

Crackerworkz Media

Gujarat Printers Building
7-Bhaktinagar Station Plot
Rajkot, Gujarat 360002
India
Phone: 91 28 1461870
Fax: 91 28 1462114
Email: tinu_13@indiatimes.com
URL: http://www.geocities.comtinu_13

Creative Film Productions

68 Conway Rd.
London, N14 7BE
United Kingdom
Phone: 44 207 447 8187
Email: awninfo@creativefilm.co.uk

DHX France

95, rue du faubourg
St. Antoine
Paris, 75011
France
Phone: 33 1 43 47 15 41

Fax: 33 1 43 47 15 48
URL: http://www.dhxprod.com

Diasaina

lot fvf 19 b firavahana fenoarivo tana 102
factories mac cann centre
multiplex androhibe
Antananarivo, Tananarive 101
Madagascar
Phone: 261 22 43858
Fax: 261 22 43859
Email: factocrea@dts.mg

Digital Video Srl

Via Sante Bargellini 4
Rome, 00157
Italy
Phone: 39 6 433620 1
Fax: 39 6 433620 22
Email: company@toonz.com
URL: http://www.toonz.com

Digitrick Gerd Wanie

Feurigstrasse 22
Berlin-Schoenberg, 10827
Germany
Email: info@digitrick.de
URL: http://www.digitrick.de

Dream Square

8-145, Yaejang-dong
Chung-ku

Seoul, South Korea
Phone: 82 2 2236 4615
Fax: 82 2 774 5576
Email: yomanstudio@hanmail.net
yoman.co.kr

Dreamheavenpictures

Chemin Coulee Pain
Quartier Long Bois
Saint Joseph, 97212
Martinique
Phone: 596 576950
Fax: 1 775 2526250
Email: alain@dreamheavenpictures.com
URL: http://
www.dreamheavenpictures.com

Eclipse Computacao Grafica Ltda.

Rua Dr. Antonio Silveira Brum Jr, 10/23
Shopping Vitrines
Centro
Muriae, MG 36880-000
Brazil
Phone: 55 32 3721 9329
Email: contato@eclipseonline.com.br
URL: http://www.eclipseonline.com.br

eee european electronic effects

GmbH
Vestische Strasse 46
Oberhausen, 46117

Germany
Phone: 49 20 8 89 90 0
Fax: 49 20 8 90 11 9
Email: contact@triple-e-vfx.com
URL: http://www.triple-e-vfx.com

Effex & Toonz

33, Jawaharlal Nehru Salai
Opp. Hyundai Plaza
Ekkathuthangal
Chennai, Tamil Nadu 600 097
India
Phone: 91 44 3727146
Email: govardon@yahoo.com

Esin Desen-Lale

Rifatbey Sok. no: 11/2 Kiziltoprak
Istanbul, 81030
Turkey
Phone: 90 216 347 5187
Fax: 90 216 347 5187

esindesen@turk.netEstudio Fenix

C/Vent 41, Bajos
Barcelona, BCN 08031
Spain
Phone: 34 93 420 40 90
Fax: 34 93 429 12 29
Email: mail@estudiofenix.com

Famous3D Animation

55 Claremont St.
South Yarra, Victoria 3141
Australia
Phone: 61 3 9826 9433
Fax: 61 3 9826 9115
Email: support@famous3D
Animation.com
URL: http://www.famous3D
Animation.com

Fanciful Arts Animation

Calle Chaparras 12
Becerril de la Sierr, Madrid
28490, Spain
Phone: 34 91 853 8681
Fax: 34 91 853 8681
Email: chdoyle@yahoo.com
pig-nick.com

FANTASIA Studios

759/102, 'Ganga Bhuvan'
Deccan Gymkhana,
Pune, Maharashtra 411004
India
Phone: 91 20 5677110
Email: fantasiastudio@rediffmail.com

FilmTecknarna Animation

Malmgardsvagen 16-18
Stockholm, 11638
Sweden
Phone: 46 8 4427300

Fax: 46 8 4427319
Email: ft@filmtecknarna.com
URL: http://www.filmtecknarna.com

Fineform Pty, Ltd.

2/29 Wyoming Ave.
Valley Heights, NSW 2777
Australia
Phone: 61 414 848 619
Fax: 61 299 931 004
fineform@pnc.com.au
URL: http://www.pnc.com.au/~fineform

Fir Bolg

The White House
Church Road
Tramore
Waterford, Munster
Ireland
Phone: 353 87 2321134
Fax: 353 51 391531
Email: firbolg1@gofree.indigo.ie
URL: http://www.paulbolger.com

Firefly Entertainment

6-3-596/90, Naveen Nagar
Banjara Hills
Hyderabad, Andhra Pradesh
500004
India
Phone: 91 40 3370504
Email: mailfirefly@yahoo.co.in
URL: http://www.fireflyworld.com

Foretell Media, Ltd.

99 Holdenhurst Rd.
Bournemouth, Dorset BH8 8EB
United Kingdom
Phone: 44 800 018 0305
Fax: 44 120 231 1502
Email: info@foretell.co.uk
URL: http://www.foretell.co.uk

Funnyazhell Animation

30 Leslie Rd.
Glenbrook, New South Wales 2773
Australia
Phone: 61 2 4739 3061
Email: info@funnyazhell.com
URL: http://www.funnyazhell.com

Futura Ltda.

Cra 15 # 76 - 27 Oficina 201
Transversal 13 A # 114-36 Apto 102
Bogota, Distrito Capital
Colombia
Phone: 57 1 2367487
Fax: 57 1 2367487
Email: filmax@cable.net.co
URL: http://www.futura-ltda.com

Fwak! Animation

P.O. Box 1068 Darlinghurst
Level 2, 319 Sussex St.
Sydney, New South Wales 1300
Australia
Phone: 61 2 9266 0809

Fax: 61 2 9267 5661
Email: info@fwakanimation.com.au
URL: http://www.fwakanimation.com.au

Global Animation Services

GmbH
Am Bachfeld 8
Munich, Bavaria 82041
Germany
Phone: 49 89 6127250
Email: greg@globalanimationservices.com
URL: http://www.globalanimation
services.com

Global Systems and Solutions

India, Ltd.
15, 3rd Cross St.
Kasturba Nagar, Adyar
Chennai, Tamil Nadu 600020
India
Phone: 91 44 4404929
Fax: 91 44 4416850
URL: http://www.gssl.net

Gobo Box

69 Stewart St.
Paddington
Sydney, New South Wales 2021
Australia
Phone: 61 2 9380 9449
Fax: 61 2 9380 7580
Email: info@gobobox.com
URL: http://www.gobobox.com

Moving Ideas Animation

13 Sutherland St., Lane Cove
Sydney, New South Wales 2066
Australia
Phone: 61 2 9427 9775
Fax: 61 2 9427 9776
Email: dsilva@optushome.com.au
URL: http://www.movingideas
animation.com

Digikore Studios, Ltd.

410/1, 411/2
Mumbai - Pune Road
Dapodi
Pune, Maharashtra 411 012
India
Phone: 91 20 714 6690
Fax: 91 20 400 1755
Email: abhishek@digikore.com
URL: http://www.digikore.com

Digital Art Media

Compudyne House
7th Mile Stone, Kudalu Gate
Hosur Road
Bangalore, Karnataka 560068
India
Phone: 91 80 5734737
Fax: 91 80 5734742
Email: info@cwlglobal.com
URL: http://www.digitalartmedia.com

Digital Artisan Pty, Ltd.

3/8 Flame Ct.
Teringie, SA 5072
Australia
Phone: 61 8 83317936
Fax: 61 8 8331 7936
Email: info@digitalartisan.com.au
URL: http://www.digitalartisan.com.au

Django Studios

Van Eeghenstraat 80
Amsterdam,
Netherlands
Phone: 31 20 3052525
Fax: 31 20 3052520
Email: dado@django.com
URL: http://www.django.com

DrFilmgood

Kingsland House
Gas Lane
Bristol, BS2 0QL
United Kingdom
Phone: 44 870 765 3734
Email: info@drfilmgood.com
URL: http://www.drfilmgood.com

DRmoi

9F ByuckSan Digital Valley
1 212-16 Guro-dong
Guro-gu
Seoul 152-848
South Korea

Phone: 82 2 2107 2816
Fax: 82 2 2107 2833
Email: drmoi@drmovie.biz

DRmovie

9F ByuckSan Digital Valley 1
212-16 Guro-dong
Guro-gu
Seoul 152-848
South Korea
Phone: 82 2 2107 2811
Fax: 82 2 2107 2833
Email: drmoi@drmovie.biz
URL: http://www.drmovie.biz

Eguzki Bideoak

Nueva 27,3
Pamplona, Navarra 31001
Spain
Phone: 34 94 8233527
Fax: 34 94 8233527
Email: inakias@yahoo.es

Emotion Studio

Balmes 156 ppal_2-a
Barcelona, 08008
Spain
Phone: 34 93 4155566
Email: rrhh@emotionstudio
URL: http://www.emotionstudio.com

Eternal Illusions Graphics

159 1st Cross, Karnataka Layout
Mahalakshmipuram
Bangalore, Karnataka 560086
India
Phone: 91 80 322 8971
Fax: 91 80 322 8971
Email: info@eternalillusions.com
URL: http://www.eternalillusions.com

FarField Technology

P.O. Box 3894
Christchurch, 8001
New Zealand
Phone: 64 3 374 6120
Fax: 64 3 374 6130
Email: email@farfieldtechnology.com
URL: http://www.farfieldtechnology.com

Farre Producciones

Cholula 1515
Colonia Maria Luisa
Monterrey,
Mexico
Phone: 52 52 8340 7519
Email: info@farreproducciones.com
URL: http://www.farreproducciones.com

Faxcination

150 Chaussee de Bruxelles
Braine le Comte, 7090
Belgium

Phone: 32 2 706 5454
Fax: 32 2 706 5454
Email: faxcination@email.com
go.to/faxcination

Flashants, Inc.

2F, No. 89, Se. 3,
Cheng-Gung Rd.,
Nei-Hu
Taipei, 114
Taiwan
Phone: 886 2 27926762
Fax: 886 2 27909215
Email: support@flashants.com
URL: http://www.flashants.com

Framestore CFC

9 Noel St.
London, W1F 8GH
United Kingdom
Phone: 44 207 208 2600
Fax: 44 207 208 2626
Email: info@framestore-cfc.com
URL: http://www.framestore-cfc.com

France Animation

14, rue Alexandre Parodi
Paris, 75010
France
Phone: 33 1 53 35 90 90
Fax: 33 1 53 35 90 91
Email: FranceAnimation@franceanim.com
URL: http://www.france-anim.com

FX Digital Co., Ltd.

10th Fl. KBI Building, 923-5
Mok-Dong, Yangchun-Ku
Seoul
South Korea
Phone: 82 2 3219 5730
Fax: 82 2 3219 5749
Email: jykim@fxdigital.co.kr
fxdigital.co.kr

fx2nv, Ltd.

24 Portland Place
London, W1B 1LU
United Kingdom
Phone: 44 020 7323 0321
Fax: 44 020 7323 0363
Email: info@fx2nv.com
URL: http://www.fx2nv.com

G-Netech VFX & Digital Post

Production
P.O. Box 4118
Level 2 The Powertel Building
Main St Varsity Cen
Robina, Queensland 4230
Australia
Phone: 61 7 5657 8007
Fax: 61 7 5657 8008
Email: info@gnetech.com
URL: http://www.gnetech.com

Galilea

12, rue Ampere
Grenoble, 38000
France
Phone: 33 4 38 12 99 0
Fax: 33 4 38 12 99 2
Email: info@galilea.com
URL: http://www.galilea.com

Grafimated Cartoon

6, G. De Spuches
Palermo, 90141
Italy
Phone: 39 9 158 2741
Fax: 39 9 158 2741
Email: grafimated@libero.it
URL: http://www.grafimated.com

Grapheus

Ma. Jaburoaluge
Janavaree Goalhi
Machchangoalhi
Malek, 20-03
Maldives
Phone: 960 781624
Fax: 960 317860
Email: grapheus@hotmail.com
URL: http://www.grapheus.com

Graphics Domain Limited

8 York Way
Crexxes Business Park
High Wycombe

Bucks, HP12 3PY
United Kingdom
Phone: 44 149 451 5500
Fax: 44 149 451 5600
Email: info@graphdom.co.uk
URL: http://www.graphdom.co.uk

Hello Films

Norrangen 1
Skutskar, 814 93
Sweden
Phone: 46 26 731 35
Fax: 46 26 731 35
Email: info@gordon.se
URL: http://www.gordon.se

Household Products

Prahms Gate 15
Kongsberg, 3613
Norway
Phone: 47 95 897172
Email: semalilla@hotmail.com

HR3D Animation, Ltd.

10 D' Arblay St.
London, W1F 8DS
United Kingdom
Phone: 44 207 598 9436
Fax: 44 207 287 1849
Email: paul.golden@hr3D Animation –
online.com

URL: http://www.hr3D Animation – online.com

Illuminated Film Company, The

115 Gunnersbury Lane
Acton
London, W3 8HQ
United Kingdom
Phone: 44 208 896 1666
Fax: 44 208 896 1669
Email: info@illuminatedfilms.com
URL: http://www.illuminatedfilms.com

Illusion Animated Productions

46 Quinns Rd.
Shankill,
Dublin, County Dublin
Ireland
Phone: 353 1 2821458
Fax: 353 1 2821458
Email: info@illusionanimation.com
URL: http://www.illusionanimation.com

INGO Multimedia Co., Ltd.

293-3, 9F-1, Fu-Shin S. Rd., Sec.2
Taipei, 106
Taiwan
Phone: 886 3 455 6083
Fax: 886 3 435 4011
Email: Web@ingo.com
URL: http://www.ingo.comtaiwan

Inidee

Brielweg 9
Jabbeke, West-Vlaanderen 8490
Belgium
Phone: 32 50 677756
Fax: 32 50 677756
Email: i.davel@pi.be
URL: http://home.pi.be/~indavel

Isearch

11 Bhaggyam Apts.
20 Raman St.
T.Nagar
Chennai, Tamil Nadu 600017
India
Phone: 91 44 8151790
Fax: 91 44 8152429
Email: isearch@vsnl.in
URL: http://www.isearchcv.com

ISKRA

Padre Xifre St., 3
Madrid, Madrid 28002
Spain
Email: iskra@nauta.es
URL: http://www iskra.es

Jiang Toon Animation Co. Ltd.

146, Fahzhan Ave., Machang Rd.
Wuhan, Hubei 430015
China
Phone: 1 514 806-2400

Fax: 1 514 289-8778
Email: alexr@bellnet.ca

Karo Toons, Rothe & Lorenz GbR

Franz-Mehring-Platz 1
Berlin, 10243
Germany
Phone: 49 30 2978 1020
Fax: 49 30 2978 1021
Email: info@karotoons.de
URL: http://www.karotoons.de

Les Films de La Perrine

1 bix, Cite Paradis
Paris, 75010
France
Phone: 33 1 56 03 90 28
Fax: 33 1 56 03 90 38
Email: production@laperrine.com
URL: http://www.laperrine.com

Levioza Toons

53/B, Tejpal Rd.,
Above Parlekar's Supermarket,
Opp Railway Station, Vile Parle (E)
Mumbai, Maharashtra 400 069
India
Phone: 91 22 6140311
Fax: 91 22 6140469
Email: info@levioza.com
URL: http://www.levioza.com

Lough House Animation, Ltd.

Jurby Rd.
Ramsey, Isle of Man IM7 2EB
United Kingdom
Phone: 44 162 481 7151
Fax: 44 162 481 7150
Email: mail@lough-house.com
URL: http://www.lough-house.com

Lovebomb

Johannesburg,
South Africa
URL: http://www.lovebomb.co.za

Magma Films

16 Merchants Rd.
Galway,
Ireland
Phone: 353 9 156 9142
Fax: 353 9 156 9148
Email: info@magmaworld.com
URL: http://www.magmaworld.com

Maximus Studios

willem van gentstraat 35A
Geldrop, North Brabant NL-5666 GA
Netherlands
Phone: 31 40 2868485
Fax: 31 40 2927257
Email: info@maximus.nl
URL: http://www.maximus.nl

Mc Camley Entertainment Ltd.

103 The Woodlands
RATOATH,, Co. Meath
Ireland
Phone: 353 1 8257841
Fax: 353 1 8257841
Email: dmccamley@eircom.net

Messilot Animation Studio

Kibbutz Messilot
D.N Bet - Shean, 19155
Israel
Phone: 97 246066428
Fax: 97 246066300
Email: omermakover@hotmail.com

Momentum Animation Studios

157 Eastern Rd.
South Melbourne, Victoria 3205
Australia
Phone: 61 3 9682 6255
Fax: 61 3 9682 2633
Email: info@momentumanimation
studios.com
URL: http://www.momentumanimation
studios.com

Monster Animation and Design

47 Lower Leeson St.
Dublin, 2
Ireland
Phone: 353 1 603 4980
Fax: 353 1 676 1437
Email: gerard@monsteranimation.ie
URL: http://www.monsteranimation.ie

Monster Distributes

47 Lower Leeson St.
Dublin, 2
Ireland
Phone: 353 1 2871167
Fax: 353 1 2871180
Email: deirdre@monsterdistributes.com
URL: http://www.monsterdistributes.com

Mont-Blanc Distribution

Vinzel, 1184
Switzerland
Phone: 41 21 824 20 45
Fax: 41 21 824 16 26
Email: info@mont-blanc-distribution.ch
URL: http://www.mont-blanc-
distribution.ch

Multimedia Production

Kopmangatan 34
Sundsvall, Medelpad 85232
Sweden
Phone: 46 60 175990
Fax: 46 60 175930
Email: elposto@mmprod.se
URL: http://www.mmprod.se

Mumbo Jumbo Animation

P.O. Box 452
Toorak, Victoria 3142
Australia
Phone: 61 3 9509 0100
Fax: 61 3 9509 0177
Email: cecileb@bigpond.net.au

Murray Freeth Animation, Ltd.

P.O. Box 13769
352 Manchester St.
Christchurch, Canterbury 8001
New Zealand
Phone: 64 3 377 6920
Fax: 64 3 377 6921
Email: free@xtra.co.nz
URL: http://mfa.co.nz

Neo Network

V. Stampa, 8
Milan, 20120
Italy
Phone: 39 28 699 6614
Fax: 39 28 901 2853
Email: info@neonetwork.it
URL: http://www.neonetwork.it

Neptuno Film Production, S.L.

C/ Sant Sebastiy, 164, 2n
Terrassa
Barcelona, Catalonia 08223
Spain
Phone: 34 93 784 1622
Fax: 34 93 784 2938
Email: neptuno@neptunofilms.com
URL: http://www.neptunofilms.com

NetDragon WebSoft, Inc.

58 Hotspring Branch Rd.
Fuzhou, 350001
China
Phone: 86 591 7519198
Fax: 86 591 7606704
Email: liudj@ndchina.com
URL: http://www.ndchina.com

NetGuru, Inc.

22700 Savi Ranch Pkwy.
E 2/4 Block GP Sector
V, Saltlake, Kolkata-700091
Kolkata, West Bengal 700091
India
Phone: 91 33 3573575
Fax: 91 33 3573467
Email: kallol2@indiainfo.com
URL: http://www.netguru.com

Ocon Inc.

Tops Venture Tower, 1591-3,
Seocho-dong Seocho-gu
Seoul 137-876
South Korea
Phone: 82 2 3444 4411
Fax: 82 2 3444 4430

Email: jihoyoun@ocon.co.kr
URL: http://www.ocon.co.kr/english

Octopus TV

2-4 Heron Quays
London, E14 4JP
United Kingdom
Phone: 44 207 531 8469
URL: http://www.octopus-television.tv

Oddbody Aps

Struenseegade 15, 3 tv
Copenhagen, 2200
Denmark
Phone: 45 3539 1700
Email: martin@oddbody.dk
URL: http://www.oddbody.dk

OTWIC

Neustiftgasse 93
Vienna, 1070
Austria
Phone: 43 6991 1339180
Email: office@otwic.com
URL: http://www.otwic.com

Pentamedia Graphics Ltd.

1/162, Old Mahabalipuram Rd., P.O. Box 9
Chennai, Tamil Nadu 603103
India
Phone: 91 41 14474317
Fax: 91 41 14474473

Email: bizdev@penta-media.com
URL: http://www.penta-media.com

Peppermint

Rauchstr. 9-11
Munich, 81679
Germany
Phone: 49 89 982470
Fax: 49 89 982470
Email: mail@seepeppermint.com
URL: http://www.seepeppermint.com

Plan B Media

Am Coloneum 1
Cologne, 50829
Germany
Phone: 49 22 1 250 1020
Fax: 49 22 1 250 1588
Email: info@planb-media.de
URL: http://www.planb-media.de

Post Logic

2, rue de Longchamp
Neuilly sur Seine, 92200
France
Phone: 33 1 46 37 77 61
Fax: 33 1 46 37 55 51
Email: info@post-logic.com
URL: http://www.post-logic.com

Ranfart

via leopoldo traversi 7
Firenze 50127
Italy
Phone: 39 349 4696550
Email: gabriele@ranfart.com
URL: http://www.ranfart.com

Realise Animation, Ltd.

87 Regent St., Suite 64 - 68
Kent House
Soho
London, W1R 7HF
United Kingdom
Phone: 44 207 434 0770
Fax: 44 207 437 1386
Email: info@realisestudio.com
URL: http://www.realisestudio.com

Reciproque.net

5 rue de la Folie Regnault
Paris, 75011
France
Phone: 33 6 64 99 04 72
Fax: 33
Email: Webmaster@reciproque.net
URL: http://www.reciproque.net

Rothkirch / Cartoon-film

Bergmanstrasse 68
Berlin, 10961
Germany
Phone: 49 30 69 80 84 0

Fax: 49 30 69 80 84 29
Email: cartoon-film@snafu.de
URL: http://www.cartoon-film.de

Roving Stage Productions

130, rue Lafayette
Paris, 75010
France
Phone: 33 1 42 46 19 35
Fax: 33 1 42 46 00 70
Roy Williams Animation
24c Hillock Rd.,
Blue Range
Diego Martin,
Trinidad and Tobago
Phone: 1 868 695 133
Email: roy_williams@hotmail.com

RRS Entertainment

Sternwartstrasse 2
Munich, 81679
Germany
Phone: 49 89 2111660
Fax: 49 89 21116611
Email: info@rrsentertainment.de
URL: http://www.rrsentertainment.de

Scratch Production

581 du Domaine
Cowansville, QC J2K 3G6
Phone: 1 450 266-1631
Email: pierre@scratchproduction.com
URL: http://www.scratchproduction.com

Screen First, Ltd.

The Studios
Funnells Farm
Down St.
Nutley, East Sussex TN22 3LG
United Kingdom
Phone: 44 182 571 2034
Fax: 44 182 571 3511
Email: info@screenfirst.co.uk

Scruffy Productions

Rathconnell
Nurney
Co. Kildare
Dublin,
Ireland
Phone: 353 87 7725633
Fax: 353
Email: tommygirl@esatclear.ie

Siriol Productions

3, Mount Stuart Square
Butetown
Cardiff, Wales CF10 5EE
United Kingdom
Phone: 44 292 048 8400
Fax: 44 292 048 5962
Email: enquiries@siriol.co.uk
URL: http://www.siriolproductions.com

Skaramoosh

Covent Garden
9-15 Neal St.
London, WC2H 9PW
United Kingdom
Phone: 44 207 379 9966
Fax: 44 207 240 7111
URL: http://www.skaramoosh.co.uk

SOB Animation Group Limited

17-19 Maurice Rd.
Penrose
Auckland, 1800
New Zealand
Phone: 64 9 622 0618
Fax: 64 9 622 4080
Email: sob.prod@clear.net.nz
URL: http://www.sobproductions.co.nz

Softamation, Ltd.

69B Green Rd., 4th Fl.
PanthaPath
Dhaka, 1205
Bangladesh
Phone: 880 2 8624780
Fax: 880 2 8117564
Email: info@softamation.com;info@biit
bd.com
URL: http://www.softamation.com

Stars Animation Services

42/10E Quang Trung Ward 11,
Govap DiSt.
HoChiMinh, 00000
Vietnam
Phone: 84 9 3966599
Email: van@starsanimation.com
URL: http://www.starsanimation.com

Stenarts Productions

Landreiterweg 51 a
Berlin, 12353
Germany
Phone: 49 30 60540978
Fax: 49 30 60540979†
Email: info@stenarts.com
URL: http://www.stenarts.com

Crow Digital Animations

8 Leverton Cls St. Ives
Sydney, NSW 2175
Australia
Phone: 61 2 94400156
Email: animator1@bigpond.com
crowanimations.com

CTECH s.r.o.

Nuselska 53
Prague, 14000
Czech Republic
Phone: 420 2 61215644
Fax: 420 2 61217764

Email: info@ctech.cz
URL: http://www.ctech.cz

Digital Dream Studios

553-3 Dogok-Dong, Kangnam-gu
Seoul
South Korea
Phone: 82 2 2140-4000
Fax: 82 2 578-0933
Email: ttaok@ddsdream.com
URL: http://www.ddsdream.com

DoMotion, Ltd.

44-2 Yatab-Dong Bundang-Ku
Sungnam
Kyonggi
Sungnam,
South Korea
Phone: 82 31 781 9616
Fax: 82 31 781 7616
Email: info@domotion.co.kr
URL: http://www.domotion.com

Dongwoo Animation

Hyundai Information Technology
Bldg. 2 8F,†
#1131-1, Kuro-dong, Kuro-gu
Seoul
South Korea
Phone: 82 2 3282 9500
Fax: 82 2 864 2701
URL: http://www.anidong.com

Dopesheet Media

8 Kathleen Ave.
Alpeerton
London,
United Kingdom
Phone: 44 797 704 5014
Email: Sagar3D Animation
ee@hotmail.com
URL: http://www.dopesheet.co.uk

Dunia Kecil Animation

Workhouse
44, 1st Fl., Taman Sri Siantan
Jalan Kuala Lumpur
Off KL-Karak Highway
Bentong, Pahang 28700
Malaysia
Phone: 6 09 221 1128
Fax: 6 09 221 1129
Email: dkmagic97@hotmail.com
URL: http://www.geocities.com/
duniakecil_animation

Dusar Star Sdn Bhd

9A, Jalan Nirwana 39
Taman Nirwana
Ampang, Selangor 68000
Malaysia
Phone: 6 03 92813887
Fax: 6 03 92813872
Email: dusarstar@yahoo.com

Dygra Films

Linares Rivas 9
La Coruna, 15004
Spain
Phone: 34 91 5213508
Fax: 34 91 5227993
Email: cristobal@filloa.com
URL: http://www.dygrafilms.com

Entertainment Rights, PLC

Colet Ct.
100 Hammersmith Road
London, W6 7JP
United Kingdom
Phone: 44 208 762 6200
Fax: 44 208 762 6299
Email:
enquiries@entertainmentrights.com
URL: http://www.entertainmentrights.com

Enxebre Sistemas, s.l.

3D Animation Production
c/San Andres 56, 3-E
La Coruna, 15003
Spain
Phone: 34 981 220524
Fax: 34 981 205046
Email: info@enxebre.es
URL: http://www.enxebre.es

EUREKA Television and Video

Martìn de Gainza 517 2B
Buenos Aires, Capital Federal 1405
Argentina
Phone: 54 11 1541820798
Fax: 54 11 1551415924
Email: info@eurekatv.com.ar
URL: http://www.eurekatv.com.ar

Evelyne Monsallier Creations

24, chemin des Bruyeres
Tassin la Demi Lune, 69160
France
Phone: 33 4 78 34 10 43
Fax: 33 4 78 34 10 43
Email: iletait1x@wanadoo.fr

Fenix Animation

Les Galeries
13, rue de la République
Arles, 13200
France
Phone: 33 4 90 52 23 63
Fax: 33 4 90 93 17 71
Email: info@fenix.fr
URL: http://www.fenix.fr

Ficticious Egg

Kingsland House
Gas lane
Bristol, B52 0QL
United Kingdom

Phone: 44 117 971 9945
Fax: 44 207 691 9558
Email: admin@eggtoons.com
URL: http://www.eggtoons.com

Fido Film AB

Stadsgarden 17
Stockholm, 118 56
Sweden
Phone: 46 8 556 990 00
Fax: 46 8 556 990 01
Email: info@fido.se
URL: http://www.fido.se

Film Export Group

Via Polonia 9
Rome, 00198
Italy
Phone: 39 68 554266
Fax: 39 68 550248
Email: info@filmexport.com
URL: http://www.filmexport.com

Flip Studio

232/3 Rayer Bazar, Pathshala
Lane, Dhaka -1209
40, New Elephant Rd., Dhaka-1205
77/1,North Dhanmondi, Dhaka-1205
Dhaka, 1209
Bangladesh
Phone: 880 2 8117025
Email: nemo@bdonline.com
URL: http://www.flipstudiobd.com

Flix Animation

66 Holtermann St.
Crows Nest
Sydney, N.S.W. 2065
Australia
Phone: 61 2 94396666
Fax: 61 2 94396066
Email: info@flixanimation.com
URL: http://www.flixanimation.com

Freestyle, Inc.

9 Elliot Ave.
Pottersville
Roseau,
DomInc.a
Phone: 1 767 448-7903
Fax: 1 767 449-9381
Email: info@gofreestyle.com
URL: http://
www.gofreestyle.comindex2.htm

FTD France Television

Distribution
1, boulevard Victor Hugo
Paris, 75075
France
Phone: 33 1 44 25 01 40
Fax: 33 1 44 25 01 42
Email: ftdinternational@francetv.com
URL: http://www.francetv.com

Gambit Film

Koenigsallee 43
Ludwigsburg, 71638
Germany
Phone: 49 71 41125 170
Fax: 49 71 41125 175
Email: info@gambit-film.de
URL: http://www.gambit-film.de

eneGony Entertainment

354-306 Toe-Gyo
875 Kumgjeong
Kunpo City, Kyounggi-do 435758
South Korea
Phone: 82 13918512
Email: genegony@hanmail.net

Ghost vfx

Thorsgade 59 3th
2200 Copenhagen North
Copenhagen,
Denmark
Phone: 45 35858192
Fax: 45 35858194
Email: mail@ghost.dk
URL: http://www.ghost.dk

Graphilm S.r.l.

via Faa' di Bruno, 52
Rome
Italy
Phone: 39 6 39742703
Fax: 39 6 39742705
Email: info@graphilm.com
URL: http://www.graphilm.com

Graphissimo

2 Myrtous St., Glyfada
Athens, Attica 16675
Greece
Phone: 30 10 898 2086
Fax: 30 10 898 2086
Email: simlys@graphissimo.com
URL: http://www.graphissimo.com

Graphiti Multimedia Private, Ltd.

3B Kamanwala Chambers
Mogul Lane,
Mahim (West)
Mumbai, 400016
India
Phone: 91 22 4441580
Fax: 91 22 4442347
Email: munjal@graphitimultimedia.com
URL: http://www.graphitimultimedia.com